RUSSIA AS IT IS
Transformation of a Lose/Lose Society

ISBN 1-59113-391-2

Published by Matthew Maly, USA.

PRINTED IN THE UNITED STATES OF AMERICA
Booklocker.com, Inc.
2003

RUSSIA AS IT IS

Transformation of a Lose/Lose Society

Matthew Maly

TABLE OF CONTENTS

REVIEWS OF THE BOOK

+++

A civilised market economy, which Russia is professedly building, calls for competition without conflict, freedom without indiscipline, ambition without envy and co-operation without coercion. These requirements clash head-on with some of Russia's most ingrained cultural and anthropological traits. Matthew Maly's scholarly elaboration of the dilemma is replete with parables, poetry and aphorisms, reminiscent at times of Thorstein Veblen's sociology of American capitalism. One could almost entitle his book, *Theory of the Thieving Class.*

Peter Oppenheimer
Oxford University

+++

Russia As It Is: Transformation of a Lose/Lose Society is an iconoclastic, provocative, politically incorrect, and probing analysis of why Russia doesn't work – and never has worked – as well as it should. Those who will influence Russia's future would do well to read it with care. The same is true for non-Russians who deal with the country, and for those who wish it well.

Lawrence E. Harrison
The Fletcher School of Law and Diplomacy, Tufts University,
co-editor of "Culture Matters"

+++
As a former professor of economics and business owner and operator active in Russia and other states of the former Soviet Union for the last 10 years, I can highly recommend this book for policy makers, international aid agencies and businesspersons.

The fundamental thesis of the book is that Russia (and other Slavic countries of the former Soviet Union, such as Ukraine and Belarus) have developed social, economic and governmental structures that are implicitly based on a psychology of lose/lose as contrasted to the general western psychology of win/win. The zero sum game is perceived as reality in Russia owing to its long history of internal deprivation and external threat. How this developed historically is one subject of the book. Because Russian institutions of law, government and society are derived from this historic-psychological base, an understanding of Russian behavior in its many manifestations requires a firm understanding of how and why this psychology has developed, especially during the Soviet period.

The basic error of western policy makers has been to ignore this important psychological difference with the result that westerners are continually surprised or dismayed by Russian behavior that appears to run contrary to what they assume to be optimal or at least predictable decision-making based on the implicit psychology of win/win. Russia is the proverbial square peg that the western world is trying to force into a round hole. It would better for those involved with Russia to read this book so that at least surprise and dismay can be replaced with understanding and anticipation.

Paul R. Thomas
President, IRE (USA) Inc.
Partner, IRE (Ukraine) LLC

+++

The advantage of Matthew Maly's book is that it manages to combine reality with theory. You get a general introduction to the basic concepts of liberalism and communism together with a lot of funny examples of how these concepts work or do not work in Russia' s everyday life. This gives you a sense of the enormous difference in the perception of the world that separates East and West; a difference that cannot be explained, as we like to do it in the West, by different stages of development of our respective civilizations. In other words, Maly's book shows that is it just not a matter of us being ahead, and them lacking behind, so that it will only be a matter of time before they catch up on democracy and market economy; no, in many ways, the Russians perceive the world differently than the peoples of western Europe. That is why Maly's examples from everyday life in Russia are as true today as they were in Soviet times and in tsarist Russia. I would have liked to have read Maly's book as a student of political science; then I would have understood these things on a much earlier stage. I had to live in Russia several years before I grasped the difference; and nevertheless Maly's book was an eye-opener for me. It may not be the final truth about Russia; but it is surely a step in that direction, and that is more than can be said about most other books on the subject of Russia. I enthusiastically recommend Maly's book to everyone who wants to understand Russia – be they scientists, students, politicians, expats living in Russia, or just curious people.

Anna Libak
Moscow Correspondent of Berlingske Tidende, Denmark

+++

Matthew Maly brings a uniquely informed and enlightening perspective to the continuing mystery of Russia. *Russia As It Is* provides a much needed insight into today's Russia.

David Johnson
Editor, Johnson's Russia List

+++

Matthew Maly's third book promises to shed more light on why Russians seems so baffling to us, and perhaps to themselves. A culture based on envy has inherent problems with economic development. I particularly appreciated his explanation of why they don't fix small things that would improve their lives: they are waiting to do something perfect, and can't waste their time doing anything halfway. Whether the reader agrees or not with Maly's provocative analysis, the book presents a stimulating array of ideas.

Susan McIntosh, MBA
charity president

PRAISE FOR MALY'S FIRST BOOK, UNDERSTANDING RUSSIA

+++

Over the past five years, Russia has acquired the superficial trappings of democracy. The country's psychology, however is much slower to change. Perhaps the best guide to this psychology is a slim volume by Matthew Maly, a Russian economic expert. His book, *Understanding Russia,* is intended for Western business investors in Russia, but it is equally useful for anyone wanting to understand Russian politics.

From the article "Russia – a country of power, not a country of law" by Geoffrey York, *The Globe and Mail*, Canada

+++

Understanding Russia, Matthew Maly: Maly was hired by USAID to write a booklet on how Russians think. He did such a great job that his USAID sponsors recoiled in horror and disowned the project. They didn't expect anything like this: a brilliant, concise, original explanation of the way Russians imagine the world. If you don't mind a little truth now and then, you may be able to stomach this wonderful, orphaned book.

The Exile (Moscow) Issue #152, 17/10/02

INTRODUCTION

Peter Lavelle
http://untimely-thoughts.com

I would like to start by quoting a sentence that illustrates the approach that makes *Russia As It Is* so different and so successful:

If a man asks a woman to come up for a cup of coffee, a good historian will not ask what brand of coffee they ended up drinking, particularly if the woman gets pregnant that day (p. 150).

Indeed, if this is a coded invitation to start a relationship, it is irrelevant whether or not they actually drink coffee at all. If the man has no coffee in his place, that does not make him a liar. What is interesting to us here is how the couple met and why they attracted to each other, and we should go directly to those questions - never mind the contents of the cupboard.

Matthew Maly's book is not a history of our (largely unsuccessful) attempts to understand Russia. Mercifully, it does not mention our numerous examinations of the cupboard, prompted by passing mentions of coffee: *Russia As It Is* reveals historical undercurrents and makes us understand the events they have driven. Yes, we were aware that these events had occurred, we marveled at them, were concerned by them, we were sad, angered, or frightened. But rarely did we understand why they occurred, and what they meant. Maly's book changes that: it reveals the logic of Russia's recent history and lets us see the causes of historical events that heretofore were enigmatic and baffling for us.

Maly's book cuts straight to the chase: I read the entire book practically in one go, because the book is impossible to put down. And when I finished, Russia as a historical and cultural phenomenon was suddenly obvious to me, as understandable and clear as if I were a surgeon looking at a patient under the sharp light of an operating room. I am a long-time student of Russia, and there were many aspects of Russia that I knew and understood, some more clearly than others, but I had never had all of Russia lit up so brightly and pinned down so tightly as when I was reading Maly's book.

Since the book is not a history of our efforts to come to grips with Russia, it does not contain one single quote from a scholarly work. This is one reason it reads so easily and respects the reader's time: it promises to make Russia understandable, and it does just that, without any of the distractions or interruptions caused by scholarly debate. It delivers, and I am afraid that many a Russia scholar will now view a shelf or two of painstakingly accumulated Russia-related books as a somewhat wasted investment. As I read, the joy of discovery was frequently mixed with sadness as the thought "I wish I had read this book years earlier!" crossed my mind over and over.

Russia As It Is does not cite any previous scholarship, but you will want to go at it with a highlighter. For this is a book that seems destined to be discussed a lot, be it in approval or in anger. Maly has thrown down the gauntlet, challenging us to disprove his many surprising assumptions – assumptions that cannot be ignored, as they appear to lead us straight to the elusive goal of (finally!) making sense out of Russia.

To make Russia understandable, Maly uses a multidisciplinary approach, which makes this book hard to classify. Is it a history book, or is it social psychology? There certainly is a discussion of economics, but it looks more like political or moral philosophy. There is a description of Russia, and yet it looks more like an explanation of it, all the examples and stories being there only to illustrate an important point. In contrast with the serious subject it treats, the book is light and often funny. *Russia As It Is* covers all of the huge cultural, political, and economic expanse of Russia, and yet it is short and very easy to read.

The book's genre is hard to pinpoint, but even its subject is elusive. *Russia As It Is* discusses Russia – that much is clear. But having read the book, I would also strongly recommend it to those who never knew they should be reading "a book about Russia": for example, to those who are working to bring democracy to Iraq or economic prosperity to Africa. Indeed, the book is not so much about Russia as it is about the lose/lose worldview found in so many places, and about this worldview's struggle with the newly emerging, astonishingly productive, and user-friendly win/win outlook. This outlook is the social discovery that brought the West unprecedented prosperity and, most recently, the apparent desire to bring its blessings, by peaceful means or otherwise, to countries that have yet to see the magic and the benefits of win/win. If this is so, then Maly also writes about the West, using Russia as a contrasting backdrop against which the West can see and understand itself.

I made this introduction short so that you can get straight to the book: whatever your level of knowledge about Russia, you are about to embark on a journey that will entertain and enlighten better than any book I have read in a long time. It may not look like a gem, but believe me, it sparkles. Please approach *Russia As It Is* with an open mind, and do not cling to what you thought you knew for certain. Let go and enjoy the ride.

ABOUT THIS BOOK

Today, political science is at a crossroads:

- America has the world's strongest military, and yet it is powerless to counter a threat posed by a few determined individuals.
- The Soviet Union has collapsed, but its peoples have failed to build true democracy and a market economy. What is holding them back?
- The superpower confrontation is over, and yet we do not feel secure; what is the bipolarity of the contemporary world, who is our enemy?
- Why do some economies develop very rapidly, while others stagnate or regress?

The answers to these questions affect the lives of every human being on Earth. As an example, we could reduce all these questions to a single, very practical one: "Will America's airports continue to help us travel quickly, or will they become places where we have to undergo endless checks and searches?" In other words, will progress and creativity continue unimpeded, or will they be slowed or even reversed?

This book lays a foundation for answering such questions, offering a new vision for the post-September 11 world

Every interaction can have one of three outcomes: a winner and a loser, two winners, or two losers. Win/lose is as old as Tyrannosaurus Rex vs. Brontosaurus. Win/win is a far more recent invention: societies that embrace concepts like ethnic and religious tolerance, or international cooperation, became the rule rather than the exception only after World War II. Lose/lose has always seemed irrational, a dynamic of interaction that neither economists nor political scientists cared to even mention, much less study. But they should have paid more attention, because societies based upon a lose/lose world outlook, from post-revolutionary Russia to Osama bin Laden's al-Qaeda, do exist. And we are still intellectually ill-equipped to deal with such threats.

A general discussion of a lose/lose society will appear strange and difficult to comprehend, and that is why this book uses the example of Russia, to make the discussion more factual and engaging.

Here is what the book offers:

It explains the origins of the modern global conflict, currently mislabeled as a "war on terrorism" or "war on poverty" (it is, in fact, lose/lose against win/win).

It offers a new explanation of 20th century European history and explains the phenomenon of such people as Hitler, Stalin, and Pol Pot.

It explains Russia's history, especially its twentieth century history.

It gives an answer to the question, "What would it take to build in Russia a western style democracy, which in turn would mean building the only possible foundation for it: a well-functioning market economy?"

It explains envy, the most powerful and the least understood psychological and economic force.

It teaches how to live an envy-free life and be creative, happy, and truly alive.

This book is about Russia, but it will develop a theory that is applicable to every country of the world. Russia is just an example, chosen because it is the country that best illustrates this theory. This book is much more than a book about Russia: poverty, envy, macroeconomics, history – if these topics interest you, this book may be quite useful.

This is not a book approved and financed by the "international development community," which sometimes appears to believe that even a stone-age tribe can have "a democracy" if we only give them ballots with pictures they can understand. No matter how many thugs you put on a ballot, a "choice" between them is still not a democracy, even if Jimmy Carter serves as an observer. *Russia is still largely a viable and self-sustaining lose/lose society, and as such, Russia is not a democracy because democracy is based on win/win.*

Another aim of this book is to destroy some of the convenient assumptions that often cause our policies to fail. Here is one such assumption: Why do we take for granted that all people want to live better? What if a particular society wants to live worse, seeing more benefits in war and destruction than in peace and creation? If you are offered the chance to run the 100-meter dash against Carl Lewis, will you run, or will you claim that "running is stupid" and that you are "not in the mood"? Have you not known people who were actively trying to destroy their lives, those who achieved their unspoken, but still obvious goal of personal catastrophe? If so, why are we assuming that people always see good as being more desirable than bad?

I am not going to propose to you a politically correct, nice, or balanced discussion. My aim is to make you think, to experience strong emotions, to call me names if you like, but, most of all, to come up with better solutions than those that are being proposed right now. For a multitude of reasons, we want Russians to live better; and it is dangerous and immoral to pretend that everything in Russia is going just fine.

Our immediate goal is to understand Russia as it is today and to propose the best course of action. To do that, it will not be enough merely to be in possession of historical, political, and economic facts: they are so numerous and contradictory that we would be left totally confused. Also, the book would have to be at least twice as long. What we need is a clear and simple theory; it may well be rough and ready, not taking into account some quirks of history, but it should be fundamentally sound and operationally useful, so that we can accomplish our goal, even at the risk of offending those historians who cannot let even the tiniest fact be overlooked.

We need to describe the trends, the undercurrents; we need to draw a bigger picture, and the historical facts will be used only for that. There are many good Russian history books, and this book is not a history book in a traditional sense of the word. My favorite historian is Alvin Toffler: Pre-industrial Age, Industrial Age, and Information Age – the whole of human history in three periods, recognized and described by a genius. We need the tendencies, the system of coordinates, the dividing lines, the major points of tension; we need classifications that a high school student would understand and recognize. And, if our theory is good, Russia as it is today, as well as the road it is traveling, should become clear.

For the task that this book sets out for itself, it is a very small book. This means that there is just enough space to state something, but absolutely no space to exhaustively substantiate the claims that are being made. The realities of life in Russia make for a better read than disclaimers. As we have very little space in which to discuss some very complicated phenomena, the only way to do it is to revert to striking symbols. Sometimes this is done not by being well-balanced. It might be that some of the statements here would not be true from the point of view of academic science: they might indeed be overstated to point your attention in a certain direction, and the goal is to do it in a way that, it is hoped, you won't soon forget.

Picasso has a painting called *Weeping woman.* This is the only painting I know that has succeeded in depicting a crying woman, and the woman happens to have two noses, three eyes, and seven fingers on one hand. My goal will be to depict the crying, rather than to make sure that each hand has five fingers.

I will try to give you the "historical instruments" to work with, the chopsticks to pick out on the plate of events the facts that are really important. Using these instruments, you will be able to understand Russia better than I do, and this is my ultimate goal. Russia is, for the moment, no longer as important politically as it used to be, but it remains a worthy object of study, a worthy object of love, respect, hatred, and fear.

Today's Russia is a product of Russian history going back at least a thousand years, and it is also a product of the Soviet period. We will start by discussing certain permanent features of Russian civilization that became apparent long before the birth of Lenin. These features may be centuries old, but they are very relevant and important today. Here, our question will be, "What made Russia susceptible to becoming a lose/lose society? Some people claimed that Lenin and Stalin destroyed Russian civilization: no, they did not. In many ways they were true representatives of Russian civilization, who only highlighted and reinforced some of its major features.

As the Soviet period played such a great role in shaping today's Russian reality, we will then propose a theory that explains the Soviet period, that reveals it for what it was. Only then will we be able to discuss Russia as it is today and to give some recommendations, and the last chapters of the book will be dedicated to that.

We will also discuss two fundamentally different ways to live one's life: the Way of Creativity and the Way of Envy. We will discuss how Industrial Age ideology destroyed traditional religion and became a new religion in its stead. We will gain a good understanding of Russia and will be able to discuss, and maybe even to influence, the choices that Russia has to make.

Another aspect of this book could be called "culture-specific translation." If Russians were to listen in as Americans discuss baseball, they would come up with many strange theories of what the game might be, but would never understand the game. My father never saw a baseball game and thought that the ball they hit with the stick was pear-shaped. Why is this so? Because those who know the game never discuss the basics: the ball, the bat, the shape of the field, or the rules. The same goes for the Russian way of life. Americans come here, see people wearing jeans, and immediately assume that this is a country that has a functioning legal system and wants democracy. The opening of the first McDonald's in Moscow was heralded as a victory of capitalism and western values, but ten years later both capitalism and the western values are still hard to find, even though the fries and the shakes are available. The dialogue between Russia and the West cannot be successful as long as both sides have different unspoken basic assumptions: Western political culture searches for win/win solutions, while the Russians mostly choose between win/lose and lose/lose.

This cultural bridge-building was one of the main themes of my first book, *Understanding Russia: A brief introduction to the psychology of Russian society for the arriving westerner* (Moscow, 1995). This book was in English, and I attempted to explain Russia to westerners, i.e. I played the role of a Russian who understands the western frame of mind. In my Russian language book *How to Make Russia a Normal Country* (Moscow, 2000 and Saint Petersburg, 2002), I played the role of a westerner, trying to explain western democracy to the Russians. In this book, I will attempt to show you Russia from the inside, to explain to you the motives of Russian behavior, to make you understand how the Russians view the world.

DAYDREAMING

There actually is only one fundamental difference between Russia and the West: Russia has never had the concept of private property. Instead of private property in the western sense of the term, the Russians have "conditional possession". We will discuss this at length, but for now I just want you to believe me that private property is not the same as conditional possession.

I assume you have never asked yourself, "How am I going to take a shower?" You just simply take it: physically and logistically the process of taking a shower is one of the simplest things you do during your day. Now suppose there was a guy who went to war in Vietnam, a shell exploded right next to him, and he lost his left leg and right arm. Now I would like you to stop reading and think how a guy like that would take a shower, and what needs to be done for him to accomplish this task. Here is a challenging problem for the technologically inclined. Take several minutes to think. What did you come up with? A harness around the waist could help him to stand in the bathtub. Or should he be sitting in a special chair? It would be interesting to visit this person's bathroom to see what kind of technological solution this guy adapted.

Russian civilization did not develop a concept of private property. When we go to Russia's "bathroom", we will not find the missing "limbs" (they are buried in the jungle somewhere), but we will find compensatory devices that allow Russia to function somehow in spite of the missing limbs.

There exists a large body of scholarship on Russia, and this scholarship is of two kinds: some fail to notice that the limbs (in this case, the rights that stem from the right to own private property) are entirely missing, and the other do notice the missing limbs, but fail to notice the compensatory devices (the harness or special chair), simply assuming that the poor guy never takes a shower. International financial institutions avoid the problem altogether, simply telling our guy, "Once you get out of the shower, wrap yourself in a nice fluffy towel". They do not realize that the guy, incited by them to get into the bathtub, may fall and badly hurt himself.

We will avoid these mistakes. We will study Russia like it really is; we will daydream, thinking of what it might take for Russia to compensate for its missing limbs, but we will not dream up a Russia that never existed and cannot exist.

Indeed, the last ten years of Russian history showed that the simplistic "manual" prepared for Russia by Western experts did not work. Russia got into the bathtub and fell so hard it almost broke its back. We need to write a personalized manual for this special customer. We should start by figuring out what limbs and senses the customer is missing and what additional support devices are necessary. And then we should write a step-by step procedure, indicating exactly where the customer should place his only foot.

As you read my book, please make frequent pauses, if only for a minute or two, and daydream about what you have just read. The worst thing about a book, any book, is that it just continues uninterruptedly, like some idiot that won't shut up. I can't wait for a high-tech book that will read your brainwaves to figure out when you have stopped understanding and somehow alert you to this fact. Pending that, I would love to be able to get you daydreaming.

This book is not about Russia as such, nor does this book aim to prove to you that I, the author, either happen to understand Russia or am an idiot suffering from self-delusions. I want this to be a book about you, you as someone who understands Russia. But it won't be a book about you unless you start daydreaming.

I use the same method in my Russian book, *How to Make Russia a Normal Country*. There are enough books that order the Russians to go in a certain direction and try very hard to convince them that the proposed route is the only one possible. I think that Russia's troubles are largely a consequence of Russians' inability to think and act as citizens, their true lives being totally private, hidden from society at large. My Russian book is a textbook of civic action, and I am trying to teach the Russians to think and act as citizens, to daydream about the Russia that they want to live in and then to act to turn their daydreams into reality. My Russian book is on my website *http://www.matthew-maly.ru/index-eng.html* , and I repeatedly invite my Russian readers to rewrite the text with me, and in the process of rewriting the text of book, to make Russia better.

HOW TO MAKE RUSSIA A NORMAL COUNTRY

The Russian book of which this one is an extensively rewritten translation is called *How to Make Russia a Normal Country.* What did I mean by that? Russia is normal, it is what it is, and is likely to be what it has always been. It is not as wealthy or civilized as France, but it is certainly wealthier and more civilized than Ethiopia, and people live in Ethiopia, too, and sincerely think that their life is normal. Moreover, all things considered, Russia is much more civilized and more prosperous today than it has ever been, and may well become even more civilized and prosperous tomorrow. Relatively speaking, Russia is doing all right, so why are we posing this question? All countries are "normal", and that includes Russia. Ethiopia is doing fine, while Saudi Arabia and China are doing just terrific. Yet we might not like everything that goes on in these countries, and we may think that it is not normal. Would we want to live in absolute poverty in Ethiopia, or to be a dissident in China? No, we would not. Now we are ready to rephrase the question of "normality:" Can Russia be made to meet western standards, and if so, how?

So why did I give my Russian book such a provocative title? I did so because today a great many Russians feel that their country is in fact not normal, and I wanted to participate in the discussion of how Russia can be turned into a more civilized and prosperous nation. Today, Russian police torture suspects to make them testify against themselves, just like they did 500 years ago. Russia is normal in the sense that Russia is the same as it has always been. But there is one great difference: if 500 years ago everybody thought that torturing suspects was normal, today some citizens of Russia no longer think so. For them, normalcy is a departure from this age-old tradition. They want the torture to end. These people have a very different standard, a standard that comes from the West, and it is that standard that represents normalcy for them. Now we see that the true title of my Russian book should have been "How to make Russia different from what it has always been and turn it into something more resembling the West." The hidden title of my Russian book was "How to make Russia more western." In other words, my book was directed at those who, even though they are Russians, feel that they are entitled to a real, western style democracy.

And here is the answer: we can try to push Russia towards the western standard, we can even partially succeed, but we should not expect to succeed fully and within a short period of time. Sixty years ago, a period less than the average human lifespan, Hitler occupied virtually all of Europe. Mass executions and genocide were commonplace, racial hatred and national hatred were acceptable. Even in America, a country that was not being bombed or invaded, Japanese Americans were interned in camps and African Americans were still segregated. Today, the pendulum has swung all the way to the other end. People of all races, creeds, and backgrounds are expected to vote democratically, drink Coke, and strictly adhere to the latest standard of behavior developed by the western court system. As a benchmark, the western lifestyle is acceptable, but it is woefully naïve, even dangerous, to expect that these standards be immediately met everywhere. Human society can adapt and change, and we are pointing it in the right direction, but it cannot just switch, because that will cause it to break down. Russia can and should have a much better system - fairer, more productive, more tolerant, more democratic, more inclusive, and friendlier towards its neighbors. But it will not have a system fundamentally similar to the western one for at least ten or twenty years. We must understand the Russian system, and help the Russians to improve it and to gradually modernize it, not to break it. If the system breaks, the Russians will only become more aggressive, more desperate, more violent and belligerent: more, not less. We should be more respectful towards our own democracy as well: it is the crowning achievement of a millennium, not a piece of chewing gum that anyone can chew without reading an instruction manual.

CHAPTER ONE. RUSSIAN CIVILIZATION

RUSSIAN CIVILIZATION AS A UNIQUE PHENOMENON

If we discuss the possibility of building a western style democracy in Russia, the first thing we must take into account is the fact that human societies are much more different than we tend to admit, and often are different not superficially, but fundamentally, in their basic assumptions.

For example, the Chinese do not use such a basic (from a Western point of view) thing as an alphabet, and to convey the term "surprise" a Chinese writer has to draw a horse sticking its head out of a window. But when we translate a Chinese text into English, the striking images that are used to convey the terms such as "surprise" get completely lost: the original text is much more colorful than can be judged from an English translation. The only thing that Westerners see are the drawbacks that the use of characters entails, while the advantages of their use remain hidden. But having to use elaborate character-images, the Chinese have developed a tendency to see things at once from many different sides. Just like their characters, a Chinese meal is always a combination of several ingredients, textures, and colors. The Chinese are not about to introduce a writing system based on the alphabet, because for them the issue here is not just the method of putting words on paper, but their view of the world, their civilization.

In the same way, Russian civilization is built on values that, while fundamental for Russians, are both alien to Westerners and hidden from them. Westerners disregard some aspects of Russian psychology, and yet assign to the Russians certain traits that Westerners wrongly assume to be universal. That often results in a clash of values and assumptions between the products of these two civilizations. And yet Russia must make a difficult transition into the unknown, must bring its civilization much closer to the West.

The concept of private property is as basic to the development of Western society as the alphabet is for the Western writing system. Western laws, Western customs, Western morality are all founded on the concept of private property. And yet, in Russia virtually every aspect of social life has been influenced and often determined by the lack of this concept. That has led to a way of seeing things that is so different from the Western one that here we are dealing not just with another culture, but with a thoroughly distinct civilization. As a consequence of one missing basic concept, everything else had to adapt, compensate, adjust, and change its nature and appearance.

The Russians can no longer survive without private property and will have to learn to accept it as a concept. There are quite a few other concepts that the Russians will have to learn to accept, while some of the notions that have reigned here from time immemorial will have to be torn out, roots and all. This is a great existential conflict, but it cannot be avoided.

A picture of a horse sticking its head out of a window is a basic unit of the Chinese language, but it is not a letter. Nor is it a word. It is a uniquely Chinese thing, a character. The same with Russia. Suppose a Westerner wants to study Russian law. In every Western country law is firmly based on the concept of private property, be it the land one owns or the rights one has. But looking for "law" in Russia makes about as much sense as looking for an alphabet in China. There is a Russian "something" that plays the role of law, that substitutes itself for law (it is called the *zakon* in Russian), but it resembles the Western law no more closely than a Chinese character resembles a Western letter.

Those who look at Chinese characters and pretend that they are letters are not going to learn Chinese. Characters must be learned as characters; *zakon* must be learned as *zakon*, not as a "weird law." Russia must be examined as it is and for what it is, and not in comparison with anything, as if making a catalogue of features that are either "weird," "lacking," or "incomprehensible."

People who live in Russia and love it are well aware of its negative, scary, revolting, and desperate features. These people see the lawlessness, envy, poverty, disregard for human life, and lack of citizen participation in determining the fate of their own country. Intelligent Russians do not need westerners to point all of this out to them. They want to change Russia, to make it better, but not to abolish or forget Russia as if it were some kind of a nightmare. Russia has a wonderful soul, a unique history and culture, a unique voice, and a very special place in the world. It also must be emphatically noted that even though Russia may be lacking something, its huge size and its history full of military victories and great achievements indicate that Russian society is fundamentally viable, a society that has learned to compensate – indeed, some would say overcompensate – for whatever it may be lacking. Here is one major theme of this book: Russia is a lose/lose society, and yet, it is viable, at times even successful.

On the other hand, today Russia is in a fight for its survival, and it may well go the way of Byzantium before our very eyes. If that happens it would be an irreplaceable loss for all of human civilization. This is what makes the recommendations we are trying to develop so very important.

TOO MUCH LAND

Russia sits on an enormous landmass, which in the past was largely covered by forest. The ancient Russians practiced slash-and-burn agriculture, where an area of forest was burned down, cleared, and the land was fertilized with ash. Such a plot was good for one or two harvests, but then people had to move on to clear another plot. There were enormous expanses of land, and a resource that seems limitless is usually free: price is a measure of scarcity. Moreover, land did not have permanent value, becoming useless after one or two harvests. Thus the concept of owning a piece of land was out of place. Instead, "ownership" was a consequence of use: if you are using it, in this case a plot of land, well, we'll assign it to you. This concept is very important because it conflicts with the permanent nature of ownership.

Slash-and-burn agriculture was very labor intensive, and the effort involved in clearing forested land counted for much more than the land itself. The key here was labor. As the population was small, and human labor was very valuable, the chiefs were keen on "capturing" it. Thus, the concept of land ownership did not develop, while the concept of slavery or other forms of "capture" of labor became the foundation of economy.

As late as 1861, a measure of a nobleman's wealth was the number of "souls" (indentured servants) he owned, not the acreage of land that he had title to. In Western Europe the situation was exactly the opposite: the foundation of the economy was ownership of plots of land. Land rights were well protected, and people were free, as if defended by the mere possibility of land ownership.

Slash-and-burn agriculture also meant that one should migrate, building new temporary housing each time, instead of building a permanent house. Russians settled in a particular place much later than West Europeans. And that is also very important: every place has its rules, "the way things are done here" - there is no law without a place where it is being practiced. But the Russians could not stay in one place, and thus could not develop law the way West Europeans did. To this day, Russians "carry their law with them, the way a turtle carries his house". We will note that Russia denies individual rights, tries to subordinate the individual to the collective; yet in Russia the law is not the same for all, as the application of law depends on who you are.

In Russia, the houses were wooden, not the stone ones like in Western Europe. It often happened that a wooden house would burn down (the wood burning stove with a proper smoke stack being a relatively recent invention), and the unlucky owner would escape with nothing more than the shirt on his back. And that meant that ninety percent of a person's wealth was in the goodwill of his neighbors. Will they build me a new hut when I shudder on the snow next to the ashes of my dwelling, will they let me to move in with them, will they lend me a coat? That was the question, and it still is, even though today Russians live in reinforced concrete apartment buildings. Proof positive that genetic memory goes back hundreds of years.

In ancient Russia, the prince owned everything, and not because he happened to be "wealthy" but because he was the personification of law, and therefore had to control everything and everybody – for the same reason that in the West everything and everybody is subject to the law. And from that it follows that it is the relationship with power that allows you to use a given piece of property, so this relationship is much more important than actual ownership. Needless to say, it is so to this day. Russian law used to be the tsar, and today Russian law is Putin.

By contrast, for the last thousand years, Western civilization was based on the principle of inalienable ownership. Property could be taken away, but this was not an easy thing to do – it was the exception rather than the rule. Even the king could not simply confiscate the land of a poor tiller: the king had to have a "reason" for that. In Russia, once the Strongman takes away his good disposition, your property flies out the window with it: confiscation of any and all property or rights is accomplished by a simple frown.

You cannot be sure that Ivan Ivanovich will be your friend forever. When we started drinking, he was; when we finished, he was not. That is why a Russian businessman does not need to obey the law, but he absolutely must go fishing with the prosecutor.

THE RUSSIAN CONCEPT OF OWNERSHIP

As Russia has no concept of private property, property is "suspended in mid-air" by the conflicting claims of possession that surround it from all sides. As a result, possession of any property can only be temporary and conditional.

First, an "owner" must repel all other claimants. A Russian owner must be willing either to personally defend his property, to hide it, or to present it as unattractive. When I was a first grader in Moscow, the first thing everybody would do at lunch was to take a quick bite of his sandwich, so that it would not be snatched by anyone else. To "possess" property, one should make alliances with Strongmen who can offer protection. And that means an immediate transfer of certain rights to this property to those same Strongmen, so full ownership of property in the western sense of the word would not last long at all.

What I am describing is similar to the behavior of hyenas. They kill an animal, but as soon as they start eating it, they can easily have their tails bitten off by their fellow hyenas. Were it not for the strict hierarchy that exists among them, more blood would be shed at the dinner table than during the hunt itself. It's the same in Russia.

Only after protection is secured can the owner try to quickly squeeze from his property everything that has any value. In the West, people get a plot of land and then plant an orchard on it. It is worth noting that in the West most of the land is inherited, while in today's Russia almost none is. In Russia, those who take upon themselves the pain of land ownership must first build a fence, then bribe some officials, and only then, if there still is any time or strength left, plant potatoes that will have to be guarded around the clock. And after the harvest is in, one will have to deal with the murderous envy of less successful, less industrious, or simply wiser, more far-sighted, neighbors. Many neighbors, who were smart enough not to plant their own potatoes, have saved up a lot of energy to fight for the ones I have planted, watered, fertilized, and harvested. As I carry the harvest home, they meet me outside with a knife, fresh, ready, and hungry. As for the orchard, it gives its first fruits in ten years, and in Russia no one has the wherewithal to hold back the siege for that long. Nor would anyone put any effort into the long-term improvement of property that is only conditionally his. Just like America, Russia is the Land of Opportunity. Only Russia's name is a little longer: it is the Land of Opportunity That Is Too Dangerous To Take.

What you have you cannot use; you can only grab something that belongs to someone else. That is why Russia has so much territory; that is why this territory is in such bad shape.

From that terrible feature of Russian civilization comes its best feature. Russian culture is not materialistic and not firmly grounded, but changeable and fluid. It is searching not for a material object to hold on to but for feeling, emotion, or spiritual connection. The Russians praise what they see as the spiritual basis of their society; they have adapted to their way of life, and feel that they have much to lose from the transition to capitalism, which they wrongly perceive as materialistic and soulless.

If there is no law, there must be something that plays its role. And what we have here in place of the law is an envy-based comparison attempting to determine what is "fair". There are envy-based methods of social control, such as the racket, various barriers to trade, and high taxes. There also are temporary personal alliances founded on the rule "you are who you know", and two ingredients that are most important here: chance and change.

Here is the crucial difference between Russia and the West: Western civilization is based on property, on hard soil, on a brick house, on a leather-bound law book, and as such it is *hard.* A German knows "how it should be" because he can touch it or look it up in a law book. In Russia, everything is *soft and changeable.* Since there is no protected private property, there are no hard rules, and the Russians hope for a fat chance or go for a big change. In a word, Russia is different.

WHAT KIND OF LAWS HAVE YOU GOT HERE?

Let us compare the map of Russia to the map of Holland. Could it be that the map of Russia has something to do with the Russian national character (and thus would help us to understand it), while the map of

Holland might have something to do with the Protestant ethic and the Weberian spirit of capitalism?

Holland is tiny and densely populated. In such a country, what would be the prevailing attitude toward the law? If people live so close together, they all have to follow the rules that make their common survival possible.

A Dutch punk throws a banana peel on the sidewalk: "I've had it with your external order, I feel strangled by your ever-present rules! I need a little freedom!" And yet, he knows that the peel will be picked up and disposed of properly, so that nobody is likely to slip on it and get hurt.

Each particular individual in Holland has rules to follow; the individual is not free, but society is. You are not allowed to throw a banana peel on the ground, but your city is clean. You get freedom from garbage, but not the ability to dispose of your personal garbage the way you see fit. Citizens of Holland are bound by laws head to toe, but theirs is a free country.

Russia is huge and sparsely populated. What if people lived so far apart that whatever they did would not seem to affect others? The idea of creating and adhering to the Law of the Land would then appear redundant. Russian law is simply an attempt to answer the question, "Who are you, where have you come from, and what do you want?" Russian law is strictly personal, and is based on exception as firmly as American law is based on precedent.

I think that the custom of using a given name together with a patronymic (your father's name) is directly related to that. If Victor Ivanov walks down the street, it is not clear where he comes from and whether he has a defender. So we can go and kick his ass. But if he is Victor Petrovich Ivanov, then the situation is different. He is the son of Peter Ivanov, and is defended by all the connections and alliances that Peter Ivanov had established. In this case, kicking Victor's ass could backfire. Indeed, in many parts of Russia it is customary to call people exclusively by the patronymic, the most important part of their three-part name. People are called by the name of their best protectors, their fathers, because there is no better protection to be had - and because what everyone needs is protection. This is certainly not unique to Russia, as every Mr. Peterson would agree: but Mr. Peterson has long since acquired another protector, the law (we can say that Peterson's "patronymic", his protector, is the word "Mister," which is also a part of his name), while Petrovich can only depend on the help of his kin.

In Russia, the law exists to oppress. The stronger you are, the more you can turn the law to your advantage, while the weak and powerless have no recourse. In the West, the law offers equal protection to all citizens, but it was created to protect those who find themselves in a position of weakness.

President Clinton was impeached (and then acquitted by the Senate) for lying about a personal matter. American law is clear: no citizen can lie to a judge. President Yeltsin shelled the Parliament without asking anyone's permission, and he was not even censured. Russian law is clear: the higher your position the more you can disregard the law. In Russia, the law is custom-made to whoever you are at the moment. If you are up, you can do whatever your position allows, if you are down, you are in a prison cell, beaten up, and cannot even get a glass of water. To go from the former status to the latter sometimes takes only a minute.

What Law of the Land can there be if you do not see anyone else, and in every direction, there's nothing but trees and grass? Trees, grass, and the sky above your head – could it be that you are a god? I realize it sounds overblown, but it would really help you to assume that the Russians believe themselves to be gods. Read on and you will understand what is meant by the word "gods," and the book will eventually convince you that the Russians are indeed such "gods". Right now, don't get scared by this word, and you will soon see how useful it is in our effort to understand the Russians.

Indeed, the first thing to do, as a god, would be to ensure for yourself total personal freedom unrestrained by any laws. In the city, I throw a banana peel right on the sidewalk. I am free, I am bound by no law; I live in a garbage dump and do not care. There is a good Russian expression, "The law was not written for me!" But others are gods, too. One assumes that the passerby's own divine powers will prevent him from slipping on the banana peel and falling, so no harm will be done. This is where the famous Russian *avos,'* meaning "hopefully," comes from. But what if you do fall? Then, it is either "A broken leg won't bother a god'," or "It serves you right, you devil".

In Holland, everyone looks at the punk with disapproval the moment he drops the peel and then, in three seconds, the peel is picked up and disposed of; thus, the result of the punk's infraction is nil. In Russia, sometimes it seems that only burning the offender at stake would impress others enough to make them observe the rules, and then only for three seconds.

The law is always connected to a certain territory where it exists, otherwise known as a jurisdiction. When someone breaks the law, the first thing that law does is to restrict this offender's freedom to move, as if saying, "You are where this law is in force." Holland is small, and there is nowhere to run. Thus, if you go somewhere, the situation is not likely to change. And so, you submit to rules and to laws. The result is that the law is permanently there. In Russia, the situation has always been different. If you did not like the way things were going in a particular area of the country, you could just move a thousand kilometers away, still remaining in Russia but no longer susceptible to the offending regulation.

OWNERSHIP WITHOUT POSSESSION, OR THE REASON BEHIND TERRITORIAL EXPANSION

When you have property, you stay put, and when the law is not arbitrary, you do not have to run away. But when you have nothing to tie you to a place, when you fear for your life but can do nothing about the legal system or about your rights, you do try to run away. Could this be the reason why the urge of the Russians to extend their borders was so much greater than that of their neighbors, so that the Russians eventually came to spread over such a large territory? We again come to the question of land ownership: when you can't have your own, you can never have enough.

Usually, people first civilize the heartland of their state, and then try to spread further. In Russia this is also the case, but to a much lesser extent. The Russians were afraid to stay in place as there was no rule of law, and left their heartland almost as underdeveloped as the new territories they moved into. Very old cities still have unpaved roads and wooden houses as if there hasn't been not enough time, for the last eight centuries, to do the roads and the houses right. Wherever you are in Russia, it seems that people have either recently settled or recently left.

If you visit a Russian wheat field, you a likely to find a huge boulder stuck in the middle of it. Why didn't anyone haul it away, during all these years? If it were Germany, this boulder would have been taken away eight hundred years ago, broken up, and used to build a house. In Russia, the boulder is still there; the peasant hut beside it is made of wood, and is already in need of repair.

If we compare a street in an old German town with a street in a Russian town of roughly the same age, we will see that the German street shows ten times the amount of human effort: stone houses, paved streets, cozy cafes, fresh paint. A Russian poet said, "We do not know our country, and our footsteps are not heard". It is like trying to reach through a glass window: since the Russians cannot own property, they cannot touch and feel their land.

A German house is built for eternity; a Russian house looks as if it was built in a way that the owner wouldn't mind abandoning it. But the Russians also care about eternity: there is a half-rotten fence around the hut so as to impede those who would try to steal some radishes, and on this fence we can read a carving of "Ivan loves Maria", or something less readily quotable.

LAW AND LAND

What if there is no law to protect your property and, as a consequence, you have no property? That would mean that you could move freely, but the state cannot allow that because otherwise there would be no one to harvest the crops and to pay taxes. Thus, the state had to tie its citizens to a particular place by force. We see that in Russia serfdom was a direct consequence of the lack of protection of private property. In the West, there is no need to attach you by force as it is your property that ties you to a particular place.

Running away from the law, to a place where this law does not apply (and yet, a place that is still located in Russia) is a major theme of Russian history. There is absolutely no notion that the law is set "once and for all". As a consequence, there is no notion that the laws are set for everyone. In Russia, a soldier does not follow the law if the captain does not see him, and this law is not a law for generals.

The Russian heartland is at the crossroads of entirely different cultures and religions: from Germany to China, from India to the Polar Cap, from Turkey to Sweden. It is not surprising that a Russian was the first man in space. Russians live between the Germans, who live in the same house for three hundred years, and the nomadic Mongols, who have never had a permanent house. The Russians have found a compromise: they live in one place, but own no property. Russia's unique culture and national character come from that: there is nothing to restrain the emotions, there is no limit, friendships and relationships count for more than anything, there is a reckless bravery because there is nothing to lose, there is envy because people do not have their own space, and as far as the western idea of law and individual rights, it has no cultural basis whatever. Instead of technical and impartial law, instead of blind Femida, there is a great literature and a very emotional heart, vacillating between total forgiveness and great cruelty - and all the time actively disliking the middle. Moderation is one quality that is distinctly un-Russian.

Russia never had good laws because in Russia no one is willing to admit that the law is written for him. The law is a genuine orphan, and nobody cares what it says. Those who write the laws are in power, and thus are exempt from laws. Their reason for writing laws is to keep the ordinary people enslaved. But the intended subjects of the law do not much care either. They have never been consulted, and feel that laws are a given, something akin to the weather. These people intend to rely on their hiding skills, connections, luck, or their readiness to run away.

When you own the land you are like an oak: you are strong, deeply rooted, you know the neighborhood and are known to it, you are respected, but you are also exposed and stationary. If you have a house standing on your land, you want to be in charge of the surrounding territory, and you insist on good and fair law.

If you are not an owner, it is not clear on what grounds (pun intended) you are trying to impose your will. You are excluded from the process of making the law, yet you are subject to it. Since you cannot influence the laws, you count not on laws but on personal connections to prolong your tenuous hold on property.

Property you do not own does not tie you down. Russians consider themselves free as long as they can run away. For them, the law simply states, "Do as we say and if you don't like it – leave". In these circumstances, running away becomes a real option. "The law is bad, to hell with it:" this is the Russian conception of freedom.

Since running away was the only salvation, people were very interested in expanding the territory where they could run while at the same time staying within their own linguistic borders and among their people. Russia is the largest state on Earth, but it did not grow that large because it was strong and advanced: it was expanding like steam in a kettle, because people couldn't stand the heat of lawlessness and wanton oppression. Indeed, the Russians were able to colonize territory that was practically unfit for human habitation – but Russian laws were still worse, and people relentlessly pushed deeper and deeper into Siberia. About Siberia, the Russians had a saying, "Here, the untamed forest sets the law." Harsh as the Siberian forest was, the Russian State would somehow always make sure that for free thinkers it was a more attractive option: those who wanted to freely work the land, those who wanted to worship as they saw fit, those who talked too much – all went to Siberia by themselves, and many of those like them were brought there in chains, with their backs bearing the marks of a whip. If it were not for Siberia, Russia could have been more democratic, as Siberia has always served as the place where the steam could escape.

Why has Russian law always been so cruel? Because even if the law were good, it probably would not be followed: the law is not written for gods. That is why the sanctions for breaking the law are so harsh: it takes a real threat to scare a god. And then, for a buddy, an exception can always be made. On the one hand, the Russians have bad laws and cruel sanctions, on the other, exceptions and excuses. Who can be blamed for not following a law that is both inhumane and arbitrary?

The Russian peasant had nothing that was his own, and that meant that he could run away. But the wheat needed to be harvested, and that meant that the peasant had to be enslaved. Note this paradox: a bountiful harvest should mean happiness, freedom, opportunity, and wealth. But for the Russian peasant, a bountiful harvest was a curse: it meant stricter measures to make sure the slaves would not run away, and the greater the harvest, the more work for each slave.

It seems that land or real estate serves as a skeleton for the body of law, with the law growing on this unmovable ownership like meat on bones. If people own land, laws appear; if there are laws, there are rights. If there are land, laws, and rights – you can make enough to support your family, and that brings independence and allows you to put down roots, to become what is known as a pillar of society. In Russia today, society has no such pillars, as those who "own" property are afraid that the conditions of ownership would be revoked should they decide to speak up.

If there are no landowners, there can be no permanent and just law. When you fly to Europe from the US, you fly over Canada, but that does not give you the idea that you should write Canadian laws. You cannot write a just and fair law unless you commit to stay and observe it yourself, and only real property can give that commitment.

If there is no land ownership, the law cannot be just. If the law is unjust, people will not be willing to observe it. If they are not willing to observe the law, the law must have cruel sanctions. Cruel sanctions do not make this law any more just, fair, or adequate: they simply add insult to injury. If there is no land ownership, and law is both unfair and cruel – people want to run away. The state cannot allow its citizens to run away, and thus, using the fact that the law is overseen and protected by no independent body, tradition, or precedent, the state changes the law at will to subjugate people still further, to take the shoes away from those who are thinking of running away. This is how we get slaves. The slaves work the land badly because the land and its fruits belong to their oppressor. Their oppressor, in turn, is just a conditional owner interested in squeezing out a quick profit, but not in developing the land. Thus, the land is not used properly, and the people who live on such land will be poor – and that comes on top of having no rights.

The expression "living conditions" allows us to make a nice play on words. You can have a nice coat, a felt hat, and a 1930 Ford car. All of these determine your "living conditions". But suppose you are a member of Al Capone's gang. So you put on your nice coat and your felt hat, get into your 1930 Ford, and go to meet the Boss. What determines your "conditions of living" now? Your relationship with the Boss. Your coat will not protect you if he decides to shoot you right in his cellar. In Russia, the expression "living conditions" has the latter connotation, not the former. Throughout Russian history, the Tsar's henchmen could, without explanation, confiscate the property of even the proudest nobleman and subject him to torture. Today this is done just as easily and just as arbitrarily: the tax police or the prosecutor's office have no laws to observe and no restraints, and they have virtually unlimited powers, provided the Boss gives them the order.

Today, there are "democratic" reforms in Russia. New "laws" are being written. They are written by an elected Parliament, and some are written at the suggestion of western experts. But laws are rules that owners promulgate for a certain territory, because on this territory they own property, own and not just "conditionally own". When you own, your concern is ownership; when you conditionally own, your concern is not ownership itself, but the preservation of conditions. If you own, your concern may be taxes, or environmental protection, or crime. When you have stolen and not yet been caught, your concern is how to bribe a policeman, how to dispose of your gun, how to color your hair and get a nose job, and none of these has anything to do with managing the property you supposedly came to "own". Democrats seem to be unaware that democracy was invented by landowners. But the Communists are aware of this, and they have been fighting against land ownership tooth and nail. This is why it was so important for the communists to destroy private farmers.

WHY DON'T RUSSIANS HAVE RIGHTS?

In Dostoyevsky's *Crime and Punishment* the protagonist, Rodion Raskolnikov, asks, "Am I a miserable creature or do I have the right?" And the right that he meant, of course, was the right to calmly kill other "miserable creatures", as he could think of no other right. Let us reread this question as it holds the key to the problem we are discussing. "Am I a miserable creature ***or*** do I have the right?" Please note this "or" very well: in the West one can be a miserable creature indeed ***but still*** have the same rights as all others. It is to "miserable creatures" that rights are granted, so that all of us can enjoy them. In Russia, a law-abiding society is impossible because miserable creatures are not deemed to be worthy of anything, and do not themselves believe that they deserve or need any rights, either because they still hope to prove their godlike nature, or because they have miserably failed to do so.

In the West, it was the bourgeois who grew strong enough to demand, and to be granted, the rights that they needed. In Russia, that would seem like a contradiction: if you are strong, then why do you need rights? Is not it that your strength allows you to do anything anyway? To get rights, you need to become stronger, but once you are strong, what do you need rights for? The Russian struggle is not for universal rights, but for exceptions: everyone only wants to say, "Nobody else can – but I can."

The Russian Attorney General once said, "I am all for violating the rights of suspected criminals." Here is his logic: what rights can you hope to have if you are even less than an ordinary citizen: if you are a criminal suspect? Tell this Attorney General that rights were invented specifically for criminal suspects, and he would have a heart attack.

LAW AND TIME

Here is a story I was told. The chief of the traffic police in the town of N. wanted motorists to follow the traffic laws. He ordered every traffic policeman in town to start writing tickets mercilessly, to all traffic violators, big and small. But the police could not work overtime for long, and in a few weeks the campaign ended. Soon after, the chief got a hysterical call from the local hospital informing him that the number of traffic accident victims coming in had greatly increased. You see, when the drivers of the town of N. were being closely watched, they followed the traffic rules. As a result, some pedestrians made the assumption that cars would not run red lights anymore.

After the traffic campaign was over, those simple souls were destined for the hospital. In Russia, if no one is watching over your shoulder, there is no law. The law has no time dimension because everyone is just a passer-by. By contrast, in the West law may well be the most permanent feature of society. What else is there in England as old as the Magna Carta? And the Magna Carta is alive and well.

WHICH LAW IS FOR YOU?

Here is the Russian legal framework: "If you are a god, you converse with other gods in order to find out, by means thoroughly divine, what would please the Supreme Deity. If you are a devil, then you have no business asking for (legal) protection from us gods."

There in fact exists a large body of written law in Russia. But the laws are not followed. Criminals disregard the law, and so do the police, ordinary people, businessmen, judges, elected officials, the government, the Constitutional Court, and the President. The law is followed only in the manner dictated by a particular situation. The uniqueness of Russia stems precisely from the fact that its entire legal code hinges upon two words: "It depends".

As there is no law in the country, each significant caste has its own law. The criminals may disregard State law, but some of them meticulously observe criminal law, called *ponyatia* ("method of understanding"). The high bureaucracy definitely has its own "legal code", which is profoundly different from the one they want ordinary citizens to follow. When a judge convicts someone of bribery, yet takes bribes himself and sees no contradiction, this is an example of the break-up and stratification of the body of law. The law in Russia is: "Tell me where you belong, and I will tell you which law is for you".

As the written law is only the "common" law, you should abide not by it, but by the law of your caste. As the "common" law exists to enslave and to control the downtrodden, it is both cruel and full of contradictions, the better to catch its prey. By following one "common" regulation, you are quite likely to break another, and if you try to follow all the existing "common" laws, you would not be able to do anything. In Russia, laws exist to separate gods from lower beings. Gods accomplish miracles, that is how the others know they are gods. Can you jump fifty feet in the air? A god can, because the law of gravity is not for him. If you can't jump that high it is because you are human, and for you there is a law that prevents you from accomplishing this feat.

In Russia everyone wants to be a god, not a human. Thus, if you are caught observing the law, it means you are a lower being, it means that you did so out of fear. The only solution is to pretend that you did so because you simply did not notice that the law existed, failing to break it by pure chance, or because you were trying to be extravagant. If you do not cross the street on a red light when there are no cars around, everyone assumes you are standing there only because you were struck by a sudden thought.

Russian law is contradictory and unfair, but it is not bad law: the law simply serves the social function of separating those who are not subject to any laws from those who are subject to all of them at once and are, therefore, permanently guilty. Again: in Russia, either you are not subject to the law or you are guilty; in the West, all citizens are subject to the law, and none is guilty until a court proves otherwise.

This is why the law is so badly formulated and is such a mess: those who pass the laws do not really care what the law is like, because should the need arise, they expect to be able to break it, not just with impunity but by flaunting and advertising the fact. Russian law is what it is because from the very beginning, those who wrote it meant to break it. And this law is cruel and demeaning because those who cannot break it are not thought of as worthy anyway: remember, a god can disregard the law of gravity, and humans are not worthy because they own no property.

In Russia, following the law is the mark of the most downtrodden, but for the sake of social cohesion, the laws are written in such a way that every citizen, no matter how low on the totem pole, can break at least some laws and get away with it. Take Moscow taxi drivers. The moment you get into a cab (and riders always sit up front, next to the driver), the cab driver says, "In a taxi, there is no need to buckle up." It is a privilege, you see, to go headfirst through the windshield if there is a collision: a right that is typical of the ones that the Russians have fought for, won, and now deeply cherish.

Even the most downtrodden can once in a while break some laws, and in so doing feel themselves to be "real human beings". Real human beings? No, gods, beings that exist outside the law.

In Russia, privilege is first and foremost a license to break the law. Here, "respected" means "able to break the law at will"; in the West, "respected" stands for "consistently law-abiding". The Russians define a right as a personalized, exclusive license to break the law, and rights are seen as opportunities to destroy and damage, not to create or preserve. Please reread the previous sentence as many times as it takes until you go "Wow!"

How do you think the western appeal for human rights is translated into Russian? A famous dissident, Andrei Sakharov, was a champion of human rights. And so, many Russians thought that being a member of the Soviet Academy of Sciences and a recipient of many awards, Sakharov was fighting for the personal privilege of disregarding censorship, for the right to break the law. In fact, Sakharov was fighting for a universal right to speak freely. But that was not understood: "What is a universal right?" If you have the might, here is your right; if you are a mite you do not need a right.

LAWS ARE MADE TO BE BROKEN

Every observer will tell you that Russian laws are contradictory and make little sense. But a western expert who then embarks on a crusade to make Russian laws logical and sensible will just betray his own lack of understanding. Russian laws are adequate and serve a purpose, the same way the giraffe's neck, though it may be too long for a professor of law, is exactly what a giraffe needs.

For those who can do anything, a violation of the law becomes a manifestation of their superiority, and such a violation is joyful. The law is contradictory on purpose, so it can be broken easily. Breaking the law is for gods, and so if a violation of the law carries a cruel sanction, it can only be significant for mere mortals, who have no business breaking laws.

And what would happen if a Russian lawmaker were to suggest a logical and fair law? The others would look at him with surprise: "It looks as if you are proposing a law that you yourself intend to follow. Do you plan to leave the government, or what?" Fairness and justice are not a part of the mission of the government in Russia: in Russia, government is in the business of subjugation. The Russian government takes upon itself no obligations before the people whatsoever: not to feed, not to clothe, not to defend, not to promote justice – none. The entire message of the government to the people is: "If you want something, it means you are alive; if you are alive, be thankful." The law is contradictory and illogical because its main task is to make sure that everyone who walks the street breaks one law or the other, and thus will be reluctant to protest.

American laws are written to protect people, and that includes protecting people from government; Russian laws are written by government to control people. I was once told, "I can commit any crime and will never be punished, because I work in law enforcement!"

Since Russian law is so personalized, it is very important to point out that before 1991 Soviet law schools were open exclusively to people who had cooperated with the KGB and/or held a significant Party or the Young Communist League position. Thus, the law students were likely to be the best connected, or the most corrupt, cynical, and immoral lot among the Soviet students. Today, these people are writing the laws, enforcing the laws, providing legal assistance to businesses, or teaching the next generation of Russian lawyers. This largely explains the catastrophic failure of Russian transformation to democracy. We have literally hired the wolves to promote the vegetarian lifestyle.

GET AN EXEMPTION OR SUFFER

Suppose we enacted a 55 mile per hour speed limit. This could mean two things:

No one goes any faster than 55 or

As no one can go any faster than 55, going at 150 is yet another privilege that we reserve for ourselves.

Russia is a textbook example of the second method of legal interpretation.

At the same time, ordinary citizens know that if they are singled out, they will be found guilty of one thing or another, so it doesn't matter what exactly the law says. What matters is not being noticed.

Take a moment to observe the work of a Moscow traffic policeman. There is, of course, a clear set of traffic regulations. Motorists tend to ignore them when there are no police around. But what if there are? The policeman does not stop those cars that break the rules: he stops the cars he feels like stopping. The driver comes out with his license, and a banknote folded inside. This driver meekly asks to be excused, but does not ask what he was guilty of and does not ask for a receipt. The cop takes the money and waives the car on. But some drivers do not need to pay: they show an ID and listen to the cop's profuse apologies, as one hundred and fifty miles an hour is not a speeding violation after all.

Let us recap what we saw:

If the policeman chooses to stop you (and no reason is necessary), you are automatically guilty, and you pay a bribe. If you argue, all kinds of laws and regulations (note their function!) will be produced to make you very sorry that you did not pay the bribe right away. And that means that the law exists to help those in power to commit the crime of extortion, and to force those who are powerless to commit the crime of bribery.

If there is no policeman around, you drive however you like. This means that there is no law at all when nobody is watching – and that is very bad, as the law has an extremely important function: it prevents conflicts and accidents, and fairly resolves those that do occur.

Regardless of what you might have done, if you produce a document that scares the policeman, he will apologize and wish you a good trip. And that means that the law is not the same for all: each citizen carries his law in his breast pocket.

If you display obvious outward signs of power (for example, driving extremely fast in a large black Mercedes), you will not be stopped at all.

Within his jurisdiction, a bureaucrat can interpret the law according to the whim of his bureaucratic superior. His superior tightly controls the bureaucrat, but the moment the chain of command breaks, there is total arbitrariness represented by the whim of the bureaucrat in charge.

A western bureaucrat who does not know what to do consults the law and follows it. A Russian bureaucrat who does not know what to do calls up his superior to find out what the superior's whim might be. At each point, the bureaucrat needs to take an agonizing decision on whether the buck stops with him.

That brings us to the particularly Russian dilemma between *poryadok* and *besporyadok* ("order" and "disorder"). "Order" means that each bureaucrat asks (or makes his best effort to divine) the whim of his immediate superior. That means that all decisions in the entire country can be taken solely by the President. (That is what President Putin calls the "vertical of power"). Even if the President were to work around the clock (and he is expected to know everything because he is the Supreme Deity, of course), there would still be total paralysis as Russia is significantly larger in terms of territory and population than a family with two children – and even there dad does not have enough time, or enough competence, to make all the decisions. Yet if everyone is allowed to follow their whims, there is total chaos.

Western law is comprehensive, clear, non-contradictory, and written down for everybody to see; in Russia, to find out what the "law" is, you must make an appointment. But Russian businessmen know that the worst thing is that in most cases you simply are not important enough to be told what the "law" is: once you're in jail, the warden will tell you. In business, the rules are often changed by fiat, but if the bureaucrat is your friend he can change the rules in your favor. The Russians have a saying about their law, stating the reality of Russian life without lament or any social commentary: "Prison and penury can befall you any day." In Russia, you can be indicted and convicted of anything, no matter how implausible, unless of course you have a passport from a NATO country or the home phone number of the Prosecutor General.

Russia is huge in territory, multireligious, and very diverse, and it has been huge and diverse for centuries. What is it that has held all these people together? I think there are two ingredients. One is fear. Fear of one's envious neighbors and of the arbitrary, envious, and vindictive Russian law. Russian society is held together by connections that people weave around themselves in an effort to get some protection. Another is a dream, a Russian dream of greatness, which is lofty because Russians are gods. The Russian dream is attractive because if America seeks to attain greatness through technology, Russians pin their hopes on what they call *podvig,* a superhuman spiritual achievement. The twentieth century will be remembered as one where the Russians had Stalin and the Americans had the Space Shuttle.

Today, citizens of advanced Western democracies have everything; but one thing is becoming more rare, and that thing is friendship. People are healthy and upwardly mobile, their property is secure, laws protect their rights, and they travel the world. Unless they are mountain climbers or scuba divers, they never truly find out that "a friend in need is a friend indeed". In Russia, the situation is different: without friends, Russians feel naked, exposed to the wind. And if you ask them what they have friends for, you will never hear the western response "to have good company". In Russia, friends exist primarily to save you: to bring medicine when there is no doctor, or to get you out of jail. A Western city with ninety percent unemployment, no social services and no savings would probably collapse: in Russia, where this is happening right now, people survive, because if a friend of a friend is guarding a potato warehouse, you get potato shavings for your soup.

Russian law is essentially the opposite of Western law, yet both the Russian and the Western legal systems successfully serve as a foundation for their respective societies. Russian society is based on the lose/lose principle of human interaction, and yet it is viable, functional, and cohesive.

While the Westerner attempts to protect himself by social action (filing a law suit, demonstrating, speaking out, going on strike), the Russian protects himself by showing ever more loyalty the harder he is squeezed. And the difference in terms of civil society is staggering: the worse the situation, the more quiet and "content" the population appears. In the West, a dictator faces an uphill struggle, but in Russia, should the government apply pressure, society appears to respond with, "We love it, give us more of the same."

Russian law is written in such a way as to be broken, otherwise the Russians would find it impossible to breathe. As the sanctions are cruel, the citizen, who was just turned into a lawbreaker, will be very obedient. Today in Russia we have a free market system, with millions of businesspeople. But since the law is written in such a way as to assure that every businessperson breaks the law and thus can always be convicted, the state is content: the situation is under its "control", it has established "law and order". With 100 percent Mutually Assured Criminality, the prosecutor can get anyone he feels like getting.

Russians have difficulty distinguishing between a law and a bear trap. They cannot conceive that laws are supposed to ease coexistence and cooperation, make people more secure and friendlier towards one another. In Russia, the law is what the general of a victorious invading army orders the frightened citizens of a just-conquered city. They see the law as a hovering vulture, not as a protective fence.

In Russia, the law is a fishhook with an opportunity dangling as bait for the inexperienced and stupid. When the Russians speak of laws, they cast themselves either as the hunted, or, should they happen to be the lawmakers, as the hunters. If you catch humans on your fishhook, you must be god; if you are writhing on a fishhook, you must be a worm. The population of Russia does not consist of people: it is made up of gods and worms.

LAWS ARE FOR HUMANS

In the West, people gradually and actually very recently realized that every human being has some worth. Maybe it was because of Auschwitz, maybe it was Jimmy Carter or Nelson Mandela, but there is now the realization that humans have value – a realization that was not there before.

Unconditional possession of private property by ordinary people is also a recent phenomenon, say two or three hundred years old. And only with private property possessed by ordinary people can we really talk of individual human rights, rights that allow commoners to force society to take them into account. If a person has nothing, it is hard for a society to enter into a dialogue with him. Such a citizen gets nothing from society, and in turn, society cannot ask him to fulfill his duties as a citizen.

In the West, an individual announces his existence to society at large by using his rights and his property. He then shows even greater strength and sophistication by accepting and publicly announcing his weaknesses: "I may be strong and independent, but still I am just a human being, and as such I need the protection of laws. Only under such protection will I be able to function normally. in exchange for this protection, I am ready to assume the responsibility of a citizen, of protector and defender of the law that protects and defends myself and others. If I am granted legal protection, I will develop myself, and others will also benefit from this development, as the law that protects me establishes between people a spirit of mutually beneficial cooperation."

The Russians would have none of that: no "weakness", no "protection", and no "responsibility". I think that this approach was best exemplified by life and deeds of Lavrenty Beria, Stalin's last Secret Police chief. For years, Beria was a god: he had his own kingdom of slaves, he could imprison or kill anyone, he even succeeded in getting an atomic bomb. And then one day he was shot like a dog, without a trial. And that is very logical: if you become a god, there is no way back to becoming a human, and if you are no longer a god, then you must be a worm. Beria did not even get a proper burial, and neither did Hitler or Lenin.

Now it becomes clear what kind of "gods" the Russians are. They do not have rights or the protection of the law: there are a few who are "above" it all and millions who are "below". By rejecting everything that is human scale, by not allowing for human weaknesses, the Russians turned themselves not into gods, but into slaves. To establish oneself as a human being, to accept the responsibilities of a citizen – for that, the Russians did not have enough strength. They behave like gods only because they are unable to behave like citizens. The Russians think, "If they abuse me, I will be able to bear it, or I may just fly away. Here, I have so many good books to read."

This explains one feature of Russia that is so striking as to defy any ordinary explanation. In comparison with the West, Russia is, and has long been, a cruel and inhumane country. Russians are educated, professional, and seem perfectly civilized. But a patient in a Russian hospital, a soldier in the Russian Army, an elderly person standing in line, and everyone else besides, on occasion, is treated cruelly or, at best, rudely. And this is not about to disappear: on the contrary, it is not even met with public disapproval. If you are a god, you would take cruelty as a sign of flattery, something like "We know you can take it", and if you are a devil, you deserve all the pain we can give you, and more.

Sometimes Russians treat strangers very kindly, going far out of their way for them, in a "we're all in this together" kind of fashion, and this again points to an inability to find the proper distance that exists between independent, self-sufficient individuals.

The Russians are fond of saying, "During the siege of Leningrad, people lived for 900 days on half a pound of bread-like substance a day, at forty below zero Celsius, and under constant shelling, and you're expecting a store clerk to be polite to you – you have no shame!" And this is an argument to be taken seriously. Russia is indeed populated by many people who have accomplished inhuman feats. People did survive the siege, and the war with Hitler, and the camps, and the lines, and the faces of their fellow metro travelers. Note that I am not saying that it was their recent history that made the Russians so rude: for the last millennium the Russians have been measuring themselves not against a human standard but against an absolute one. In the twentieth century the Russians brought their troubles upon themselves by, once again, reaching out for the absolute. In good or bad, Russia continues to reach for the extreme, unable to stop halfway and just be human.

The New Testament says that God sent his Son to the world as a Man. God could have sent his message Himself, or through a burning bush, yet, He selected a Man. And that means that for God, Man is a fitting vessel for His message. Yet for the Russians a man is unfit for anything: Russia's greatest poets were never recognized, the concept of human rights simply does not exist, and the law is a travesty. Russia is a very religious country, a very Christian country. But for the Russians, serving God means sacrifice, not service to others or glorification of humanity.

Russians who visit the West say that Westerners are not "warm" people. Westerners will smile at you, talk to you in a bar, but they would never share "the shirt off their back," as their friendship has definite limits. In Russia, friendship has no limits, and this feeling of genuine warmth and unreserved commitment attracts many westerners. Indeed, many westerners were healed by Russia and have found a new purpose here.

But this warm, kind, and compassionate country, which Russia unquestionably is, just recently killed tens of millions of its best citizens, and is conducting a cruel civil war right now. A contradiction? No, two sides of the same coin. In the West, every person is seen as having a private space that is off limits to strangers. In Russia, the individual does not have any private space simply because there is no concept of ownership, and that is why he will gladly give the shirt off his back to get the fleeting feeling of being protected by this link to others. Yet, if all a person has in terms of protection is the goodwill of (envious) neighbors, that person can be easily destroyed. People are not the law (in the western sense of the word): people can forget or betray, they can get scared, or they can just go shopping, and the bad guys could come after you at this very moment.

One Russian guy I knew was very well protected: he had the phone number of a general. So when the police arrested him for hooliganism, he was not scared. But the general was on vacation abroad, and no one answered the phone. So the poor guy found himself in jail, beaten black and blue for insisting that he had to make this one phone call. But he still does not agree with me that the Miranda Rule is better than the phone number of a general. The general will come back. Then this guy will be able, for example, to rape a girl he met on the street, and then call the general, and the police will let him go. Sometimes the guy may suffer because western laws are not protecting him, but there is no protection for the girl either. If she can't run faster than the guy, or call a general of her own – she is out of luck.

In Russia, people will lend you their last ruble, and if you are attacked may risk their lives protecting you. Individuals get no protection, but instead there is a "community of all people, united by a single purpose", a social unit, known in Russian as *mir*. Thus, individual Russians often behave in a way that shows that their goal is not personal success, but a universal harmony, a feeling of spiritual oneness with the other members of the community. The idea of the spiritual oneness of all people, a core idea of Russian Orthodox religion, has played a very tragic role in Russian twentieth-century history.

If Russian civilization were to define a person as a respected entity that needs to be supported and protected, Russian daily life would not be so cruel. But Russia simply has not discovered the concept of "person" yet, and as cruelty is defined only in relation to persons (I have killed cockroaches, and am not ashamed), Russia is not a cruel country.

It is exactly like the campaign against wearing fur: one day killing foxes for fur was considered natural, and then some people came to define it as cruel. The Russians simply have not yet come to define the individual human being as an entity deserving special consideration: humans have characteristics, the way roaches or horses have them, but no special place in the Russian heart.

And the most important thing here is not that the Russian thinks other people can be treated like dirt: it is that he accepts that by virtue of being merely human, he himself can, and probably should, be treated like dirt. The problem with the Russians is that none really feels that they deserve better, no one protests that their government treats them as an occupying army would.

Democracy is a society of people who came to think of themselves as worthy of rights, and therefore fought to get the rights they have, and fight to have their rights preserved and expanded. As Russia is populated with people who have not yet realized that they deserve any rights, it is difficult to make western-style democracy the basis for Russian society.

Westerners living in Russia are often confused because of their inability to make a sharp distinction between the concepts of "law" and "power". They think that power flows from law. In the West, the President has power because he was lawfully elected, and the law both allows the President to do things, and directs that whatever he does should serve the interests of the people. But Russia is a country of power, not a country of law, and the law simply serves to explain why the power is always right. Since that is so, power has no limit. Its subjects suffer and try to escape; to combat that, the power becomes more cruel; to become more cruel, it has to be even more arbitrary. While the level of cruelty and arbitrariness in Russia tends to increase, there is no gain in manageability. The tug-of-war goes on until one of the warring parties, the power or the people, simply disintegrates, and then there is a general breakdown.

WHO ARE YOU?

In Russia, you do not have to look at how things should be by law, but you should carefully study the correlation of power, knowing that the strongest always wins. A cheetah may catch an antelope, but then a lion may come along, and it will no longer be the cheetah that is having dinner.

As the function of Russian law is to help the strong subjugate the weak, even a strong person needs alliances. If an American enters a bureaucrat's office, he says, "Hello, I am Peter Johnson", but if a Russian enters a bureaucrat's office, he says, "Hello, I am from Victor Ivanov". "Oh, if you are from Mr. Ivanov, you can come in, indeed," says the bureaucrat, "and how is Mr. Ivanov's health?" In Russia, you cannot even go by your own name: you are a nobody unless you a member of an alliance, in this case you are just "one of Ivanov's guys". But if this is so, how can we talk about individual rights, which are the basis of every democracy? Ivanov's gang has a "right": Mr. Petrov himself has given them permission to control all the hot dog stands in the city. But this is not a true right, as the rights are given to all citizens equally. And how can you write a democratic constitution if most of your citizens do not really have their own names?

A SUPERHUMAN EFFORT

In Holland, if you decide to plow your field, you go ahead and plow it: it's only a thousand square feet anyway, right? In Russia, you have a field the size of Holland, and the decision to plow it takes some spiritual strength, even for a god. So what do you do? You either do a godly thing, such as daydream or drink some vodka, or you collect all your superhuman strength, and actually do it. In Russia, you will see a landscape that is adequately described by this paradigm: it is either a complete wasteland, or a huge super-project.

Westerners are bound by commonly known rules and regulations, and that allows their society to be free. Russians tolerate the rule of no law over them, they are complete anarchists, and it is possible to keep them in line only with a combination of cruelty and arbitrariness. When the Russians find themselves living under such a regime, they start looking for instructions that, in this context, are no less than instructions on how to survive. Only the logistical challenge of day-to-day survival can hope to control anarchic Russian gods.

The essential difference between Russian and Western culture stems from the aspiration of almost every Russian to achieve "greatness", to rise high above it all. Here, being "great" does not mean being a superachiever, it simply means "one who disregards the small". This is a striking contrast to Westerners, who are usually content to use the normal human scale as the measure of their interests and achievements. They may live well or very well, be successful or very successful, somewhat spiritual or quite spiritual. But for a Russian, the human scale of interests and achievements is deeply embarrassing. Because of this, some Russians do indeed achieve greatness, but the great majority, feeling themselves unable to achieve it, lose any respect for themselves, opt for no effort at all, or try to achieve greatness in evil.

Many Russians drink themselves to death, and the average life expectancy of Russian men is the lowest in Europe. Could it be because Russians unconsciously set for themselves a task that is much harder than the task of average Westerners?

And here we again come to laws. There are some small animals that attempt to scare their adversaries by appearing larger: cats can make their hair stand on end, and there are gerbils that can suddenly grow huge red ears. It may be that Russians feel the need to appear larger than life because their laws offer them no protection.

The Russians feel that they had their wings cut off, while people in other cultures feel content to live without wings, and are therefore more successful than the Russians in building all kinds of "flying devices" – devices that simply make their lives easier and more comfortable, devices that only a god would spurn.

The Russians attempt to achieve greatness, but this task requires more strength than they have. In the West, people tend to accept who they are and set themselves a task they can achieve. For them, pretending to be larger than life is not a condition necessary for physical and mental survival. In Russia, setting a task you know you can't achieve is simply a method to avoid doing whatever is achievable.

The Russians have very often succeeded in actually doing what nobody thought possible. But the Russians have also failed to do what everybody else assumed was doable ages ago.

Since they are gods that live forever, Russian chronology all mixed up: Russia is correctly called an African country with nuclear missiles, Stalin used to take people whose minds were in the 21st century and turn them into 14th century slaves. Today, Russia is in the process of converting to Orthodox Christianity, after the apparently failed attempt they made back in 988.

A god lives forever, and for him there is always tomorrow. That is why tomorrow is a cornerstone of Russian life. A Russian field that has been cultivated for centuries can have a boulder sitting right in the middle of it. If a German were to see such a field, he would be startled: "How could you have failed to take the boulder out: it makes it so much harder to plow!" Well, one reason is that Russians cannot believe it is really their field, but another reason is that there is always tomorrow. A German is human and lives but one life. For him, who lives in a house built by his great-grandparents, not to leave his son a well-kept field would amount to a disgrace that would be remembered for several generations. In Russia, no one was able to put down such deep roots:

nobles could easily be disinherited, and peasants were sold like cattle. In this respect, Russia is a country of great freedom: you can go a thousand miles in every direction and still be in Russia, and you also are not beholden to your family tree, especially now, when the granddaughter of a nobleman who served in the Communist secret police marries the grandson of a peasant exiled to Siberia. People come as if from nowhere in terms of history, geography, race, class, religion and social status, and they do not know how to relate to the country they live in.

Russia today resembles America in that it is genuinely classless, as people of all strata have equal access to wealth and positions of power. But the huge difference between these two countries is that America has its laws, and the laws establish and safeguard certain standards. In America, a person of mixed race or undistinguished origins can reach a high position in government, but this person cannot be a devil worshipper, a murderer, or someone who cannot put together a coherent sentence. Russia selects those who are cool under fire, unrepentant, cynical, loyal, and reasonably efficient – there are no other criteria.

NO STRENGTH TO BE HUMAN

A German who works the field considers himself a farmer, and knows that he will be judged by his harvest. He is a human who lives one life. A Russian god has many lives to live, simultaneously. A Russian who works a field is a poet, a thinker, a drunkard, a womanizer – everything but a farmer. The Russian probably has more varied interests than his western counterpart, but would resist being described by his profession.

A perceptive Russian writer, Vassili Rozanov, once noted, "Englishmen make good suitcases; in Russia, folk sayings are good." Here is how the Russians think: "What kind of a person would you be if you actually make good suitcases, if you put your mind to such a lowly task as suitcase making? A boring, narrow-minded one." A Russian who had the bad luck and permanent embarrassment of being a suitcase maker in real life would purposefully make bad suitcases. In doing so, he (in most cases, unconsciously!) would be saying: "Look how bad my suitcases are, me, a poet who has been put to suitcase making! Believe me, I pay these suitcases no heed at all, thinking of nothing but poetry! Okay, I do not actually write poetry, but I would, if I did not have to occupy myself with these goddamned suitcases... All right, I am an illiterate drunk, but at least my suitcases are bad; I may be a good-for-nothing, but at least I am not a suitcase-brain."

The "German" love for making good suitcases, German pride in craftsmanship, is one of the traits most foreign to Russia. To make a suitcase you could pack the Kremlin in – that is another matter. This is something for the Russians. Russian literature and art are obsessed with the theme of inhuman, overblown greatness. Alexander Solzhenitsyn is a good example. He fought in World War II, was arrested and sent to the camps, had cancer that was thought to be terminal, recovered, wrote books that made him world-famous, was arrested again, expelled from Russia, went on to write several volumes on the history of the Russian revolution, bitterly criticized the West, and then came back to Russia, touching down in the very Siberia he had become famous by describing, and immediately announced still more plans and projects. Would you not agree that the description of a life similar to this one could only have come from the classical Greeks, that Solzhenitsyn is a modern Odysseus or Jason? As for how "German" his work is, that is another matter. Are his statements well balanced and fair? Would his historical interpretation stand to scientific scrutiny? Most likely, not always, but that was not his aim anyway. The Russian way to open a locked door is to kick it in, frame and all. Using a key is not for giants.

As a practical matter, it seems that Russians would be most happy making a product perceived to be "the best in the world", though treating Russians as "blue collar workers", in the Western sense of the word, would probably be counterproductive. Work should be presented either as an achievement, or as a hard necessity that buys an exciting and fulfilling life outside of work.

On to the next characteristic of God. It is that God created the world in six days and rested on the seventh. A westerner plants an apple tree and gets a harvest of apples. If there are not enough apples, he plants again, probably a better tree, or more of the same trees. It is a never-ending story, and the result could always be improved. To the Russian psyche, this is very alien. In Russia, nothing is done step by step in order to achieve a limited goal. A Russian lies on his bed dreaming of the day when all people will have their fill of wonderful apples, knowing that as this is impossible to achieve all at once, it is better not to start. Many talented people do not start anything because of that. In Russia, the choice is clear: it is either the whole world or a long rest, and it is no surprise that the task of making the entire world over was indeed attempted.

There is form (how it should be) and there is essence (what there should be). Western countries are countries of form, while Russia is a country of essence, a country of the ultimate goal, which should be achieved regardless of the means. After all, Russia let half of its population perish for the sake of universal brotherhood. And there is no contradiction here: killing a person is form, therefore it is nothing, but what was meant (and this is the only thing that matters) was to have brotherhood.

Russia wanted to build a society based on the ideal of universal brotherhood. This didn't quite pan out. But this is not a problem: the Russians often have a problem with technical details, they're not Germans, after all. The point is to have a grand dream. It's the same with God. Surely, when God was making us, He did not realize we would be building Auschwitz or killing off the tigers: the idea didn't work out quite right, but it was a good try. The same with Russia. It was a good try, grand enough, and many Russians are willing to let the Communists try again.

The process is unimportant, but the goal cannot be lost. In the 1996 presidential elections, the Communist candidate took almost half of the vote. And this is after more than five years of constant discussion of Communist crimes in the media (to say nothing of the fact that the Russians lived out the Communist disaster). The Communist candidate never apologized for these crimes, he simply said that the ideal was good, and the next time around the Communists would do it better. The Russians bought the argument, in large part because they are accustomed to dreaming up an ideal rather than doing routine daily work. And this is very important, because this explains one of the reasons why the Russians have no law. The law assumes imperfection, and it calls for impartiality, for removal of personal preferences from the process of reaching a judgment. And this is not Russian at all: they say, "Why be imperfect: be perfect, and be as emotional as you can." In a Russian courtroom the suspect sits in a metal cage, so that the judge will not strangle him with his bare hands before the start of the trial, and 98% of all criminal cases end in a conviction. There is no due process (though it does exist on the books), while torture and falsification of all kinds are commonplace because a torturer can always say, “I was just being emotional, acting for the greater good of the country.”

Another quality of God is mysterious knowing, as God does not need directions. Here is how one Russian woman gives directions to her apartment: "When you come into the elevator, press a button that says '18'." Well, what do you think, how many stories does her apartment building have? "At least 18" would be the wrong answer. The building has nine stories, and the lady lives on the fifth floor. There just was no button with the correct number, but this does not bother the Russians: they get to her apartment just fine. And then, it is not the process that matters, but the goal. “Why don’t you change the button for the correct one?” you ask. “But you got here”, says the woman. A German would not have gotten to her place, but a Russian would, because a Russian can ignore reality, keeping only the goal in mind. For a German, a button with a wrong number on it would be an insult, but the Russians just follow the directions or their intuition. Many readers of the Russian version of this book faulted the text for “not being obscure”, thus minimizing the logistical challenge involved in understanding the book. Russians give challenges to one another as if to say, “I know you are a god”. How else would you explain a street with an open manhole and no warning sign whatsoever? It’s not that the Russians want you to break your leg: they’re just greeting you as an omniscient god.

Another feature of God is universality. A God does not carry a toolkit around, and neither do the Russians. The Russians never tire of pointing out that their beautiful wooden churches were built “with an axe only”, even though for some it would indicate backwardness, as there are many more useful carpentry tools. One distinguished Russian war veteran, a fighter pilot, philosopher, and writer, sang praises to the Russian Makarov pistol, stating that it was ready to function under any circumstances, never needing repairs or cleaning. You could also use it as a hammer or a bottle opener. The Makarov had only one drawback: it could not shoot straight. In the same breath, the veteran faults German pistols for being capricious and unreliable: “useful only for target shooting". Now, this is meant absolutely seriously, and we should not laugh, noting that if you use your gun as a hammer or a bottle opener, it is bound to lose its aim: the point here that the Russian gun was handy and reliable in many circumstances, while the German gun was good for one thing only. It should be emphasized that that writer fought for several years as a fighter pilot and came back alive, never having been wounded or shot down. In the air, he probably showed the Germans a few things they had never seen before.

Russian business contracts are written in exactly the same way. In the West, the contracts are between the Parties, and the responsibilities and obligations of the Parties are carefully listed. To sign such a contract, it is not necessary to be friends (and maybe better not to be), and after the contract is finished, the Parties do not turn into enemies, as conflicts are solved by the contract itself or by the courts. In Russia, there is only one question: "Ivan, are you my friend or not?" The relationship is much more important than the business reality, or to put it better, it is the relationship that is the real business. In a real business the benefits go to the producer; in Russia, the benefits go to those whose connections are right. And if a contract is simply an extension of a friendship, the breach of such a contract is a personal insult that calls for bloody revenge. You were wrong, Ivan, and now you are dead.

In Russia, crimes are often committed to finally bring justice (don't you wish there were fair laws!). As you are a god, people are rude to you so that you hear them better; they kill you out of pity, and take away your property to set you free. As you are a god, you should be able to take anything calmly, even your own unjustified execution, as no permanent damage is apparently being done. It is only later that the Russians discover, to their amazement, that the tens of millions executed, tortured, wasted, and sacrificed compatriots have chosen not to come back, laughing and showing their bullet-riddled bodies, even after the Supreme Deity stated that they were now "rehabilitated".

THE DRIVE TO ACHIEVE GREATNESS

Russia also differs from the West in the way that people formulate their goals. In the West, people start with whatever is good enough, and proceed from there. First they build a good house, and then, learning from their mistakes and benefiting from their experience, improve it. In due course, the house can be improved, enlarged, or even completely rebuilt, but there is continuity, a never-ending process of learning. People do not think themselves omnipotent or omniscient: they learn at their speed and on their scale. It should be noted that this method does not preclude greatness: on the contrary, it eventually makes it possible. There are several cathedrals that were under construction for seven hundred years – but look at them now.

Westerners plan their tasks on a human scale; they want them doable and achievable. If the first generation builds a simple house, the next generation adds a veranda.

The Russians start from the largest house their imagination permits, they start from an uncompromising ideal. Instead of building a comfortable house, they dream of a palace. But a palace cannot be built overnight, so they build a temporary hut. They move in to that hut, and, as building a palace requires some preparation and mental readiness, they end up living in this temporary hut all their lives. And of course, beside the hut there is, at best, no physical evidence of any preparations for building the palace. Why "at best"? Because often there is evidence of just such a preparation. No visit to the Moscow Kremlin is complete without a moment besides the Tsar of Bells, the largest bell of all times, that did not ring once, because it fell and broke as it was being lifted. The Cathedral of Christ the Savior, itself a huge structure, was blown up to make way for the Palace of the Soviets, that was to be the tallest structure on Earth with a colossal stature of Lenin on top. The architectural drawing of this structure shows planes flying below Lenin's head. The Palace was never built, and the largest outdoor swimming pool was fashioned out of its foundation. Khrushchev's time saw an attempt by a starved and impoverished country to be first in space, and indeed to compete with the entire western alliance for world domination. Brezhnev built the Baikal-Amur Trans-Siberian Railroad that was never used, while Gorbachev attempted probably the craziest thing in the entire history of Russia: an outright ban on the production and sale of alcoholic beverages. And of course, the greatest example is Russia itself: the ruins of the world's largest empire, the most far-reaching and the bloodiest revolution, and the near-successful attempt to destroy the entire planet. As the Russian saying goes, "Our midgets are the largest."

It looks like the westerner moves into his house forever, but in fact he is there only temporarily, as his house constantly improves, and may in fact grow to the size of a palace. A Russian moves into a temporary hut, built next to the construction site of his intended palace, but he ends up living in this temporary hut his entire life, while the palace of his dreams is never built.

The rapid industrialization of the thirties caused explosive growth in many Russian cities. The collectivization of peasant land made a job in the city the only way to avoid hunger. As the population of the cities grew, new housing was not being built, and that gave raise to the phenomenon of communal apartments, with thirty or forty people sharing the seven-room apartment of a pre-revolutionary doctor or engineer. The war only made this phenomenon worse, as entire cities lay in ruins. When Khrushchev came to power, he embarked on a huge construction program that aimed to give each family an apartment of its own. Brezhnev continued this project on an even larger scale, thanks to the influx of oil revenues. It should be noted in retrospect that nothing contributed to the eventual fall of the regime more than the housing program: as soon as people were able to close the door and separate themselves and their loved ones from the outside world, the normalcy of day-to-day human life would overtake and belie the collectivist communist ideology. But here's why I'm describing this: the apartment buildings built by Khrushchev and Brezhnev are crumbling and soon will start collapsing: they were built to stand twenty years, and some of them have been standing for thirty five years or more. Yes, they were built cheaply and fast, because so many of them were needed. That may be one reason why the concrete is crumbling and the pipes have rusted all the way through. But there is another reason: in the early sixties Khrushchev announced that "within one generation" full Communism would be built in the USSR. And under Communism, people were not supposed to live in cheap apartment buildings: they were supposed to live in Moon cities, fly to work on their own spaceships! And if so, why build housing that would last? The entire Russian housing stock today consists of these concrete "temporary huts" built next to the palaces that were not to be. Russian buildings built forty years ago are in a state of collapse, while the beautiful houses of Amsterdam, built four hundred years ago, are still functioning as if they were new. If Amsterdam were populated by Russians, all the money would be spent on building a bridge from Amsterdam to New Amsterdam, and the residents of Amsterdam would be living in cardboard boxes near the ruins of it.

But we are not just talking about the quality and the permanence of the dwelling: it is very important that a westerner accepts the housing he lives in as his, while the Russian cannot emotionally accept his home. A western house is neat and clean, and everything is in good order. In a sense, it is like a business suit: something you feel comfortable in, something you deserve to wear, and something you are going to be judged by. A Russian dreams of living in a palace, but lives in a temporary hut. For him, his dwelling, which is of course by far the most important personal possession of every Russian family, is like a prisoner's uniform, something that he is cursed with and refuses to own. To get a one-bedroom apartment, a typical family would wait for ten or more years, and/or pay a fortune for it. Imagine how desirable it should be! Yet the stairwell of the apartment building is covered with graffiti, full of swear words and hatred, the light bulbs are smashed with stones, everything that is plastic is burned with matches, and the elevators are broken. A Moscow apartment building populated by upper middle class professionals looks no better than a New York slum. And these are not punks or local hooligans: the people who live in a building simply refuse to identify with it. In the West, it is commonplace to attach one's name to the entrance bell, but in Russia this is almost never done: people are embarrassed. People live elsewhere, in their dreams, in their books, but not in their building or on their street.

Do you know what the Russians were doing while the Communists made a serious attempt to destroy the world? They were reading – Hemingway, Gabriel Garcia Marquez, you name it – they were not really there. They were not living in their apartments, and they were not living in their country. Whatever their country was doing had no relationship to them, exactly the same way as no Russian housewife is ashamed of the stinking entrance to her apartment building. But she is ashamed not to have Hemingway on her shelf. What dirty entrance? A god lives everywhere, and if you have Hemingway you can be a god and just fly away.

Russia is depopulated, empty as the Sahara. The statisticians will tell you that at one hundred fifty million Russia has more than half the population of the United States, and the cities are bustling, but in terms of their social impact, the people are nowhere to be seen. There are hundreds of thousands of homeless and abandoned children; yet the private citizens willing to help them number in the dozens (and of course, the state barely keeps these children on a bread-and-water diet). It is quite likely that Russia has the world's highest percentage of people who would say that their country is the world's worst place to live. Unless the Russians succeed in putting down roots, their country will remain ungovernable.

BEAUTY, HONOR, GREATNESS

What separates a human from an ape? A human studies the world around him, finds causes and consequences, and formulates definitions and theories about everything he sees. He gives the world a certain order, establishes what is "right" and what is not, and thus starts to consider the world esthetically, with whatever is "right" giving him satisfaction, and whatever is "wrong" causing him to feel anger or sadness. But what if something is more right than you expect? Then you experience joy, and as it takes place in the emotional sphere, it is called "beautiful", or more emotionally gratifying than the person expected. Beauty is an emotional surprise that something is better than one expected, and its impact is so strong that humans want it to be repeated.

Thus, when a human seeks to establish a certain order in the world, there appears something that is much greater than the satisfaction that everything is working out fine, and this is a sense of beauty. A primitive man can see a deer, and this is good, it means that his hunt will be successful and he will have enough food. But he can also feel gratitude towards this life-giving deer and appreciate the beauty of its movements or the round shape of its body. He draws this deer on the wall of his cave because this deer is beautiful. What did he do to deserve to see this deer, what kind of person should he be to see this deer again? Beauty is an uplifting esthetic surprise far beyond one's expectations; so much so that you feel you need to earn its repetition.

But how could that be done? To see something, you need to have good eyesight; to hear something, you need to have a good ear. But beauty is an emotion, and to experience that emotion you need to have a pure heart. The appreciation of beauty is a message from God: it tells a person his heart is pure. That is why those who cannot experience beauty seek to pretend that they do. This gives birth to kitsch, a substitute for beauty for those who lie to themselves and others, something that can help them get even farther away from themselves.

Since beauty can be appreciated only by those whose hearts are pure, people soon realize that to experience it again, to deserve it, they need to undergo a certain internal cleansing, to become "ready for beauty and worthy of it", or, in a word, honorable. A person can be "honored" for many things, and "honorable" is also a title, but that is not what I mean: my point is that only someone who is worthy and pure inside can justly be described as "honorable". In this sense, "honor" can be described as the internal purity necessary to find, appreciate, and be worthy of beauty.

As beauty always exceeds our expectations, widens our horizons, it allows people to expand their standards of what is good and right. As the standards grow, civilization strives for greatness, the highest standard of honor and beauty. As some individuals achieve greatness, the standards of civilization rise as well.

Thus, evolution can be said to proceed in three stages: Beauty, Honor, Greatness.

AIMING TO BE GREAT

Russian civilization has a very attractive distinguishing feature: it consciously sets out to achieve Greatness through Honor and Beauty. Western civilization is built to human scale, people there do not "set out to achieve greatness", they set out to be the best they can, and their neighbors usually do not interfere with the process. In Russia, the situation is different. Russian society gives an artist an incredibly heavy cross to bear, but the artist, oriented towards greatness from the start, often proves ready to bear this pressure, and sometimes turns into a diamond at the end. We can cite probably a hundred examples of this, just from this century. Solzhenitsyn is the first that comes to mind. He was just a young military officer, but Russia was not satisfied with that. It gave him an opportunity to visit the Gulag, to learn about life there, to take upon himself the task to survive and to tell the world about it, and Solzhenitsyn did it. Akhmatova was a promising young poet, but her writing improved considerably after the Communists shot her husband and arrested her son. A Swiss writer needs to wait for a sunset or look at flowers to see some beauty, but Russia gives its artists its horrible beauty by the truckload, and expects them to take all of it in. Many do. Russian culture was never stronger than in the period of totalitarian pressure, 1920-1960, and it may well have been the greatest cultural period the world has ever known, just a few men and women who were daily afraid of arrest. In literature, poetry, and music this period will never be equaled anywhere, because Stalin, the greatest artistic manager and enabler in the history of humanity, is dead.

Stalin fostered an official culture, manufactured by assorted toadies and hacks, but his real work was behind this curtain. He succeeded in scaring Shostakovich, Bulgakov, Platonov, Akhmatova, and many others to such an extent that they started to take energy directly from the stars. Stalin's "art management company" subjected Solzhenitsyn to such suffering that he admitted an undeniable fact: there was nothing he couldn't do, and indeed, after Stalin was through training Solzhenitsyn, Solzhenitsyn did ten lifetimes worth of work, and still continues working. The point here is that Stalin had the appropriate working material: the Russians, a race of people culturally and emotionally ready to be turned into diamonds, as they don't have to waste any time keeping their houses neat.

During World War II, the Germans experienced this phenomenon as well. First, the Germans quickly wiped out the entire Russian army and came to the outskirts of a virtually defenseless Moscow. But at that very moment of German near-victory, Stalin held a parade and made a short appearance. The German situation immediately became hopeless, and they lost the war! A moment ago, Russia was just a piece of soft pencil graphite, and then suddenly it was a diamond.

But the challenges of Russian life are way too much for most people, and many people just break. Among the Russians we see many people who are not content with "bourgeois" existence and yet cannot achieve "greatness," i.e. realization of their intended mission.

To put it in stark terms, when Yuri Gagarin was making the first ever space flight, he was a Russian who felt just fine, just like a Frenchman after a gourmet dinner. But space flights are not a daily occurrence, nor are they for everyone, and so the Russians suffer. This suffering has little to do with their material conditions, lack of rights, or whatever else a westerner could think of: the cause of this suffering is a yawning gap between the ideal of greatness and the grim reality of daily life, the undeniable and cruel realization of being merely human.

Suffering is a cornerstone of Russian life, and indeed of Russian religion, and the next logical step that the Russians make is to find greatness in suffering, to suffer greatly, or to help their neighbors to take this route. Russian Good Samaritans are often the ones who come to inflict suffering so that others do not stray from the road of greatness. As the Russians say, "We are here to make sure that your life does not taste like honey." Later, we will talk about greatness through suffering in more detail.

In this sense, Russian life is wider in scope than western life, as there are many heroes who were able to do the impossible as well as millions of those who are broken or lie to themselves.

The West had very many great people, but that was not because their society called upon them to be great, or caused them to make a choice between greatness and death. A great person in the West is mostly someone whom his society did not impede, who was free to develop, and whose development was far above the average. In Russia, society almost makes greatness a precondition for survival, and the initial crop of people with great potential is large. Then Russian society proceeds to break or destroy most of them. But the remainder, the few who defy death, sometimes achieve real greatness.

Why is it that in Germany, the streets are paved with stone and the houses are neatly painted, while in Russia there are dirt roads and ruins? Where is all this labor that in Russia is not in evidence? In Russia, most of the labor is destroyed to reach an unreachable goal. If you admit a thousand people into an aerobics class, in a year those thousand people will notice an improvement in their health. But if you force a thousand people to attend a school whose aim is to produce a hockey superstar, in a year you will have three hundred broken bones, two hundred concussions and three deaths. You may also have one or two good players, or you may not. But this is the bet that Russia is making, time and again. The Russians go for broke every time.

The Russians are not content to live their lives going for gradual but steady improvements: they constantly go for a revolution that ends in disaster. Most Westerners think that there were but two major upheavals in Russia in the twentieth century: a revolution in 1917 and the World War Two. But here is a list of them:

TABLE 1. RUSSIA'S TWENTIETH CENTURY

1905	Failed revolution against the Tsarist regime
1917	Tsar is overthrown (February revolution)
1917	Communist revolution (October revolution)
1918-21	Civil war, wholesale confiscation of harvests, widespread hunger
1923	New Economic Policy (small enterprises permitted)
1929	Collectivization, confiscation of land, prosperous peasants sent into exile
1932-33	Man-made hunger in Ukraine, Ukrainian peasantry wiped out
1936-38	Stalinist purges. Lenin's Communist Party members and Red Army senior officers are shot or sent to camps almost to a man
1940	War with Finland
1941-45	War with Germany and Japan
1945-52	Still more Stalinist purges, huge Gulag empire with millions of inmates
1953-61	Stalin dies, Beria is executed, Khrushchev delivers his "Secret Speech", millions of Gulag prisoners are released. Khrushchev's "thaw" delivers a profound shock to society.
1960	Khrushchev decides to plant corn instead of wheat everywhere; an agricultural disaster
1961	Khrushchev promises that Communism will be built within one generation, i.e. by 1980

1948-89	Cold war
1980-85	War with Afghanistan
1986	Chernobyl nuclear disaster
1985-91	Gorbachev's reforms, including a virtual ban on alcohol
1991	Putsch against Gorbachev, breakup of the Soviet Union, several regional wars begin shortly thereafter
1992	Gaidar's reforms, privatization
1993	Parliament is burned down
1994 to present	War in Chechnya
2000	Putin brings back the Soviet anthem, puts other branches of the government under his control

Well, this is twenty three (!) wars, revolutions, or huge disasters within one century, costing at the very least sixty million (!) lives.

Russia is a veritable boot camp for greatness, but you would not know it from the outside, as very few people actually succeed. Why not? Because Russian society is both aware of greatness as a real possibility, and an envy-based society, totally devoid of laws that offer personal protection. Once a talented person becomes known, almost a formal decision of the government to let him be (or not to be, as is most often the case) becomes necessary. This decision would offer personal protection, but at the price of obedience and censorship. And it is not just Lenin and Stalin who made such life and death decisions: we may recall Brezhnev's decisions to expel Solzhenitsyn or to exile Sakharov. It is only under Yeltsin that the Russian state stopped claiming outright ownership of talented people. It was a protection racket in the literal sense of the word: if you grew up talented in Russia and were not destroyed, you must have been protected, and your protector must have been the state; therefore, you owed the state your allegiance. In America, nobody says, "Here, by the grace of President Bush, go I." But in Russia, every single citizen feels the hand of President Putin on his shoulder. Today, the hand happens to be permissive, busy with other things; for some, it is even comforting and fatherly. But it is a hand on your shoulder, the hand of an unrestrained powerful man whom you personally do not know, and with this invisible hand you cannot walk. And of course, as far as business in Russia is concerned, this happens to be the Russian version of Adam Smith's invisible hand: whoever has the hand of power on his shoulder wins the "market competition" every time.

BEING GREAT VS. BEING NICE

The West does not force people into a superhuman effort, but it lets them be, and many people become successful of their own volition. These people have rights and laws that protect them from the envious. Moreover, at some point western civilization moved from merely tolerating talent to actively promoting and rewarding it. There are other ways, very elaborate and quite efficient, to combat real talent and to stifle dissent, but the talented people can often find their niche anyway. Many westerners are now financially independent, and they can do what they want without fear.

When an individual tries to achieve greatness, this is one thing, but when an entire country tries to achieve this goal, it's another: the results are the exact opposite. Beauty turns into nightmarish renditions of "equality" and "order"; honor is reduced to a desire to be "one of the guys", and greatness turns into a Big Lie.

Yet this desire to achieve greatness at any price makes Russian civilization worthy of respect; Russian civilization is impossible to like, but it's perfectly natural to love or fear it. Western civilization is likable and convenient, but it shuns strong emotions and thus becomes impossible to love. Adolf Hitler seems to be the only Westerner whom a western newspaper would describe as something worse than "very controversial" or "unacceptable", and Hitler cannot sue because he is dead. Western society demands no more from its members than to be fashionably dressed, tastefully undressed being also acceptable. If a Western man sees a woman being assaulted, the only thing that society demands of him is that he calls the police. The West aggressively demands that everyone in the world should be nice, and assumes that all conflicts can and should be immediately solved through a process of gentlemanly negotiations. September 11 showed that not all the guys who matter wear ties, and not everybody strives to make the world a nicer place.

The word "beautiful" is being replaced by words like "nice", "exciting", or "cool", and these words have nothing to do with beauty. Beauty is being replaced by convenience, a shallow emotion aimed at combating boredom, and above all, self-congratulation and self-gratification. This is not real beauty: indeed, most of the time, it is edible.

As far as honor is concerned, it has been entirely replaced by fame and money. But a rock idol cannot be "a hero": heroes are those who did not come back from Vietnam. With the notion of honor removed, women battle for "respect", while men see their duty as making money. These are blind alleys that destroy many lives. As the number of people who already have everything they could possibly think of buying goes up, this problem will grow even more acute. Without beauty and honor you cannot achieve greatness, and without greatness you feel you are missing something very important in your life.

Russian civilization has got it right: people were meant to achieve greatness. This could be the quiet greatness of parenthood or professional success, but a person must reach the level that would not have been reachable without beauty and honor, without love.

Russian civilization has beauty, honor, greatness, and love, but does not have private property. Some Russians feel that there is a contradiction between these four on the one hand and private property on the other, and our aim is to prove to them that it is not so. But our aim is *not* to convince the Russians to abandon the search for beauty, honor, greatness and love in favor of lawnmowers, designer jeans, 24-hour sports channels and pre-nuptial agreements. The Russians propose to us all the theory that human life has a higher purpose: let us not shout them down.

THE RUSSIAN ATTITUDE TOWARDS TECHNIQUE

Russia and the Russians can be described in a very few words: aspirations are *big*; the economy is based on *envy* (about which more later); law and personal relationships are *informal and soft.* Another extremely important term is *technique.* What is it? Technique is a set sequence of actions that allows us to accomplish a certain pre-determined goal. There is a technique that car companies use to build cars, and this technique is used to build every car that follows. Another example of technique is law as it is understood and practiced in the West.

Russian civilization has a very strong tendency to reject technique in favor of the attitude of the moment, or as the Russians say, "do as your heart directs you".

For example, there is a universal principle that guilt is determined only in a court of law. Until the verdict is rendered, all parties are supposed to suspend their judgment. But here is a typical quote from a Russian newspaper: "A young woman was assaulted and robbed today. In connection with this crime a young man was apprehended. The scoundrel told the police that he was just an innocent passerby unaware of what had happened. The lowlife came to Moscow by train." It is natural to wonder why we should have a trial if the newspaper has already convicted the poor guy. Indeed, this very newspaper has written many times that the police simply pick up those who look vulnerable and then torture them until they confess, all to improve their crime-solving statistics. Yet if you were to protest that the newspaper "convicted" the young man without a trial, the newspaper would respond that you condone crimes against women. Indeed, if an indictment is tantamount to conviction, what is a function of a trial? And indeed, 98% of all trials end in convictions, and almost all convictions mean a long jail term. Needless to say, all Russian investigations and trials grossly violate western standards of due process: police torture and falsification of evidence are widespread, and the suspect is usually convicted on the basis of his own forced confession.

I am writing this on a personal computer connected to the Internet. Yet I am aware, though it is hard for me really come to terms with it, that somewhere in the world men go hunting with bows and arrows. If I were to show them my computer, I suspect they would come up with a theory that hardly anything could be more silly than to bang on a keyboard all day, and that I should go with them to trap a monkey. The same could be said about the Russian legal system: it is as firmly based on the order from above and on somebody's personal decision as it was centuries ago (with the notable exception of the 1870-1917 period, even though the judiciary of the period showed too much sympathy for revolutionaries). As with the hunters, the Russians have a theory about why their judiciary is better than the western one: "Why hold a trial if at the end you find a suspect not guilty? What a waste of the judge's time!"

LEFTY THE MASTER

There is a famous story by the Russian writer Nikolai Leskov (1831 – 1895) called Lefty the Master, which best describes Russian attitude towards technique.

A group of Englishmen presented the Russian tsar with a tiny mechanical flea. The flea, visible only through a microscope, after having been wound with the tiniest key, would perform an elaborate dance. The tsar wished to find a Russian master who could top that English mechanical feat and uphold Russia's reputation. It was reported to him that in a village somewhere in the backwoods of Russia lived a master who could do something about it. Off went the tsar's messenger, and, after a long search, found the master.

In England, such a master would have lived in London and owned a shop at a fashionable address, but in Russia this master was found in a small village, living in a peasant hut and wearing old, ragged clothes. In Russia, if you are good at something, you have to hide from the envious. And that is why it is not surprising that Lefty the Master lived in a hut and wore rags: he was a real Master.

Lefty the Master is a piece of fiction, but the Soviet regime made this fiction a reality: night watchman, elevator attendant, street cleaner, schoolteacher, translator – these were day jobs, or better to say, these were disguises of the Soviet cultural elite, including several people who were worthy of Nobel Prizes.

But let's get back to the story. The tsar's messenger gave the mechanical flea to Lefty and asked, "Can you do something with it?" "Yes, I can." "What will it be?" "How do I know? Leave the flea with me and come back in a week. I'll do something." "Here is the microscope that comes with it." "I do not need this *tinyscope* of yours as my eye is quite a *straightshot*." (Note how the Lefty rejects the technique that is embedded in language by inventing his own words.) So the messenger leaves the flea with the Master, returns for it a week later and brings the Master and the flea back to the tsar. The tsar takes out the microscope and looks. The flea lies there, but there is nothing else. "You broke the thing!", shouts the tsar's messenger, and gives the Master a good whack. "What have you done?" asks the tsar. "Well, says the Master, your *tinyscope* is just not strong enough to see." The tsar called in the

Englishmen, who brought the strongest microscope they had. And then the tsar saw that on each of the flea's legs there is a little horseshoe, and on each nail it says "A Left-Handed Master from Russia". Fine job, indeed!

Then the tsar puts in the key and winds the flea up, but the flea does not dance. And the Englishmen explained that the mechanism was calculated so precisely that the additional weight of the horseshoes made it impossible for the flea to raise its legs.

There has never been a better description of the Russian attitude towards technique. The accomplishment of the English is purely technical: the flea is designed to dance, the microscope is used to assemble the parts, and the names of the craftsmen are nowhere to be seen. The Russian Master puts horseshoes on the flea (horseshoes that the flea never needed) and puts his name on every nail. As he works without a microscope, with the naked eye, his accomplishment, taken as such and considered from the point of view of an individual human achievement, is much greater than that of the English masters, but the flea can no longer dance. All the better: to the judgment of God, as it were, the English present but a mechanical device, while the Russian Master proved that his human eye is inhumanly sharp. By carelessly breaking the flea, the Master shows that in the larger scheme of things, the flea plays a role that is less than negligible. For him, what matters is the achievement of an individual: and that is why the *tinyscope* was rejected with such disdain.

The Englishmen presented to the judgment of God an ingenious device. To make it, they combined science, engineering, technical skills, patience, and care. The flea corresponds to the English conception of beauty. Lefty the Master presented to the judgment of God his inhumanly sharp eye and manual dexterity. And what is Lefty's conception of beauty? It is to break the English conception of beauty, to reduce it to a useless piece of metal. Lefty is reminding God to concentrate on the human being, as opposed to mechanical devices that tend to push human beings to the background, and I find this message very relevant.

The story of Lefty the Master is typical, and therefore it is not surprising that similar stories happen often in Russia. I once visited a Russian factory where I saw a very advanced and expensive computerized Swiss precision machine tool. This machine tool required absolute cleanliness, lack of vibration, and quite a few things besides. But very soon a heavy jackhammer was dropped on it from a high catwalk. You see, the machine tool had a counter that showed how many parts were made in a day, thereby preventing its operator from heading off to a cigarette with his friends. This factory now makes do with a venerable piece of equipment whose plaque says John Brown Works, London, 1903. The level of precision may not be the same, but the workers are happy.

Russian society is based on connections between friends and relatives. This is what Russians cherish the most. Next on the list comes mastery. But mastery is seen in a different light in comparison, for example, to the Japanese way. In Japan, a person is subservient to his own mastery and has an obligation before his own skill: to behave in a certain way, to perfect the skill, to adhere to the highest standard of quality. In Russia, a person is subservient to nothing but his all-encompassing dream, a dream that only a God could turn into reality. Mastery is important and prestigious to most Russians only if the human dimension of mastery is placed first, before the technical one. A Russian saying states this very well: "Be a good person, and everything else will come with it." The role of money in Russian society is increasing, and yet money still occupies only the fourth position. To recap: a lofty dream, friendship, mastery, and money. As for duty – it is not high on the list.

The Russians have their substitute for technique, though, and it is smarts. As you are reading this, some American army recruits are learning electronics, others – avionics. They sit peering into a computer screen. Their Russian counterparts, however, have just received an order to sweep the floor. But with what? There is no broom, no dustpan... A bunch of twigs and the visor of one's cap? Or maybe a toothbrush will do? The soldier can carry out this order only if he is inventive and able to use the available resources imaginatively. But please do not think that this is some kind of specially invented, touchy-feely exercise, aimed to make the soldiers more creative: as far as the officers are concerned, the goal of this exercise is simply to degrade the soldier. Russian creativity is not an art form, but a consequence of lack of resources (and lack of resources is a consequence of envy). Russians have to be creative because they cannot produce anything, and this is because they dislike doing whatever is human in scale and/or requires a step-by-step approach. Moreover, when one lacks resources and has to make do, quality suffers: a floor swept with a toothbrush is never clean. In Russia, unfortunately, it is all right not to be a real professional. The point is to be able to do everything, to be able to make do with what you have. And there is always a lingering suspicion that if you do anything really well you are probably somewhat narrow-minded, dependent not on your own smarts, but on some technical devices.

So, if you do do something well, you should apologize... Hey, wait! First hide (or better destroy) whatever you have done well, and then apologize, begging those who saw what you did to forget it and not to take it personally. The hiding or destruction is so important that when I realized I had almost forgotten it, I broke into a cold sweat: indeed, I almost advised you to turn yourself in without destroying the evidence.

THE RUSSIAN ATTITUDE TOWARDS WORK VS. THE PROTESTANT ONE

The Russian view of labor and the Russian assessment of labor's goal are very different from those which exists in the West. Protestants believe that the soul manifests itself and is strengthened in the process of productive labor, while Russians believe that the soul develops through suffering, through not succumbing to obstacles. And that amounts to a world of difference.

Jesus Christ, who could do any miracle, allowed Himself to be crucified, and the Russians believe that it is in His suffering, not in His achievement, that His religious legacy lies. Here we come full circle, as it were: a society with no private property, a society that is based on envy, gives an ample opportunity for suffering and little opportunity for achievement. That is why the Russian Orthodox church came to emphasize that which was accessible to people: they could easily serve God through suffering, while the avenue to serving Him through achievement was mostly closed.

Work is supposed to create material things, the more beautiful and sophisticated the better. But the Russians suspect that such things can lessen, or even altogether extinguish, suffering, and negate the benefit of encountering and overcoming obstacles. The problem that Lefty had with the flea was religious and philosophical in nature. One who does not encounter obstacles has no opportunity to suffer, and so his soul remains undeveloped. If you have a mechanical device that makes overcoming an obstacle easier, how can you derive the suffering necessary for the soul?

In a "German" culture, one considers a well-made gadget to be the result of a spiritual effort, as so much careful and loving labor went into it. In Russia, a gadget is an anti-spiritual thing: if one is not at peace with one's surroundings, one uses a gadget as a shield or as a means of escape. Also, once the gadget is made, the labor is over, and as labor is seen as suffering undertaken with an aim of spiritual elevation, the act of finishing the gadget signifies the end of spiritual effort, the rejection of it. One seems to be saying, "I no longer seek to come closer to God, I've got this shiny new gadget." Alexander Pushkin (1799 – 1837) said it best:

The long-awaited moment has come
My work of many years is done.
Why does this inexplicable sadness
Now distress me so?

Trans. by Matthew Maly

A thing done well has something of the devil in it: it puts a stop to the process of labor. It signifies a rebellion that claims that the suffering that was the labor can end, as if the soul does not need to be developed any further. That is why a real Russian product is always left somewhat unfinished and, ideally, clearly bears the marks of its maker's suffering or rejection.

The Russians value not the result of labor, but the process. The process of labor brings the suffering necessary to be a better person, while the result, i.e. the appearance of the final product, means the end of the process of labor, the end of suffering, a rebellion against God.

If we visit a Russian village, we would see that a wooden fence surrounds each house. A fence is far from being a high technology product: any grown human being can make a wooden fence. But look at Russian fences: askew, rotten, and unpainted, with holes and gaps, with a screeching and rusty gate. Why is not this fence like a German fence, straight and freshly painted, with the name of the owner written in big letters on the mailbox? Because the Russian fence (just like every fence in Germany) shows: an upstanding gentleman lives here. Indeed, the ugly Russian fence is proof positive of the spiritual achievement of its owner. First, there are holes in the fence, so that the esteemed neighbors could see that the chickens that walk around the yard are few in number. And then the fence itself. The Russians say, "Jesus suffered, and He bequeathed us to do likewise." The owner sees that his fence is ugly and suffers: he is working towards his spiritual salvation.

No one should doubt that Russians, especially villagers, can make a beautiful fence: by necessity, most Russian men are good handymen. Yet the fence is a horror to behold. And then, if your fence is ugly, you can always dream of fixing it up one day, and then by never doing it, turn this task into a lofty dream.

Let us recap the reasons why the Russian fence is so badly made:

I live no better than you do, so I am not to be envied. In fact, if push comes to shove, I am entitled to envy you, so beware and give me some respect;

I am a Russian Orthodox Christian: "Jesus suffered, and He bequeathed us to do likewise". You can see how I suffer;

I am a poet, not a fence maker;

This is not my house, this is just a temporary hut I have been living in (all my life): I am about to start building a palace;

I am building a better fence, but it takes time: once I am done with it, what am I going to do, what will be my future? (Indeed, God could have created a perfect man right from the start, but then He would have had nothing to do for all these years. But since we are far from being perfect, we are giving God something to do.)

We will discuss it later, but this idea is so important I will state it here as well. It is not an accident at all that I chose fences for such a detailed discussion. A fence is extremely important as it symbolizes the law. Indeed, it separates my property from society at large, it protects my privacy, my family, my land. The fence is also the "face" I show to the outside world. And it is not surprising that Russian law has the exact same characteristics as a typical Russian peasant fence.

For a Protestant, a well-made product is like a prayer: "Look what I have done working to the limit of my abilities". A German shows God his shiny Mercedes and says, "This is the result of my lifelong labor, and this is a perfect, expensive, well-respected car." A Russian crawls out from under his rusted out barely functioning Russian car to say, "I am suffering just like You did. Who else would buy this clunky piece of junk? I am surely putting spiritual values above material ones: it would be hard to put this car of mine above anything that has any value."

It is the absence (preferably, the total absence) of material things that Russians have always considered a mark of spiritual strength, goodness, and, most importantly, freedom. In Russia, it was the man who had nothing who was considered blessed.

A Russian saint is always a single old man living by himself, far away from other people. His dwelling is called a *pustosh'* which means an empty or deserted place. Indeed, if a man has nothing and is attached to nothing and nobody, he would think only of God. This man never works, but lives on whatever the pilgrims who desire to witness his saintliness or benefit from his advice bring.

Again, Russians apply to people standards that can be applied only to God. People need food and clothing, and hungry people will not think of God: they will think of stealing food from others, they will hate those who do have enough to eat. And yet, Russians believe that only the lack of property, lack of attachment, gives real freedom. Westerners think otherwise: their constant quest for material possessions is actually a quest for freedom. In Russia, the rich have always been seen as suspect; in the West, the rich are respected as those who have achieved their dream of freedom.

Moreover, it is not thinking of God that makes you a saint: not being envious or destructive towards other people is more like it.

We see that it is hard to call Lenin and Stalin anti-religious in the Russian context: they confiscated everything and caused untold suffering, turning many Russians into the very kind of saints they had venerated for centuries – turning them against their will, but this is even better. The Russians had saints that starved, tortured their flesh, tied themselves with ropes, beat themselves with whips: Stalin did his best to impose just that on millions of Russians.

Seeing Russian youths giving the Nazi salute, commentators talk about nostalgia for a strong hand in a country whose economy is collapsing. But I think that unconsciously many Russians love Stalin and even Hitler (!) because they made the Russians suffer, and suffering lifts you up above it all. Today, many Moslems venerate those who killed themselves while committing a horrible and senseless crime against innocent people. What is there to venerate, what was gained? Suffering is what was gained.

Furthermore, this attitude provides an ideal cover-up for the offspring of envy: general indiscriminate hatred of one's neighbors. If we recall our banana peel example, we could see that throwing a banana peel on the sidewalk "has a good side to it" as "it could give someone a chance to suffer by slipping on it". What fertile ground Russia was for a cruel dictatorship, and now it is just as fertile for a state run by criminals.

If in Russia labor is a process that one undergoes to suffer, in Germany, the fruit of labor is its result, and the result is joyous. Thus, labor is fed by anticipation, it is pleasant, and to finish work well is a moral act. In Germany, a good person makes good suitcases, while a bad person makes ones that are not so very good. Since in Russia to work is to suffer, and a person who aspires to greatness should be prepared to suffer greatly, to commit oneself to labor one must gather a great deal of spiritual strength. Not many people are able to do so, and the most respected are those who never start working. In Russia, a good person is forever engaged in attempting to make a suitcase, while the best person spends years simply collecting his strength in the hope that one day he, too, will make a suitcase. Not a normal suitcase, of course (we recall how embarrassing that would be): a suitcase, into which, for example, "one could put everything that is bad on this Earth, lock it, and throw away the key". The result is that a German can make anything; a Russian can endure anything.

Note how Russian a project it was to build a Communist state, and how stupid were those who asked what this state would be like. Building it was everything, and this was exciting precisely because it was not likely to end in anything.

Now, here it comes. Just like Lenin predicted, Communism in Russia was built! It is here today! Look at it: a total ruin! Unfinished! And sure enough, the Russians are suffering!

Here is how this difference in approach can be used in business: a Russian can successfully solve a most difficult theoretical problem or find an ingenious solution in a daunting situation. As an inducement, the process, such as an interesting problem or a pleasant work environment, works better than the result, such as the money. Russian workers tend to want to put a bit of their personality into the product they make, and value human effort and ingenuity more than the quality of the final product. The Russians seek beauty and greatness, and see them as somehow in opposition to being finished or being high quality. If it is either finished or high quality, it must have been too easy or attainable, too human in scale, unworthy to be presented to God.

POVERTY AND SPIRITUALITY

What kind of freedom could poverty possibly bring? The lack of a pen does not give freedom to write: it deprives you of such freedom. The only freedom that poverty does give is the freedom to run away, freedom to leave the land. Russian society envies success and begrudges property, and in this respect, poverty is a blessing: you will not be destroyed by the envious, you will not have to pay for your possessions with your life.

A pauper does not arouse envy, and in Russian eyes this makes him a holy man. Western social invention was to make everyone self-supporting, and it was hoped that this would kill envy as a rational emotion.

In other words, the saints in Russia are saints first because they are not the object of envy, and second because not being the object of envy, they arouse not pity but veneration. Note how difficult that is: if you are poor, you will not be envied, but you might be pitied instead. Pity is a consequence of insecurity or superiority, it is not the same as respect, and therefore pity can be a destructive emotion. If instead of pity people feel veneration, then they venerate the human spirit "in its pure form". The question remains whether they really do so and why they do so.

While those who were sanctified by the Russian Orthodox Church lived alone and mortified their flesh, there were people who achieved "sainthood" among the Russian people. I can think of five such people:

Pushkin, Tolstoy, Akhmatova, Shostakovich, and Solzhenitsyn, two poets, two writers, and one composer. All five of them are people of tremendous artistic accomplishment, and all five have suffered for it.

On the one hand, it appears that the Russian Orthodox version of saintliness is very destructive and misleading in terms of building a civil society. On the other hand, Solzhenitsyn and Shostakovich are not the same as Michael Jackson or Madonna. There is something to the Russian idea that a man was created by God to be better than he actually is; there is something to the idea that one is never good enough.

Protestants proclaimed that private property defends your freedom, including your freedom of worship. When Russians decided that private property interferes with worship, they created a perfect ideological defense for laziness and envy. Indeed, what is a Russian doing when he burns down his neighbor's house? He is proselytizing! He wants his neighbor to go barefoot and free in search of spirituality. We will see later that in Russia the Communist ideology was able to substitute itself for the Orthodox religion, and indeed, the Communists burned down everyone's house.

Well, here is a Russian man who works, gets tired, suffers. Will he be fulfilling his task of getting closer to God? No, because he gets paid for his labor. You cannot "suffer" if you get paid for it. OK, if you work but do not get paid, will that do? No, it will not: you obviously like what you are doing, a human being was made to work and to create – this is joy, not suffering. In order to suffer, and thus, according to this theory, to grow spiritually, one needs to do, without pay, something that one hates to do – something that goes against one's nature, something that is meaningless. Or better yet, something destructive, ugly, inhuman. It is in the course of such labor that, according to this logic, a man grows closer to God.

I do not know how to emphasize the previous paragraph enough. The more you reread it, the more grotesque it appears. How could meaningless and destructive labor be the goal? There obviously must be a mistake in my logic. Yet the reality of Russian life proves me right! Serfs, who were not freed until 1861, criminals at hard labor, tens of millions of prisoners at the Gulag, collective farmers dying from hunger in their fields, workers who today, in "democratic" Russia, do not get paid the wages they have already earned, the tax police that confiscates the businessman's entire income, the racket that makes an entrepreneur regret he ever started his business – all of that proves me right. The Russians simply have not yet accepted the idea that labor must be free and its fruits can be kept, that labor is uplifting and liberating, that it is creative labor that brings a human being closer to God. Unconsciously, the Russians hold a different opinion, thinking that only unpaid and destructive labor could be uplifting, as it creates and spreads suffering; whereas one who has created something beautiful and useful has thereby committed a sin.

Since I used a new term, "destructive labor", the term that will be discussed later. I want just to point out for now that destructive labor does not mean destruction. Destructive labor can produce things, such as tanks. In fact it can be very efficient: Hitler mobilized so much hatred and destructive energy that Germany quickly overtook both France and England in its productive capacity.

In April 1945, Hitler's army controlled only Berlin. The Western allies knew that Berlin was heavily defended by fanatical troops, and they did not want to storm Berlin, fearing heavy casualties. But Stalin ordered his troops to take Berlin at any price by May 1, as this was the major holiday, the Day of Workers' Solidarity. And the Russians did take Berlin by May 1. Yet because the assault was unprepared (and probably unnecessary, as the German situation was utterly hopeless) three hundred fifty thousand Russian soldiers died within a week of the final victory. The Russians took Berlin in the bloodiest street fighting in human history, and promptly turned half of the city over to the Western allies. Why did Stalin need all these casualties? Yes, a victory by May 1 was an important symbol; yes, the storming of Berlin was a symbol of victory; yes, Berlin was strategically and politically important. But I believe there was yet another reason, one that the Russians did not voice, and that westerners would never believe. Here it is: the German machine guns were about to fall silent, and the Russians wanted to suffer some more, they wanted thousands more of their solders to die days, hours, and minutes before the ceasefire. And indeed, after the war was over, Stalin did not slow down, as millions more went to camps, executed, exiled, or starved to death. Only Stalin's death saved Russia from the planned "final solution of the Jewish question": exile of all the remaining Jews to an uninhabited and uninhabitable corner of Siberia, the so-called Jewish Autonomous Republic.

THE INVENTION OF WIN/WIN

In the West, Christianity can be reduced to the words "Love thy neighbor as thyself". Gradually, people learned to love (and that includes educating, understanding, and managing) themselves, and as they were doing so, they increasingly realized that loving your neighbor is the best policy. They have gradually come to make an exceptionally important social discovery, currently known as "win/win".

Here again I would ask you to slow down, as this is a crucial point. The "lose/lose" and "lose/win" types of relationship are well known even to animals. When two male deer fight for a female, they will get one of those outcomes every time. But to establish consistent mutually beneficial cooperation – this is not something deer can do. That is why a human society that consciously wants to augment the benefits of every member, a society with no losers, is such a significant (and very recent) discovery. Indeed, Karl Marx's prediction of the eminent demise of capitalism did not come true in large part because Marx was not aware that a human society based on the "win/win" model was possible.

Russia is among the many societies that have not yet progressed to "win/win," as it is a very recent social invention. And yet "win/win" is the only possible basis for a democracy and a market economy as we see them today.

The real problem is that the Russians (consciously or unconsciously, but it does not really matter) reject "win/win" as sinful and dangerous and instead passionately go for "lose/lose" as a way to what some of them see as religious salvation.

CHAPTER TWO. THE WAY OF CREATIVITY AND THE WAY OF ENVY

This chapter may be difficult to read, but it is the most important chapter of the book, without which the book simply cannot be understood. There are no special terms, but there is a certain logical thread, which needs to be carefully followed. If at all possible, it would be best to read this chapter without interruptions.

The communist revolution was not a revolution of individuals, but a revolution of the united masses, a fact that is evidenced by the very name *communist* – and that means that we should look at how the outlook of a single individual differs from that of a member of a collective.

There are two methods that people can use to assess their situation: a person can compare his situation as it is today with his situation as it was yesterday, or he can compare his present situation to the present situation of his peers.

Method of comparing today with yesterday

This method has the following characteristics:

1. There is only **one person** involved.

2. This person is aware of **time**: there are such things as "today" and "tomorrow".

3. The time dimension means that one is equipped to deal not only with material objects, but also, and even primarily, with things that **develop and change**. For example, one can see things not the way they are "right now", the way a cat sees things, but can trace events and things as they transform. A cat knows whether its master is happy or sad, but it cannot think "What was it that made him change his mood?"

4. In order to be able to evaluate one's progress, one has to have a **memory**. Memory and the sense of time give a person the ability to think.

5. A person remembers his situation as it was before, and compares it with the current or imagined situation. If he wants to make some changes, he needs **freedom** to do so and the ability to tell whether the change has been **good or bad**. And that means that we talk not only about obvious changes, such as "the fish was here and now the fish is gone", but about changes in the inner world of this person. If yesterday

he had one perception of the world, today he might have another. When one makes a comparison between them, one develops preferences, that is, introduces the notions of "good" and "bad". And these comparisons are possible not only between physical objects, such as "chicken is better than red meat", but between two abstract notions, such as "Better to be kind than angry".

6. When one observes change in the situation from one moment to the next, one forms a certain system of preferences. The next step would be to form a method of achieving these preferences, that is, a certain method of **self-management**, a method that will be guided by a person's **character** and **morality**. If you hit a cat, it will be angry or scared, and if you are kind to a cat, it will respond with kindness. A cat can be taught and it has a mechanical memory, but it cannot remember, compare, and analyze its behavior and thus cannot modify it of its own volition. It makes a world of difference that a human being can decide that a certain behavior pattern is better than the other. When we eat candy, we often hear an inner voice advising us not to eat it. When a person thinks, someone inside him (not always, by any means, but at least sometimes) is looking at him as if from the sidelines, unmasks his motives, and offers corrections. People are able to simultaneously hear their own voices and critically evaluate them, thereby correcting and modifying their behavior. We each conduct an **internal dialogue** within ourselves, organizing our thoughts in a certain system, managing our behavior, developing our character. This dialogue can be called **moral** as it seeks to answer the question, "What is better for me?"

7. If we say that a person is conducting an internal moral dialogue, then the language in which this dialogue is being conducted develops under the influence of this dialogue, in a way that makes it possible. This language has to be capable of change and development and must be able to express spiritual ideas, i.e. it should be **a living language**. Language is usually defined as a means of communication between several people, while here we have one person, but there is no contradiction. We are discussing a person that lives in society and communicates with others. But language does not live "in society": it lives within each individual member of society, and each person analyzes his life, conducts an internal dialogue, develops his character, tries to formulate what is best

for him. Without this internal dialogue, language could not have developed: while birds can say "danger" or "come here", they cannot say "beautiful, kind little birdie", because the lack of internal dialogue makes it impossible for them to develop such abstract, changeable, comparative notions.

8. In the course of this internal dialogue, a person comes to certain conclusions, accumulates certain experiences that he then seeks to share with others. As all people conduct their internal dialogue, in the same way they can converse with others. And the word "converse" is important here: the "language" of animals imposes a reality that, like a stone, is not open to discussion or modification. When one gazelle cries "danger", the others do not think "what a coward", or "why do I care?"; this cry is perceived just like any other immediate physical fact. Humans do not just exchange their opinions as if these opinions were cast in stone: they have the capacity to modify, adapt and develop them. If a herd of a hundred gazelles loses one member to lions, the herd has lost nothing at all, but with a loss of one human being, some **unique and transmittable** knowledge, experience, and perspective is inevitably lost. Each human being could therefore be described as an irreplaceable contributor to humanity's process of learning. That is why it is logical to declare that to kill, or simply to ignore or exclude, a human being will cause incalculable damage to all humanity. As this person's experience cannot be replicated, this exclusion will hinder us in pursuing our common goal of understanding the world. From this comes the idea that each person should be allowed to exist. And finally, we come to the realization that human beings should be helped to develop their talents to maximum extent possible. Each person now sees himself as valuable and important, and formulates an extremely important concept, that of the **individual self**.

9. Let us return to the internal dialogue that people conduct to evaluate their changing situation and to distinguish good from bad. A dialogue is conducted between two participants. Who are they? One participant is one's own self, while another is an internal entity that can influence that self to change his opinion, to modify his thoughts or indeed to modify his character. In other words, there appears to be an imaginary entity that conducts an internal dialogue with one's own self.

As the person is alone, this substance is either inside him or is guided from the outside, but it is definitely immaterial, spiritual, and imaginary. Trying to define this substance, human beings developed such terms as **"soul"** and **"God"**. The dialogue with this substance is conducted by means of a language, and therefore this language should be adequate to this dialogue. It means that this language should be able to change, to develop, and to express abstract ideas. As this language exists inside one's self in a dialogue with a substance that one has never seen and cannot describe, this language is based on animate or metaphysical terms, tending to use them even when describing inanimate objects. Animals do not have "home, sweet home", to say nothing of such words as "beauty" or "truth". As early as the Stone Age, humans realized that a root of a tree can resemble a bull (resemblance being an abstract concept); moreover, this root could then symbolize a bull, play a role of the bull. Humans were used to abstract concepts because they were talking to somebody unseen in their heads; they were conducting a dialogue. The next step was the appearance of art: the ability to transmit a feeling and a mood, to transmit the indescribable from one person to another. This art may well be abstract, as a person is now capable of imagining whatever is not evident in the painting. Thus, it is the imaginary world of the human being that now becomes the foundation of his existence, and people see the material world through the filter of their imaginations. **The material realm thus becomes subservient to the spiritual one.** Through the notions of "God" and "Beauty", humans come to a realization of something that is eternal and ever-present. In this context, humans come to worship **life**, and assign life-like qualities even to inanimate objects. Thus, the interest in one's own self, in one's own development, turns into a worldview.

10. The internal dialogue means that one must choose what is good and reject whatever is bad or evil. To separate good from evil, and resolutely and consistently **choose the good**, there needs to be an internal control, and this is known as **conscience.** If a human being has a conscience and can make an informed choice between good and bad, we can say that he is developing a **character**, a certain predictable and consistent model of behavior, which is nevertheless open to change.

11. All that we have discussed so far takes place **within** each particular human being, and there is no need to get other people involved.

12. Character means that one is making choices. But you cannot make a choice unless you have freedom and independence. Thus freedom and independence become fundamental human needs. On the other hand, one is able to strive for freedom and independence precisely because one is alone, precisely because one's dialogue is internal. That brings freedom and independence within reach, and once they are attained, they permit further development. A person liberates himself, but in the process he loses the ability to blame others for his failures; he thus has to assume **personal responsibility** for the outcome of his actions.

13. This method allows to create something that was not here yesterday; there is **development and growth**. If reality is always changing, it means that one can never be sure that one is right in its representation. There is a **lack of finality** in the knowledge: new facts can always come to light and influence one's view of reality. People collect known facts, build a theory on the basis of them, but can never stop learning or declare an existing theory to be the final and unchangeable truth. This principle of uncertainty is a foundation of **science**. In the social sphere, the principle of uncertainty translates into contested elections between several candidates, a system of separation of powers, a method of checks and balances. In other words, the principle of uncertainty is a foundation of **democracy**, a social system under which each citizen is seen as uniquely valuable, but none is considered to be all-knowing or all-powerful.

14. Now that we have introduced such terms as independence, free choice, democracy and the unique value of each human being, we should ask ourselves, "Where do other people come into this process?" In the same way as a person "talks" in the context of an internal dialogue, a person can talk with others. If I can ask a question of myself, I can also talk to others; if I have a conscience that controls my behavior, I can also ask others for their advice, which I would then subject to an internal examination. One becomes able to experience **friendship** and **love** because they create bonds similar to those created by the internal

spiritual dialogue. It is the internal spiritual dialogue that makes respect, friendship, and love possible.

15. Now a person's life can be represented as a process of distinguishing between good and evil, and attempting to choose the good. I will call this method of evaluation of one's situation Individual, and note that it is absolute, "animate" and growth-oriented, that is, "**vertical**". It can also be called the Way of Creativity.

Method of comparison with one's peers

The characteristics of this method are as follows:

1. In order to make this comparison, there must be at least one other person or a **group of several people**.

2. Since the situation can change with the passage of time, a comparison can be made only in a particular moment, meaning that we need to **stop time**. Right now, I have $20 and you have $5, so I have more money, and this conclusion cannot take into account the fact that yesterday you spent $300 to buy a TV set, whereas I bought a sofa five years ago. To make a comparison, we need to agree that only the second when the comparison is made matters, while both the past and the future are irrelevant.

3. The lack of a time dimension means that one is not equipped to deal with things that develop and change. Therefore, in order to deal with things that are alive or metaphysical one must **represent them as inanimate**. There are several ways to achieve that. First, there could be a law that prohibits a change that could interfere with the comparison. Or the moment can be somehow fixed. If you kill a man, the amount of dollars he has in his hand will no longer change. Or, you could attach to a man a permanent label, such as “a bourgeois” or “an enemy”. Note that “an enemy” remains one long after the reason for the quarrel is forgotten. Yet it is as if once the label is attached, life, with its constant change and re-evaluation, is killed or suspended. An enemy may now want to be a friend, but it is too late as the label is already there.

4. To evaluate one's progress, one does not need to have a memory, but must be a member of a group of people whose present situation can be compared to one's own. To make a comparison possible, each member of the group should be denied an opportunity to change his situation of his own accord.

5. Now one is unaware of one's own situation, because one's eyes are directed towards others. By directing one's attention away from oneself, one stops one's personal time, and now one is unable to recall one's past or to control one's future. One is no longer able to improve one's situation by changing it; instead, one expresses oneself by **changing the situation of others,** the situation that one sees well and can control. By **worsening** the situation of others, one achieves an illusion of improving one's own situation (not in absolute terms, but in comparison). Two guys stand on a bridge. Then one pushes the other off. Now he can think: "A minute ago, I was just standing on a bridge; now I am also not drowning."

6. This means that members of the group should have an opportunity to change the situation of each individual member. To achieve that, everyone must be stripped of his privacy. But the loss of privacy is now painless, as the group member is no longer aware of his own situation: he sees himself only through the eyes of others. The only thing that the group member can do is to ask the group how it sees him, i.e. what **label** does it attach to him today. The label is crucial for the group member, as this is how he finds out what he is. This is a very important point. Since you write poetry, you could have been seen as a poet, but since your label is "enemy of the people", you are not a poet but an executed prisoner. To obtain the desired label, you must become an inseparable part of the group, faithfully carrying out its will. You must work on your character to extinguish all those personal qualities that interfere with unquestioned and automatic readiness to carry out the will of the group, regardless of what it might be. The goal of this work is to develop a **social morality**. Social morality concerns itself not with changes in the behavior of a particular person during a period of time, but with each person's conformity to the opinion of the group at any given instant. Each member must know what, according to the opinion of the group, is good or bad. His own opinion, if any, is no longer relevant; thus, instead of a personal morality, there is now a social one.

7. To combat the internal resistance to social morality, one needs to develop a language of an entirely different kind. This language has an astonishing capacity to spread instantaneously and impose itself on all the people it reaches. It is not a language that records change and

development, not a language of ideas, but a language of fixed images (known as slogans or clichés) that remain unchanged until, in an instant, one image is replaced by another. Here is an example: the word "Jew" invokes various emotions and associations; it can be seen in a wide variety of contexts. We can talk about Jews in the framework of history, religion, science, art, humor, Israel, personal experience. We see that there can be a multi-dimensional and never ending discussion. Now, let us consider the word "kike," which describes exactly the same human being as the word "Jew". And suddenly we have absolute certainty and finality. Kike means "one to be killed". Can one kike be kinder, better, or more interesting than another kike? Of course not, as their character is no longer relevant. A change in one word brought about the end of all discussion. We needed volumes to describe a Jew, and we would never all be of the same opinion. But we know with certainty who the kike is, and more importantly, we know what should be done to a kike. A kike must be turned into an inanimate object. A kike is a Jew who has lost all its personal and temporal characteristics, lost his future and his past, lost his memory and experiences, lost his personal language. When you say "kike" you mean "execution", and that is the only word and the only action that now remains of the entire world invoked by the word "Jew". This is the magic of the new language. Each cliché and slogan has such characteristics. Let us compare the slogan "Communism is our goal!" with the sentence "What are you going to do tomorrow?". Both sentences have the same topic, the future. But the first sentence tells us that millions of people have suddenly acquired a common goal – a society that they cannot even describe, a goal so far removed none will ever see it realized. Why live if your goal is something that you do not understand and will not see? Isn't that like death? Why mark time, why have memory: your future is known, and it is "communism". By contrast, the second question allows for an infinite number of answers, all perfectly natural and understandable, human and time-sensitive.

8. Individual morality is now out of the question: one's eyes are directed away from oneself, and time has stopped. But the social morality is no less well developed than the individual one; it is just that the two moralities are absolutely different. The social morality considers it a given that each person is completely similar to those from whom he

is supposed to take his cues. The social morality does not see any human being as precious, but is able to tell a member of an execution squad that he is acting immorally if he does not kill efficiently enough: indeed, such behavior creates more work for other members of the squad. A group unified by a social morality is no longer just a group of people, but an entirely new entity that has a special name – **a collective**. The goal of a collective is to make sure that each of its members abandons the personal morality and accepts the social one, developed by the collective, as his own. One is no longer free and independent and can exist only as a part of a collective. Now one strives to maintain the bonds that connect one to others, the bonds that restrict one's freedom. Thus, one's desire for freedom constantly diminishes.

9. In order to conform, one needs to have as current and complete an idea of the opinion of the collective as possible. Thus, one must continuously look "around" and can no longer afford to look "within" or "above" oneself. Furthermore, to be able to instantly conform one's behavior to the will of the collective, one must remold oneself in such a way that there is no internal resistance to whatever the collective might do. One now uses a language in which history appears not as a movie, but as a stack of photos, which are not necessarily connected to one another. (If the Communist Party's newspaper, *Pravda* ("The Truth") contradicted what it had written the day before, it did not lie: *Pravda* always accurately reflected the current point of view of the Party, and this view did not have to be connected with the past. Thus, today's issue of *Pravda* always tells the truth, while yesterday's *Pravda* is a contradiction in terms. That is why in the Soviet Union, which lived according to today's issue of *Pravda*, past issues of *Pravda* were hidden from sight and were never quoted. This language can use only material and inanimate terms to describe what is animate or metaphysical. *The spiritual realm becomes subservient to the material one, to the degree that the very existence of the spiritual realm is denied.* Yet this language, which seems to be materialistic and matter-of-fact, is absolutely mythical. A social language would describe a goal, for example, an Arian type of man: blond, tall, strong, and blue-eyed, and at the very same time present the personification of the Arian type, Adolf Hitler, who was neither blond nor tall. Such words as "Communism" or "kike" are the

words of magic. For example, unlike Jews, kikes are everywhere. Even Boris Yeltsin, who does not look Jewish at all, was rumored to be a kike. The mythical nature of this language becomes understandable as soon as we realize that the slogans are created by a collective that, while it appears to consist of human beings, in fact consists of beings that have stopped their personal time.

10. Now the responsibility of a member of the collective lies in conforming to this collective's will. One is forced to conform until one loses one's separate and distinctive personality and becomes but a **nameless and replaceable** part of a social organism. Individuals disappear, but at the same time this new social organism with its own laws, goals, and mode of behavior makes its appearance, and soon establishes itself as the only entity capable of social action. It becomes immoral to be different from others. Now there is a process of constant comparison, but only inanimate objects can be compared. And that means that human beings must also be viewed as inanimate, lest growth and development make them no longer susceptible to comparison. This means that humans must be labeled, represented as fixed images, so that the metaphysical aspects of life could be denied outright. Thus creativity, development, growth, and life itself fall under the direct control of the collective and become impersonal. Each member of the collective, unable to evaluate himself, peers into the faces of others in an attempt to determine whether he is still distinguishable in any way – so that he can immediately destroy this distinction. As one diligently works on destruction of one's own personality, a **ritual suicide** can be said to have taken place, as a human being gradually turns into an **inanimate object.**

11. As one's behavior is determined from the outside, one no longer feels responsible for one's own actions. Personal responsibility is replaced by a social one, and one is now guided not by a personal morality, but by that of the collective. In return, one gains the right to blame "outside influences" for personal failures. Now every accusation is tantamount to conviction: it is impossible to accuse a person without first singling him out; the fact that he has been singled out proves that he is different from others, and being different makes him guilty. Common as it is, this guilty verdict is not to be taken lightly, for it is no longer immoral to kill: the collective has no member that it considers unique

and irreplaceable. On the contrary, dead people play the role of inanimate objects better than live ones do.

12. Yet the collective is not the only killer: the habit of looking at everybody but oneself in order to determine the direction of one's life is a rejection of self, and it is this mass ritual suicide that is responsible for the fact that both the collective and each of its members acquire certain inanimate characteristics. The collective continuously violates each person's privacy, and it becomes impossible to be better off than others. In return, one asks for the assurance that the others are no better off than oneself. This leads to further destruction of the notion of privacy, and eventually human beings melt into the collective and disappear in it.

13. The collective designates what should be considered good, while declaring that evil has been conquered forever, or shortly will be. One's only duty is to conform, and one's life becomes static, but in return one no longer has to notice evil, let alone to struggle with it. One is no longer able to experience friendship and love, and one's relationships are based on dependency and envy.

14. People create the collective themselves, from what looks like a very small concession: from a loss of personal responsibility for one's own destiny, from succumbing to envy and fear. But time stops, and there appears a monster of which each of them is a part. They forget themselves totally, but they are born anew as something else (they only need to read the label). They experience strong emotions, fear and elation, stronger than they have ever experienced before, and yet they cannot influence their reality: they are captives of it. Suddenly the screen says "The End", the light comes on, and the people stand up and go home. The collapse of an ideology takes exactly one second: however powerful it may have been, it is just an illusion. Today Russian youngsters can no longer remember the name of the country they were born in, the USSR.

15. When a human being loses control over his life, his life turns static. But life is not supposed to be static: it is growing and changeable. Thus, there is a need to destroy life, to stop all living processes. Human beings now actively seek death and wear skulls on their black SS caps. Something immense is being built out of human bodies, yet one day it disappears in an instant, leaving millions of corpses in its wake. This

method of evaluation of one's situation should be called Collective, and we note that it is comparison-oriented, relative, and inanimate. I will also call this method **horizontal**, as one's eyes are directed away from oneself and towards one's peers. As this method is based on self-rejection and on envy-based comparison, it can also be called the Way of Envy.

We will be using the word "**vertical**" to designate the terms having to do with the first method, and the word "**horizontal**" for the second. Here is a table of keywords pertaining to the vertical and horizontal methods of evaluation of one's situation.

TABLE 2. VERTICAL AND HORIZONTAL METHODS

VERTICAL METHOD	HORIZONTAL METHOD
One actor, individual citizen.	Collective, or an entire society based on comparison.
A sense of time. Memory, one thinks about tomorrow.	Lack of a sense of time; personal memory is not taken into account. There is only an abstract "distant perspective" that never becomes a reality.
Desire to develop and change.	Desire to preserve the status quo. Readiness to act forcefully against change.

VERTICAL METHOD	HORIZONTAL METHOD
Serving the needs of living, actual persons. Social actors are living individuals.	Serving the needs of social structures; needs and desires of actual persons are not taken into account, and only the decisions made by a collective are considered valid. Individuals are not able to become social actors: only symbolic individuals can play this role, but then they are assigned the characteristics that make them inhuman, such as "an immortal leader".
The spiritual aspect is more important than the material one; each citizen has his own morality that he developed himself and continues to develop.	The material aspect is more important than the spiritual one; morality is developed by the collective and serves only its interests. The only social actors that this system recognizes – collectives – are charged with enforcing this morality and instilling it into everyone. This morality cannot be questioned and thus cannot be developed, but it can suddenly be drastically changed. Yesterday's beloved leader suddenly turns out to be a hated spy. And it is not you as a person who came to this conclusion: you took it as yet another directive and unquestioningly obeyed.

VERTICAL METHOD	HORIZONTAL METHOD
The "leading role" in society is played by the personal qualities that an individual citizen has; his memory, experience, desire to work and succeed. The law forbids violation of privacy.	Society is governed by decrees that are always directed against legitimate individual activity. Consider a 90% tax on profit: you thought that each entrepreneur is different as far as his skills, desire to work, geographical location, and product are concerned, but now all of them are equal, as none of them produces anything. As the individual is not a social actor, there is no notion of individual rights, and violations of individual rights go unchallenged.
The individual has the right and the opportunity to improve his situation in the way that he sees fit. In return, he loses the opportunity to blame others for his failures.	The individual cannot improve his situation other than by becoming ever more subservient to the collective. In return, he is given the opportunity to take away the rights of others, so that they will be as enslaved by the collective as he is. As an individual, one is helpless, but one is rewarded with the opportunity to have a claim against others and can watch with glee as the powerful collective enforces this claim, even though the collective does so not on any single person's behalf, but on its own.

VERTICAL METHOD	HORIZONTAL METHOD
Creation as an inner need of human beings.	Everything that is produced is not produced for human beings, or at least not directly for them, but for a Higher Purpose, for the Collective. People may be dying from hunger, but construction of monuments to the Great Leader never stops. The Collective believes that goods will appear mystically, as soon as the Leader wills it, rather than as the result of productive work. People wear rags and prepare for prosperity by remaking themselves, rather than by producing.
Production is rational, it can be economically evaluated, and products have a price.	Production is subordinated to the task of social remodeling; products are distinguished not but their price but by their social impact. Production cannot be evaluated economically, but is evaluated politically.

VERTICAL METHOD	HORIZONTAL METHOD
Whatever is good for an individual is considered to be good. And when you know what is good for you, you can get organized with other individuals who have the same interests to protect and advance your common interests together.	Whatever is good for the collective is considered to be good; the desires and rights of particular individuals are never considered. You are part of the collective, but the collective will never protect your rights or be responsive to your needs: it defends only its own needs, which are the opposite of your (personal) needs and are in irreconcilable conflict with your (personal) rights.
Personal growth and development, desire for independence and self-sufficiency. Self-sufficiency causes goodwill towards others, and this goodwill becomes the foundation of society.	Internally, one invents excuses; externally, one submits claims.
Paying attention to yourself, your inner voice, your moral principles. Control over your physical and moral condition.	Physical and emotional dependence on the collective: "they" owe me love and care, "they" have to help me and lead me. "I" am just a list of claims that I can present to others, and even my body is no longer under my control.

VERTICAL METHOD	HORIZONTAL METHOD
Collecting information about oneself in order to improve oneself.	One listens carefully to the collective in order to be able to follow any order at a moment's notice. One looks at others with suspicion and is ready to blame them if they do not follow orders fast enough.
Sincerity and honesty are vertical: a human being has no need to hide himself from others.	Deception is horizontal: a liar looks at you in order to determine what you will believe, so that he can say it. Instead of stating his truth, he constructs a trap for you.
Self-sufficiency.	Total dependence on the collective.
People cooperate for mutual benefit.	Collectives destroy all that is human in people.
Living language.	Clichés, slogans, verbal codes.
Conscience.	Political correctness.
Human individuality.	Similarity, fashion, grayness, conformity.

VERTICAL METHOD	HORIZONTAL METHOD
Personal success is possible; it is expected, and is rewarded.	Personal success is extremely dangerous for personal survival, and is made impossible to achieve. The defeat of individuality is expected and rewarded; destruction of one's own individuality is the only way to achieve social acceptance.
The development of society moves by way of granting new rights to individual citizens, rights that they are spiritually ready to use not just for their own benefit, but for the benefit of other individuals that make up the society.	Development of society moves by way of inventing new methods of controlling individuals, convincing them that they do not need personal freedoms and mean nothing without their collective, even to themselves. The goal is to create a situation when no individual would want to have any freedom, and would in fact beg that it be away so that it would be easier to be part of the collective.
One feels responsibility not just for oneself, but for one's neighbors, one's city and country. Blaming others for one's own faults is not an option.	No responsibility for anything but carrying out an order. The right to blame others or "the environment" for one's own faults.

VERTICAL METHOD	HORIZONTAL METHOD
Self-development, ability to listen to oneself, understand oneself, and be truthful to oneself.	One remakes oneself in order to be able to submit instantaneously to the will of the collective.
Murder and theft are not just outlawed: everyone has a profound understanding that they are deeply repugnant. On the other hand, private property and privacy are not just protected by law: citizens consider them sacred.	Decisions of the collective are sacred and always right. There is nothing that cannot or should not be done if the collective wants it.
Society is held together by strong ties of mutual respect, common heritage, friendship, and love.	Society is held together by strong ties of dependency, envy, mutual hatred, amnesia of their heritage, and lack of any alternative.
Life is seen as a process; hope for further improvement is natural.	Life is static. No matter how bad the situation is, citizens have justifiable fear that it could be still worse.

VERTICAL METHOD	HORIZONTAL METHOD
Good and evil exist and are in constant conflict; an individual learns to understand them on an ever-deeper level. There is no notion of finality, no notion that evil has been, or will ever be "conquered forever". There is a tendency to find something good in those who only yesterday seemed to be evil. The death penalty is used less and less.	The collective knows all that is evil, and much is. The collective knows that evil can be defeated only by establishing "order". Furthermore, even though the collective deals with the evil it discovers with absolute ruthlessness, there is always more evil around, not less. The collective knows that one day it will be able to defeat all evil, but for that, every human being will have to stop breathing. Many people do not care whether they live or die, and some of those who are alive envy the dead.
I am a human being. I have some knowledge, but I do not have certainty.	They know it all. They know very well, who I am and what I am all about. Should there be a need for me to know who am I or what am I to do, they will tell me. But myself, I do not want to know anything: when the time comes, they will tell me all I need to know.

VERTICAL METHOD	HORIZONTAL METHOD
Individual action. Every action is born within the person who does it, and is then judged by this person. The individual is a real social actor, who ultimately determines everything.	Predictable reaction. Every action is taken in response to an outside order, and is controlled by the collective that gave this order. The individual had no voice in the decision that led to this order, and carries it out as if he were part of a machine.
The individual's view of life is absolute. In his analysis of life, the individual uses the notions that are eternal.	The individual's view of life is relative. The individual is nothing without the collective and is under the collective's total control.

Take fashion as an example. The idea that a person can dress differently from others and in so doing express character and individuality is obviously vertical. But the assumption that a person who is dressed differently from us is therefore an enemy or a loser is ideological. When we want to use clothes as an art form, it is one thing, but when we fear that not being dressed fashionably will be seen as a character flaw, that is another. A fashion show tries to express human personality through clothes, and therefore it is vertical. A column of soldiers is dressed in uniform to hide their distinct personalities, and therefore it is horizontal.

It is very important that certain words can be used for only one of those two methods. One of these words is "religion". I think that only a teaching that prompts us to adopt a vertical outlook can rightly be called "religion". Indeed, religion is based on self-development, spiritual growth, and primacy of the spiritual world over the material one. Any "religious" teaching that promotes the horizontal outlook I propose to designate as a "cult". Another such word is "ideology". Ideology promotes the horizontal outlook and seeks to destroy human personality, so that a philosophical construction that promotes the vertical outlook should be called a "worldview" or "system of ideas". Thus, there was Stalinist ideology, whereas the American system was built on a worldview proposed by its Founding Fathers.

Religion teaches us that there are so called "mortal sins", the sins that turn a living human being into something that is unworthy of life, into a being whose soul no longer guides it, into an inanimate object. The principle that not all humans who walk and talk are in fact alive is very important for this book.

The description of the two outlooks shows that each of them creates its own, completely different, realm of existence. Thus, in order to understand the Communist system (or any other lose/lose system, for that matter) we should study the realm to which it belongs – the realm determined by the horizontal outlook. To understand contemporary Russia, we need to be aware of both realms, as we will be tracing the transition of Russia from the horizontal to the vertical realm, from the right side of Table 1 to its left side. It is very important to treat both of those realms as separate, without mixing them up and evaluating events that take place in one realm from the point of view of the other.

The system of coordinates

Our description showed that the vertical realm can be characterized by the following keywords: Animate, Individual, Future (or Time). The horizontal realm can be characterized by the opposite keywords: Inanimate, Others, Past (or Time Stops).

If so, we can organize these keywords in pairs of opposites:

1) Animate – Inanimate;
2) Individual – Others;
3) Future (or Time) – Past (or Time Stops).

Now it becomes possible to draw a three-dimensional system of coordinates to organize the space in which all human activity might be said to take place. We could assign each set of opposites to an axis, and get the three axes that we need.

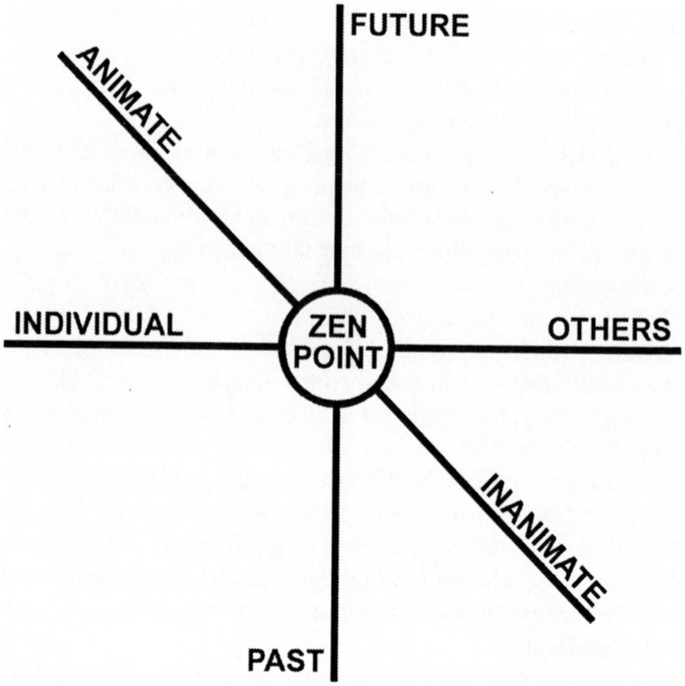

DRAWING 1. THREE AXES, EIGHT OCTANTS, AND THE ZEN POINT

Our three axes divide the space of human activity into eight three-dimensional "open cubes" called octants (see the drawing). Each of these octants is determined by three half-axes, or by three right angles that make each of these octants up.

Let us consider the angles for the octants that represent the horizontal and the vertical outlook respectively.

Here we will need to use our imagination. Stop to think why the names fit the angles.

For the "horizontal" octant ("Others, Inanimate, Past") the angles are:

a) Others, Past. This angle is called “Custom” or "Do Whatever Others Do".

b) Others, Inanimate. This angle is called "Goods Go to Everyone" or “Equality”.

c) Inanimate, Past. This angle is called "Cemetery" or “Everyone is Dead”.

That is why the octant itself is called "Collective".

For the "vertical" octant ("Individual, Animate, Future") the angles are:

a) Individual, Future. This angle is called "Tomorrow".

b) Individual, Animate. This angle is called "A Person Has Rights and Opportunities".

c) Animate, Future. This angle is called "Creativity".

That is why the octant itself is called "Life".

A preference for the "vertical" outlook over the "horizontal" one translates into a preference for

1) "Tomorrow" over "Custom", that is, individual growth and development over stagnation and social dictates;

2) "A Person Has Rights and Opportunities" over "Goods Go to Everyone", that is, the creative and private needs of an individual over the impulse to redistribute the goods and to turn the state into the arbiter of everyone’s fate.

3) "Creativity" over "Cemetery", that is, individual aliveness and uniqueness over sameness and prohibition of "unauthorized", individual activity.

Overall, the vertical outlook means a consistent preference for (individual) "Life" over the (social) "Collective", a preference for the first method of evaluation of a personal situation over the second one. These octants can also be called "horizontal" and "vertical", and this is what we will be calling them in this book.

I will call the point of intersection of the three axes the Zen Point. Indeed, its distinguishing features exactly correspond to the teachings of Zen. When a person passes through the Zen Point, he is not beholden either to his past or to his future, not determined either by his mind’s representation of what he supposedly is or by the ideas of other people of what he should be, he enjoys life and accepts death. This person can be said to be experiencing his life to the fullest, yet this is achieved simply by "being there".

When we consider the two methods we have described, we realize that to be conscious of one's situation, one does not necessarily have to make an internal (vertical) comparison or an external (horizontal) one. One can "just know" one's situation, be "fully aware of the present moment". Well, this is our Zen Point.

Thus, in principle, we can evaluate each human action from nine points of view: one for each octant and one for the Zen Point. Each of these points of view will be biased as far as the other points of view are concerned.

If one prefers, in thought or in action, animate to inanimate, the individual to others, and the future (or time) to the past (or time stops), then one can be said to have a "vertical" outlook. If you observe a social event and give it your interpretation, it will not be the only possible interpretation, but a vertical one. There may be a horizontal interpretation of the very same event (as well as a Zen interpretation and possibly the other interpretations).

The vertical realm has its logic, which happens to be the logic of life and development. But the horizontal realm also has its logic, which happens to be the logic of fear, envy, self-rejection, and death. This is the most important point this book has to make.

All the angles are named in the Appendix to the book, and when we know the names of the three angles that make up an octant, the name of each octant becomes apparent. Since only two of the octants are important for our discussion, here we will simply list the names of each octant. Please refer to the Appendix if the names of the octants are not self-explanatory.

1) OTHERS, ANIMATE, FUTURE; THIS OCTANT IS CALLED "HUMANKIND".

2) OTHERS, PAST, ANIMATE; THIS OCTANT IS CALLED "CIVILIZATION".

3) OTHERS, FUTURE, INANIMATE; THIS OCTANT IS CALLED "PRODUCTION".

4) OTHERS, INANIMATE, PAST; THIS OCTANT IS CALLED "COLLECTIVE".

5) INDIVIDUAL, ANIMATE, FUTURE; THIS OCTANT IS CALLED "LIFE".

6) INDIVIDUAL, PAST, ANIMATE; THIS OCTANT IS CALLED "KNOWLEDGE".

7) INDIVIDUAL, FUTURE, INANIMATE; THIS OCTANT IS CALLED "MIND".

8) INDIVIDUAL, INANIMATE, PAST; THIS OCTANT IS CALLED "DEATH".

CHAPTER THREE. TWO METHODS AND THE TWO REALMS THEY CREATE

TWO OPPOSITE OCTANTS: HISTORY FROM TWO POINTS OF VIEW

Every socially-significant action may be evaluated from two points of view: ideological (horizontal, or H-realm) and individual (vertical, or V-realm). It can be creative (or destructive) from one of the two points of view, and would likely (but not necessarily) have the opposite meaning when evaluated from the other point of view. The GULAG is a good example: from the individual point of view, this was destruction of millions of individuals, but from the social point of view, this was the creation of the Soviet people.

Consider the members of a firing squad. The first soldier thinks about his new belt, the second would rather be drinking, the third feels strong sympathy for the condemned, the fourth likes classical music, etc. This is the description of the squad in V-realm. But in H-realm the soldiers know that should they refuse to shoot, they will themselves be shot. Thus, in this realm it is totally irrelevant what any of them thinks or feels in private. As to the private thoughts and feelings of the condemned, they matter even less, as all we see now is his dead body.

When the West learned about Ukrainian famine of 1932 – 1933, it could give only one explanation: bad harvest. But the 1932 harvest was excellent. Stalin simply wanted to get rid of Ukrainian peasantry, which he saw as potential opposition to his regime. That is why all grain and seeds were confiscated by the Army and sold abroad. From the ideological point of view, everything was done right: ideological enemies were destroyed (about 10 million peasants starved to death in Ukraine in 1933), and the grain they did not get to eat was sold for cash. It would be impossible to find a reason for these actions in the individual realm, where it looks exactly like what it is, a premeditated genocide.

During the Kosovo conflict, the western allies were bombing Serbian bridges and thought that Milosevic would give up, unwilling to "inflict further damage on his country". But bridges and people are not present in the realm of ideological considerations. For a death-worshipper, there could be no better monument than mountains of corpses.

Only the dead vote unanimously, and the ideologues are primarily concerned with transforming humans into an (inanimate) ideological realm. Hitler killed many Jews, but he killed even more Germans. Stalin killed many Germans, but he killed many more Russians, Pol Pot never killed anyone but his fellow Cambodians, of which he killed about 30%, in three short years. And these are not murders in the usual sense of the word: this is making people more suitable for the ideological realm because, again, ideology happens to have inanimate characteristics.

PERSONAL RESPONSIBILITY

The vertical method of evaluation of one's situation is based on developing one's individuality, and its "drawback" is that it puts on each person a heavy burden of responsibility: one must think for oneself, develop oneself, create for oneself, and should the results be unsuccessful, one has only oneself to blame. It is easy for us to say, "Take personal responsibility for your actions, develop your character." But can every person successfully do that? It seems that not everyone can.

The horizontal method poses a different problem. This method allows people to simplify their lives, because there is no longer any need for independent thought or action. Instead of an individual, now the only social actor is the collective.

We define the collective as a group of people assembled for the purpose of ideological remodeling of each of its members.

One cannot improve one's situation without obtaining permission from the collective, but one can work for the good of the collective or to worsen the personal situation of other members of the collective relative to one's own.

THE TWO METHODS AND GOD

Both methods exist within each person, constantly battling with each other for influence on each person's behavior. Yet we know that in certain groups or in certain countries, or under certain political systems, one method clearly dominates over the other one. If in the US we see the values of personal responsibility, private enterprise and individual rights, in North Korea we see the domination of the opposite set of values. If we tune our radio to America, we will hear America talking in millions of voices. But if we tune our radio to North Korea, we will only hear the voice of the leader interrupted by nothing but the thunderous applause of those North Koreans who are still alive.

How did it happen that in the 20th century the horizontal method could so supplant the vertical one that entire societies were organized solely on this one method?

When a person chooses the vertical method of evaluation of one's situation, one often comes to realize the existence of a perfect Being (a perfect State of Mind or a perfect Condition), which is totally free from human weaknesses and limitations. As God is all-encompassing, every human being can relate to Him. As every individual has a personal connection to God (or to the values that God represents), all of them find themselves assembled into a community, thus solving the problem of creating a human society. The vertical method can only be chosen by individuals, but they all come together and form a human community: they come together in the idea of God the Creator, whom all those who choose the vertical method are trying to emulate.

Our description of a society built on the vertical outlook shows that it would be a productive society. But productivity creates inequality, which in turn creates unhappiness and engenders envy, giving rise to the horizontal method. How would the vertical method deal with the impulses that create envy? It becomes possible thanks to the realization of the existence of God. The absolute standard represented by the Supreme Being shows that no human being, no matter how successful, has anything that makes him comparable to God. This makes envy meaningless, and those who acquire superior skills or possess more than others are not seen as offenders. Furthermore, the vertical method teaches us that moral values are incomparably more important than material possessions. The poor can engage in the pursuit of morality as readily as the rich; thus material possessions lose much of their importance.

All of us are weak and vain, and talented and successful people arouse envy in all of us; yet creators treat each other at least with grudging respect, if not with love and understanding. By contrast, the envious person reacts to creativity with hatred. The main object of this hatred is the envious person himself, and that is why the envious person cannot be a believer in God the Creator, as this God gave him a life of constant suffering. An envious person hopes for the magical destruction of everything that is alive.

If you envy a person for having something you lack, it would be more logical to envy God. The envious person hates God not because God did not give him the material possessions he craves, but because God gave him life, and yet the envious person is unable to live it: the horizontal method of evaluation of his situation turns him into a walking corpse.

The vertical method leads to an awareness of the existence of God. But there is a "God" in the realm created by the horizontal method as well; this method also has its Creator, its Unifier of people, and its ideal of spiritual development. We will be discussing this shortly.

TWO SETS OF LAWS

A human being developing in accordance with the vertical method exists independently of others; how then can such a person be a part of society, how can he coexist with other people? The goal of such a person is self-sufficiency based on his own labor and spiritual development. If you fulfill your basic needs yourself, then your role in society is no longer based on a claim against someone else's property: there is only a need for unhindered development.

If you can develop freely, you will work productively and joyfully; this labor is bound to produce good results, and this success will result in spiritual growth; spiritual growth will bring harmony with God's world on the basis of the spiritual brotherhood of all creators, and this sense of harmony will allow you to truly appreciate beauty; appreciation of beauty will open the door to happiness, which is a joy that is not based on suffering of others, joy that is non-contradictory.

And if there is all that, then there is bound to be a gang of envy-ridden detractors around, armed with a plethora of instruments of torture: after all, no man is an island. And that means that every creative person needs a fence made of rights to defend him from envy.

DRAWING 2. FENCE OF INDIVIDUAL RIGHTS WITH A FLOOR OF SOCIAL SECURITY

Communism destroys the fence of individual rights; instead, it promises a solid floor of social security. But we know that this floor is usually a sham: ordinary citizens frequently go hungry and lack basic social services, which is not at all surprising in a state that fights individual creativity and thus tends to be poor. As for "enemies of the state", a description that can fit anyone, their "social security" takes the form of a bullet to the head. The Communists promise the floor under people's feet but instead build a ceiling so low that people bow their heads, drop to their knees, are reduced to crawling, and eventually get crushed.

DRAWING 3. CEILING (PERSONAL GROWTH IS IMPEDED BY LAW)

The only "guarantee" you got was against achieving personal success. In the Soviet Union, even a dissertation in physics started with the words, "Our guidance came from the Party", thereby naming the real author of this particular scientific discovery. The slogan went, "The Party is the architect of all our victories", and it was indeed so, as the creator could survive only by hiding under the guise of a nameless assistant, a mere tool. One Soviet song went, "When the country orders us to be heroes, everyone becomes a hero all at once." This "everyone" is very important. The Party ordered its scientists to make an invention, and you should make no mistake: if you present yourself as the inventor, the Party will destroy you and appoint another person as inventor (official, artist, writer, live human being) instead.

It is very important to note that stifling individual growth, creating a ceiling for individuals, does not necessarily mean a lack of growth in the social realm. Indeed, under Hitler the German economy grew faster than the French or the British economy: but it grew faster in large measure because new lands were occupied, Jewish property was confiscated, concentration camps were established, and strict wage and price controls were enacted. And of course, the economy grew faster only in production of weapons, without, to put it mildly, the corresponding development in culture and art. Hitler was able to mobilize the economy because people were willing to sacrifice themselves, to diminish themselves in favor of a larger whole, in favor of the social realm that Hitler was constructing.

The lack of a ceiling and the existence of a fence of individual rights create the conditions necessary for individual growth (people grow wealthier, more self-sufficient, they grow kinder to others and more attentive to themselves). But the existence of a ceiling and the lack of a fence of individual rights may create short-term growth in the social realm: while individually people are frozen in horror or abandon themselves in self-denial, there are more and more tanks, and the columns of soldiers march in perfect lockstep.

In the vertical realm, the law is oriented vertically and protects an individual from other people's envy. An individual can grow, has an "unobstructed view" of God located "overhead" and yet has his feet firmly on the ground (the ground representing an opportunity to produce, the tools of production, as well as history). That compensates an individual for having to be responsible for his actions.

In the horizontal realm, the law is oriented horizontally and separates the individual from God and from the land. But in return the people are all together. Personal responsibility is no more: where are all those individuals who served as guards in concentration camps, wrote millions of denunciations, screamed their approval for the cruelest acts in human history? There is just a blur.

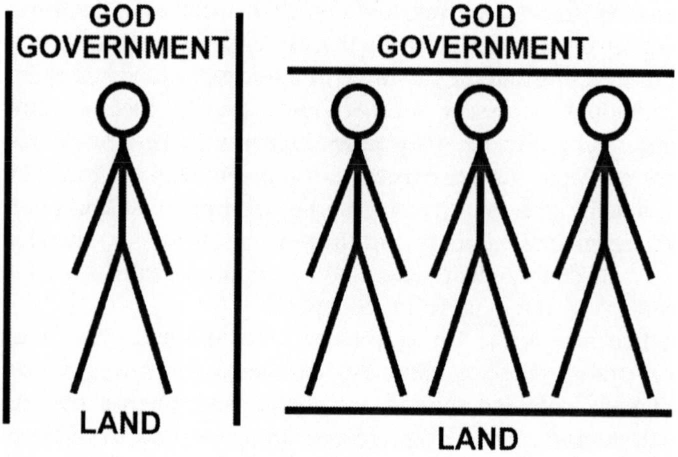

DRAWING 4. GOD, EARTH, AND VERTICAL AND HORIZONTAL LAW

The drawing shows that whoever builds a fence of law around himself also builds this fence for others. This is important to note, because in Russia people continuously confuse rights and privileges, or, to put it better, having no rights under oppressive laws, are reduced to fighting for personal privileges (exemptions). By definition, rights are given to all equally, and that is why one who fights for one's rights is at the same time fighting for the rights of others. The main feature of the vertical society is that it has a set of laws identical to those that a vertically-oriented individual would have set up for himself.

A law-abiding society is not one where there are a lot of policemen around: a society that includes a large proportion of people who want to break the law will never be law-abiding. A law-abiding society is one where citizens recognize the law as fundamentally fair, necessary to protect their rights, so that people abide by the law for exactly the same reason they want to have breakfast in the morning. Just as people do not need to be force-fed, citizens will develop and protect such a system of laws of their own volition. The goal of this system of laws is to free up the creative potential of every citizen to the maximum extent possible.

But when we talk about citizens' support for laws, we must emphasize that a horizontally oriented society also can build such a system of laws and create such an atmosphere that the citizens will show (or genuinely feel) enthusiastic support for the system. Indeed, popular support for Stalin or Hitler was immeasurably greater than that of any conceivable democratic politician. We will discuss the reasons for that a bit later; for now, we simply need to avoid the common misconception that democratic laws are supported by people while totalitarian laws are not.

THE CHEVY AND THE MERCEDES

Suppose that there are two individuals, one of whom has a cheap Chevy, and the other of whom does not have a car but has enough money to buy an expensive Mercedes. If he buys it, his condition will be a little better than that of the other person. But if he wanted to make his condition drastically better, he would use his money differently. He would hire a hoodlum to destroy the other person's Chevy, even though after he pays for that service he would be left with only enough money to buy only a second-hand bicycle. Yet relative to the former owner of the Chevy, his condition is now much better – he can ride, while the other guy has to walk.

From the horizontal point of view, the behavior of the bicycle owner was rational, and it brought him a tangible comparative benefit vis-à-vis the former owner of the Chevy, who is now a pedestrian. This sentence may look crazy to you, and if it does, you should stop reading and think about it until you make yourself aware of the mindset under which it is not crazy at all, and indeed is perfectly natural. Maybe you know some people who are ready to damage themselves just to damage others? Could it be that you yourself have thought about acting in this fashion?

This behavior led to the large-scale destruction of property, one's own as well as that of other people; yet this path was chosen because from the relative point of view it offers the largest benefit.

We should not forget another important participant in this story: the hoodlum. He destroyed the Chevy and got for his service the price of a Mercedes minus the price of a bicycle. Now the hoodlum knows that crime can pay off handsomely, and he becomes a permanent feature of the neighborhood. Other car owners can pay to have the neighbor's car destroyed, or they can pay not to have their own car destroyed.

The hoodlum eventually takes the bicycle as well. After all, the story here is not about bettering one's neighbor by overtaking him on a bicycle: the story is about violence, about a claim against property of others. As this is what the hoodlum does best, in the end he's the one who comes out the winner.

We started with the envy-based idea as to what means of transportation the former owner of the Chevy should have. But we ended with a large scale destruction of property, of the Mercedes as well as the Chevy. Is there a contradiction? Now we realize that an envious person not only wishes the destruction of the property he envies, but also is himself an object of envy, a victim of the social contract he himself helped to establish. That is why an envious person can never grow rich: his actions can lead only to destruction.

When the Russian poet Boris Pasternak was awarded a Nobel Prize in Literature, many Soviet writers rose to criticize him. Criticism presupposes that the critic knows better. But these writers were not intending to write better poetry than Pasternak: they simply wanted to destroy him, and in that they succeeded. All they wanted was to lower the standards so that they could be seen as accomplished writers, too. An envious person always combines cruelty and a mask of personal modesty, two defense mechanisms that allow the envious person to function in an envy-based environment.

TWO ECONOMIES

Why did the pharaohs build the pyramids? Why waste all this enormous labor on a useless building when there were irrigation channels to be dug, houses and schools to be built? I think the pyramids were built because the pharaohs were afraid that should they allow excess labor to be used productively, people might grow too rich, and their next question would be why they needed a pharaoh. Productive use of labor would have enriched not only the ordinary Egyptians, but the pharaohs as well: the greater the tax base the more taxes there are to collect. But absolute wealth was not what the pharaohs were after: the key was how powerful the pharaoh was in relation to the population, the level of dependence of population on the pharaoh. And in this respect, the population would have benefited much more from the productive use of this labor than the pharaohs would. From the point of view of the pharaoh, the "excess" resources needed to be destroyed. That could be done by starting a war (note that a rational ruler does not necessarily start a war to win: there are situations where it would be just fine to lose an army, especially if he can use the war to rally his people around himself, to redirect their anger away from himself). Another good solution is to initiate factional fighting, and the relatively bloodless solution is to build a pyramid. There are ways to destroy "excess" resources in the modern economy as well: one such way is high taxation.

The pyramid example is not unique: in the seventies the Soviet Union got such a financial windfall from the 1973 oil embargo that it built thousands and thousands of tanks, many more than could conceivably be used in battle. At that time, a tiny Russian car cost more than a medical doctor earned in three years, and there was a five-year wait to buy one; yet tanks were being built around the clock. Why? Because a well-to-do population would be harder to control.

It is often said that the main problem of the Soviet system was the lack of efficient management. But efficiency in what? In stifling dissent and in producing the warheads, the Soviet economy was quite efficient. Soviet achievements in space, in military technology, in spying, and in destructive diplomacy are impossible to deny. But there were some efficient managers in the consumer sector, too. These managers did not quite understand the system they were living in, as sooner or later they found themselves serving long prison terms. What were they punished for? For efficiency as such? No. For profiting personally? No. Some of those who were punished most severely did not take anything for themselves, while their enterprises flourished. They wanted labor to be used productively, while the Communists wanted it to be used destructively (or, to put it another way, productively from the point of view of an inanimate, envy-driven collective). The Communists knew that those who worked productively, in a flourishing enterprise, were bound to feel the wind of freedom.

A capitalist economy makes better and better things, makes more and more of them, ever more efficiently. And the consumer is always dissatisfied, as there always is a better product. Under the totalitarian system, the consumer is always happy: he has a crust of bread and he is overjoyed since he is going to live another day. Only ten years ago, in Russia getting a chicken on your table required so much skill, success, social status, and perseverance that if you applied it all in the US you would have a fortune. And here is the benefit for the collective: instead of a rich and powerful political opponent, you get a person whom you can buy for a chicken.

In the vertical octant, the material world is ruled by spiritual considerations, and that means that rational possession of property is possible, that the material world can exist in harmony with the spiritual one. The horizontal octant appears materialistic as it has to do with redistribution of physical property. But in fact this realm is neither spiritual nor materialistic; it is mythical, as expressed in the rationally incomprehensible ideological statement, "If you are rich, it means you are bad". And that means that real ownership of property in the horizontal octant is impossible. This is a very important point, and it will be discussed extensively later.

A capitalist economy satisfies the vertical needs of the population: it allows people to develop and create, but disallows oppression and discrimination, even though for some people that would be very pleasant. To gloat at another person's misfortune, to cause other people to suffer, is something that many people desire, even live for. It's just that in a democracy, their preferences are not satisfied. If a starving person finds a crust of bread, he will remember its taste for fifty years; to blow someone's head off is much more exciting than watching baseball on TV. Under democracy, the height of excitement comes from buying a diamond or from making a scientific discovery; in a totalitarian state the excitement comes from surviving and from trying to kill.

In Cambodia, Pol Pot's regime killed about three million people out of a population of about seven million, and did so in three short years. As most Americans have never seen a murder, American movies show a lot of shoot-outs to make the plot more exciting. What would a Cambodian blockbuster be? "Cooking a big bowl of rice"? "A boy finds his mother"?

That which grew out of the vertical method should be considered from the vertical point of view. Whatever comes from the horizontal realm should be evaluated from the horizontal point of view, lest it appear irrational or incomprehensible. For example, as Saddam Hussein clearly had a horizontal outlook, it was irrational to expect that he would try to minimize suffering of the Iraqi people: he was working tirelessly every day to maximize it. Yet during the first Gulf war, the coalition was bombing anything but Saddam, hoping that deaths of the ordinary Iraqis would cause Saddam some discomfort. Nothing of the sort: when the West stopped killing Iraqis, Saddam depopulated several Iraqi cities and continued to execute people daily for another decade. We tried to scare a fish by throwing it in the water.

Attempts to evaluate vertical phenomena from a horizontal point of view are equally misguided. When Joseph Brodsky, who was later to win a Nobel Prize, was on trial for "avoiding work", he claimed that he worked as a poet. The prosecutor replied, "Who gave you permission to call yourself a poet?" Needless to say, Brodsky was convicted and served out his term in Siberia.

If we avoid mixing the two realms and start considering them separately, the political dialogue will clear up enormously. Here is what we have today: "Mr. Putin, do you want democracy?" "Sure. I have accelerated building a democracy in my country by giving my government two months to silence all political opponents. Our people have spoken out for democracy; so we are abolishing elections." And this is not mockery: it is simply that being in one octant you see the phenomena that happen in the other octant through a distorted glass. Distorted, but in a predictable and understandable way; we will learn to recognize and correct this distortion.

NOT TO LIVE A LIE

Here is another example of mixing the two realms together and getting an unworkable result. Alexander Solzhenitsyn, another Russian Nobel laureate, appealed to the Soviets "not to live a lie". It is clear what he meant: most Soviets knew that the government lied to them, but out of fear of repression they had to look like believers in these lies. But the clarity ends right there, and Solzhenitsyn's slogan becomes politically and morally dubious. Truth and untruth, justice and injustice exist in both realms, and most people live according to the truth that exists in the realm that guides them. You have your money because it is your money, and this is your truth. A thief takes your money because he wants your money, and this is his truth. These truths are opposite because they come from opposite realms, but both of them are the truths. Hitler did not live his life thinking he was a bloodthirsty monster: he thought himself a heroic visionary, and a hundred million people were of the same opinion. Solzhenitsyn's appeal is misleading as it makes us believe that fascists, communists, or common criminals "live a lie": most of the time, in their own minds, they do not. In fact, they are the ones whose convictions are the hardest, simply because they are not animate.

The appeal "not to live a lie" is directed towards those who live under a totalitarian system yet know that this system is wrong. But if someone lives in a western democracy and all he wants to do is to rape and kill, should he not live a lie, should he act out? The appeal presupposes that people know the real truth, but for some personal reason reject it as a guiding force in their lives. Many people do not bother to discover what the real truth is and get their truth ready-made, from their favorite newspaper, and this substitution does not make them aware that they are using a counterfeit product: they think it's the real thing.

To be correct, Solzhenitsyn's appeal should be rephrased as follows: "Do not take somebody else's truth, but find your own. Take full responsibility for your actions and find the truth that is free of claims against others, the truth that you can be a success, not a victim. And find the inner strength to live according to this truth, do not betray yourself."

What is necessary for people to "not live a lie"? They need an opportunity to formulate their own claim-free truth, and they also need the rights that protect them when they live according to their truth. The truth cannot be separated from rights: it is not enough to learn to live without claims against others, not enough not to betray oneself. "Not to live a lie" is not enough: one needs to turn the concept of personal responsibility and the claim-free truth that comes with it into the foundation of society.

TWO LANGUAGES

Before the Industrial Age, things were created from scratch by one master. The Industrial Age saw the great advance: a method of assembling a product from identical pre-fabricated parts. The first real pistol was the first one that did not have a gunsmith's name engraved on it: prior to that there were just sculptures that could shoot. The same process happened in the language. Before the Industrial Age, each word was extremely valuable, as it was a part of a prayer or a pledge, and books were handwritten. Now a word is often just a part of a cliché. Today a word seems orphaned if it is not a part of an advertising slogan. Yet the language of clichés is fundamentally different from a medium that creates and organizes the inner world of a thinking individual.

The language of clichés is an enormously effective means of communication, much more effective than the normal human language. Jeans are worn in Canada and in Korea, and we instantly know that the person who is wearing them is cool. By contrast, Korean poetry is unknown and incomprehensible in Canada: the language of thoughts loses out to the language of clichés and images. The language of thoughts can communicate everything, but it is not efficient: often, people do not understand and do not hear each other. The language of clichés is efficient, but it communicates nothing. A commercial wants you to believe that a cup of a particular brand of coffee will cause you to experience bliss; try it and see if it works.

If we ask ourselves the question, "What is God?" a striking similarity between language and God would become apparent. Language turned us into humans, it created everything, it lets us understand everything and, as we learn and develop, it makes us conscious of Time. The Bible starts by mentioning the Word. Now it is clear why language was the main target of the Communists.

The Industrial Age brought about such an information explosion that major European nations started to see themselves as culturally self-sufficient. The chauvinism and nationalism that grew out of this were one of the causes of World War I. Hitler's teachings about the supremacy of German culture were the cornerstone of his ideology. By contrast, the Communist ideology was based on the *Internationale* – the unification of all workers of the world against all of the world's capitalists. The only way to achieve understanding among cultures that were so diverse was in effect to have a two-word language: worker or capitalist. And that language was understood in countries as diverse as Russia, China, Mozambique and Cuba.

There are two very distinct languages: one is personal and the other is national and international. These languages are interconnected, but they are very different nonetheless, and serve a different purpose. One is a language of personal spiritual growth, while the other is the language of unification of people. Compare a face and a flag, a greeting and a military salute, walking and marching, clothing and a uniform, the natural rhythm of human life and a schedule. Switching from one language to the other, people change their facial expressions: from lively and emotional, they suddenly become stone-faced and distant.

A medieval knight had his name, his motto, his emblem, his personal history, the lady to whom he dedicated his heroic deeds – all distinct and intensely personal. Compare such a knight with a modern tank: we can tell one tank from another only by its number, and we see no humans at all.

TWO MORALITIES

If the vertical and horizontal realms are so different, it follows that in each of these realms the definitions of good and bad will also be very different. One morality defines "good" as that which allows an individual to grow and develop, while the other approves of everything that allows the collective to take control over the actions of the individual.

If a person has a vertical outlook, he cannot do evil while thinking that he is doing good (he can still do evil, but he is aware that what he is doing is evil). The vertical outlook is not a guarantee of moral, or even predictable or rational, behavior. But it does allow people to consistently identify good and evil. An unthinking soldier or a robot can do good simply by following an order, but the next order may cause him to do evil. The vertical outlook allows a person to make his own determination on the basis of the appropriate criteria.

The vertical outlook does not allow a person to be self-righteous, as certainty contradicts growth and development. By contrast, the horizontal ideology is free of any self-doubt, as "everybody" cannot be wrong. We will see that this actually makes the ideology always wrong, and there are two reasons for that. The first is that you cannot be right if you exclude the possibility of ever being wrong, if you suspend your doubt. And second, because whatever "everybody" accepts was actually conceived and formulated by nobody. We will shortly see that ideology has no single human author, that nobody can take responsibility for it, and that it fundamentally contradicts human logic or whatever humans need to make their lives a success.

TWO TYPES OF RIGHTS

Let's suppose that I create something for myself. I act independently, and so I should look at the event from my personal point of view. The relevant facts would be:

1) I advanced my position in the world;

2) I did so through my personal effort;

3) I got a feeling of personal satisfaction;

4) The ability of others to compete with me has been reduced.

As a result of my action, my situation improved. From the vertical point of view, the situation of others has also improved, as we benefit from success of our neighbors through job creation, an increased tax base, the services they provided to achieve their success, the use of the product they put on the market, and simply from their smile. However, from the horizontal point of view, the situation of all my neighbors has (comparatively) worsened. Since I have improved my situation, I got a competitive advantage and can count on prettier women and faster cars. Thus, is it not surprising that I provoke envy in others.

Now suppose that somebody got killed. I did not act; we saw it only as observers, so it is natural to consider this event from the point of view of "the people" seen as one unit. Each "part" of "the people" would interpret this event as follows:

1) Since the number of contenders has decreased by one, I (as well as everybody else) advanced my position in the world;

2) I did so expending no personal effort whatsoever;

3) My (and everybody else's) competitive position has improved, especially if the victim was talented or attractive;

4) I shared a feeling of satisfaction that everybody experienced.

As a result of this occurrence only one person's situation worsened (and, being dead, this person is no longer a social actor!), but the situation of all the others improved. And do not forget that each constituent part of "the people" benefited without expending any personal effort whatsoever. The conclusion is obvious: the more they kill, the better – as long as it is not me.

Now we know why the Great Purges engineered by Stalin enjoyed unanimous popular support. Victims of the Purges were killed or sent to camps and thus were unable to oppose the Purges. And those who remained could now move into the victims' apartments and get their jobs. I would again like to mention Pol Pot – in his own way, the greatest world leader. In three years, without war, he reduced the population of Cambodia by at least a third, using nothing but Cambodians whose turn to die would come tomorrow. Had the Vietnamese not interrupted this social experiment, Pol Pot could have been able to reduce the population of Cambodia to one person – himself. So, the logic that I have just articulated is no idle mental construct: it has been proven in the field. Here is this logic again. The more they kill the better (better!) it is for me. But when they kill me, I no longer can express an opinion: put me down as the supporter that I was when I was alive. As for the leader, the fewer the clapping hands, the louder the applause. Witness the tumultuous applause given to Stalin at the 17th Party Congress: all these people were killed hours or days later, their hands still sore from clapping.

Let me give you another example, just to make sure that you get it down pat. In the Middle Ages there were only a few writers. Not all of them were good, but their profession made them exceptional, and they were respected accordingly. Today there are thousands of writers, only a few of whom are any good. Being a writer is no longer exceptional, so bad writers have nothing for which they can be respected. In the West they have nobody to blame but themselves. But the Soviet system worked differently: it quickly discovered the best writers (of whom there are always only a few), silenced them, and destroyed their work. Then the remaining thousands of writers got to be the best writers around. And they felt great. They praised the Soviet system for its kindness: by killing a genius it had made thousands of talentless people happy.

We should note one quality of envy-ridden people: they have exceptionally sharp eyesight, which actually characterizes all vultures. When the future Nobel Prize winner Joseph Brodsky was just a young man writing his first poems, he was already recognized for what he was, and promptly sent to Siberia.

THE MYTH OF POVERTY

Western social science is in the grip of an extremely destructive paradigm: the paradigm of poverty. Sure, if people are afraid to produce or if they destroy their own harvest, the result they get is poverty. But physical inability to produce should not be confused with man-made conditions that impede production. The correct paradigm should concentrate on envy, as envy is the true cause of poverty. Triple the US tax rate, and the US will instantly be poor. Protect Russian producers from envy – and Russia will soon be rich. In fact, Russia is so rich in natural resources that the majority of the population does not even need to work: all they need is to stop destroying resources, stop negative interference.

There is only one reason why we are not living in the Stone Age: we did not burn at the stake all our Giordano Brunos and did not send to Auschwitz all our Einsteins. Slowly but surely, it became possible to be Galileo – and yet remain alive. The most beautiful building in Russia, by all accounts, is St. Basil's Cathedral in Moscow. Once the Cathedral was built, its creator was blinded so that he would not reproduce this beauty anyplace else. And if the Cathedral were not in Moscow, it would probably be razed to the ground, so as not to upstage the capital, just as Novgorod Kremlin was. This is the cause of Russia's poverty, not a lack of architects or a lack of stone.

It should be noted that destructive labor can be very profitable. Racketeers and bribe-taking bureaucrats live well, even though they destroy twenty times more than they take for themselves. There are simpler methods as well. One bulldozer owner told me a simple trick. In a pouring rain, he simply goes to an unpaved road. There he digs a ditch, right on the road. Soon the ditch is filled with water, and now he is in business. He waits nearby, smoking a cigarette. The car comes and gets stuck in the ditch, as the water conceals how deep it is. By pure chance, the bulldozer driver happens to be nearby. He pulls the car out of the ditch with his bulldozer, but only for a handsome fee. By playing this trick, the bulldozer driver was able to triple his monthly income: the ditch paid twice as much as his regular job.

Dear reader! You should know that there is plenty you can be loved for: you are beautiful, kind, successful, knowledgeable, you have a sense of humor, and you simply are who you are. But you can also be hated. You smile when I am suffering, you have more money than you deserve, some people like you more than they like me. Your kindness and your success insult me, I hate you for your honesty, and I would like to have your stuff. I hate you because you disagree with me, because you are not like me and thus may be better than me, and I hate you just because you exist. These are the vertical and the horizontal methods in their simplest and purest forms. Please do not mix them up, but consider them separately.

THE HORIZONTALLY-ORIENTED INDIVIDUAL AND THE VERTICALLY- ORIENTED GROUP

We said that for the horizontal method there must be a group of people. But can a single person be horizontally oriented, even if he has no reference group from which he takes his cues? Yes, this is very possible, and in fact is often the case. One simply adopts an envious and comparison-based view of oneself. Now a person behaves not according to his internal moral dialogue, but according to the desires of an imaginary collective. He starts loving (or hating) himself, striking poses even though there's nobody watching. This is clearly seen in art: some artists seek to express their inner world, their feelings, while others seek to express what the customers might want them to express. There are three types of paintings: what the artist wants to draw, what the artist thinks the customer wants to see, and what the customer specifically describes and orders. The first is called art, the second is called kitsch, and the third is called a paint job. There can also be any combination of the three. But the vertically oriented person is guided only by his personal, claim-free assessment of his actions.

Even though the vertical method requires only one person, it is usually practiced in the context of a group. (We define a group differently from a collective. A group is several people assembled together because they have a common cause. A collective is several people assembled together with the aim of the ideological transformation of each of its members). The vertical method starts with a dialogue that takes place within a human being. There is a second participant: the conscience, an ideal, a real or imaginary friend, or God. This second participant can be external, such as a friend, a loved one, a book. In battle, the bravery and sacrifice of one's fellow soldiers can uplift and motivate everyone. Art is another uplifting and cleansing force. Most people have in fact been motivated by the example of others. If the internal moral dialogue is not being supplanted, if a person learns to live without claims, his method of evaluating his situation remains vertical even though there are other people involved. The group helps, rather than destroying, this process. The vertical method is destroyed only by blind imitation, by loss of self-control.

CHAPTER FOUR. THE NUTS AND BOLTS OF THE MACHINE

REVOLT AGAINST THE INDUSTRIAL AGE

We have already noted that there are two diametrically opposite sets of rights. The first set of rights gives us the opportunity to create, even at the expense of an increase in inequality. This set can be called Creative Rights. The other set of rights gives assurance that no one's relative position will worsen, even if he is unable or unwilling to create. (Please note the importance of the word "relative" here, as such a society, as a whole, if we observe it from the outside, always experiences a sharp economic and cultural decline). This set of rights should be called People's Rights. Note that every society based on this set of rights calls itself a "People's Democracy," as it defends the rights of the people as a whole at the expense of individual creators.

A train can leave the station, meaning those who came too late will miss it, but also allowing those already inside to reach their destination. In the alternative, the train can just stand there with its doors open, never going anywhere, but accepting all comers for the sake of equality.

With the start of the Industrial Revolution, fewer and fewer people could deal with the growing complexity of life as individuals, and so the number of people who needed creative rights grew relatively smaller. At the same time, the majority of people became conscious of the other set of rights, the one that makes sure that everyone is equal. These rights could not be given to people individually: you cannot be "equal to someone" without this other person's participation. The right to equality can be bestowed only on all people together, on "the people" as opposed to all the individual citizens living in a particular country. The conflict between these two irreconcilable and antagonistic sets of rights threatened to cause a social explosion.

The Communist system promised to give people the following rights:

to make envy irrelevant for all, which was accomplished by making everyone's situation unenviable;

to make people equal to one another. Usually people earn their money by producing something that other people need; now one would be considered useful and be fed not in accordance with how one meets the needs of other people, but in accordance with how one serves ideology. Since in an ideological state, every person must submit to ideological dictates, now nobody can be said to meet the needs of other people. Everybody is equal, as there no longer are masters and servants, just slaves to ideology;

not to think or draw one's own conclusions. With the rapid development of industry and science, many people fell behind and could be considered "stupid". But ideology saves everyone from this embarrassment: as ideology always tells you what to think or do, everyone can be considered of average intelligence. In the ideological state, the illiterate worker tells the scientist what to do, and teaches the poet to write poetry. One person is able to do things, while the other is able to teach him how these things should be done; thus they can be considered of equal intelligence;

to live without exercising full responsibility over one's own life, and yet, to always have an excuse for living this way as everything is restricted, forbidden, denied, impossible, or mortally dangerous;

to be an adult, yet to have society treat you like a child or even a household pet, carefully measuring your food and your knowledge, and walking you on a leash;

not to study, and yet to know all that society wants you to know. To be emotionally involved in the heroic struggle of the people of Angola against the imperialists without knowing where Angola is;

not to succeed in anything, and yet to enjoy respect that is not any less (and often more) than that which goes to those who do succeed. When Boris Pasternak won the Nobel Prize in Literature, his work was viciously criticized; fortunately, the work of the remaining tens of thousands of members of the Union of Soviet Writers was beyond reproach;

to always have the right "facts" and clichés (conveniently printed in today's newspaper) to be able to "answer" every question;

not knowing what freedom is, to remain content as a slave;

not to have a historical memory, and to vote yet again for those who have just recently attempted to wipe you off the face of the Earth;

and, most importantly, to always have an explanation for why you did not become a true human being, a creator, a success, an envy-free and happy person.

Western readers may see these rights as tremendously negative and think that I am just being facetious, using this list simply to highlight the horrors of the totalitarian regime. That was not my intent at all. I simply described a set of instruments necessary to accomplish a different task. We could try to build a society that consists of individuals, of people who have opportunities and are securely protected by their individual rights, or we can try to create an anthill, which is also very functional under certain circumstances and where every ant has a set of rights – significantly different from the set of rights enjoyed by your average Westerner, but a set of rights nonetheless. The rights that Communism gives people are not inadequate, counterproductive, or wrong: they are simply entirely different. At one point in human history, for some people, they were very attractive. Now, thank God, they appear crazy and delusional, but they still have to be evaluated on their merits as opposed to just being dismissed.

It would be too easy to just proclaim that Western democracy is good and totalitarian regimes are bad. But our topic is not trivial: we are discussing why people worshiped Stalin, Hitler and Mao and why, ten years after the inglorious demise of the Soviet Union, 35% of Russians vote for the Communists while the "democratic" parties struggle to get a combined total of 15%. The events of September 11 showed that the West can still be mortally threatened by envy and hate.

Please reread the list of rights above until you understand how they can be viewed as a genuine achievement and a cherished possession. You need to be able to answer the question, "Why is it wonderful to be powerless, abused, even tortured, or enslaved?" Until you are ready with the answer, "Because it absolves you of personal responsibility for your actions and gives you a limitless right to blame someone else", you should not read further. But when you do give this answer and understand its internal logic, you have made a giant step forward in understanding what this book is about.

The words "communism" and "fascism" both came from words that have the same meaning, "together as one" (commune is "belonging to all" and *fasci* are branches that are tied together). Let me repeat that the social systems based on these ideologies are called people's democracies, and they are indeed just that, provided that "the people" is seen as one unit. If all the country's population is seen as one, creator's rights are no longer relevant, as they are rights for individuals. A people's democracy takes the people's rights for its basis, but it does not cease being creative; on the contrary, it starts producing handcuffs and tanks faster than Picasso could draw.

The most totalitarian word in the Russian language that has a Russian root is the word *Edinstvo*, meaning Unity. Indeed, Unity means "my opinion is no longer relevant, I am not an independent social actor; if the thousands agree as one, why should I be voicing my opinion?" By sheer coincidence, of course, Unity is the name of Russia's current ruling party (and in fact, this word is simply a good translation of "communism" – a word with a foreign root – into pure Russian).

"The people as a unit" is a social actor whose development proceeds according to the horizontal method, and that allowed the Communists to realize the dreams of those who were afraid to define their own views, to take personal responsibility for their actions, who thought themselves too weak to face God's judgment on their own. Again, the Communists fulfilled people's dreams, but these were dreams of a life based on entirely different principles, dreams for life after suicide.

The communist system defended the interests of the collective, of those who had given up on their destiny as individuals and opted instead to become just one part of a social unit.

The communist anthem said, "We shall build our own, new world; he who was nothing, will be everything". "Nothing" is a very apt self-description here, and "everything" is just as great. Please note, it does not say "Those who had little, will have more" or "servants will become barons and princes". There is no "career" or "gain" in this promise. You are not worthy of anything if you are a "nothing", and you can become "everything" only when your ashes are scattered to the wind.

The Communists gave power to the weak, dependent, controlled, nameless, and personally powerless (acting as one unit, of course), provided that personally, one by one, they would forever remain so. The communist system has nothing to do with empowerment: on the contrary, it gives the microphone only and exclusively to the mute. The communist system does not teach the mute to talk, but it makes absolutely sure that those who can speak do not have a voice. And you cannot deny that since the mute do exist, this is equality. But the mute are not happy: since the blind also exist, the mute must have their eyes plucked out. That is why under Stalin, for one wrong word you would get tortured and shot, together with all your family, friends, relatives, and those who once stood next to you at a cocktail party. All power belonged to the Party, and what the hell it was – no one knew. Read on, and you will know.

INDUSTRIAL AGE REALITIES

The advent of industrial technology brought about fundamental changes in the structure of society. Instead of manufactures, i.e. production by hand, now there were factories that used the power of steam or electricity. Machine tools were much more efficient than people, and owning a factory was very profitable. At the same time, many peasants were no longer able to support their families: they had to migrate to the cities and become factory workers. Thus they lost the relative independence that the land had given them: they stopped being independent participants in the economic market. As a result, common people lost hope for personal economic success at the very time when the upper classes had new economic opportunities opening up for them and started getting rewards that the dispossessed could envy.

The rapid technological and scientific progress of the Industrial Age opened wide horizons for those who were talented and educated. But the great majority of people were not educated, and now without education even talent was useless. Thus, the majority of people started to feel envious because they were being left behind just when there appeared breathtaking opportunities for those who could take advantage of them.

Ordinary daily life was becoming more and more complicated. Some people took advantage of the virtually unlimited economic opportunities. But most lost their way of life and saw their position in society worsen relative to the achievements of others. These people felt that in the emerging society only the fittest were equipped to survive. As a result, the lowest strata of society came into conflict with the economic and social realities of industrial capitalism, with the rapid and uncontrollable progress of civilization, and with those who could, in such circumstances, maintain their independence and achieve success.

In absolute terms, life for the great majority of people in the industrialized countries was much better. But in relative terms, the situation of the great majority grew worse. There was now a greater gap between the rich and the poor, the empowered and the powerless.

Yet since humans were now rapidly reshaping the world, the social structure no longer seemed pre-ordained: on the contrary, just as the landscape was being rapidly rearranged, it now appeared logical to reengineer the social system as well.

From the relative point of view, there appeared the greatest irritant of all: the opportunity for self-determination. In a feudal society, you were born into your class and into your stratum, and had to bear your cross. Now a peasant could become rich even though he had no divine right to his wealth, and regardless of whether the wealth was obtained through hard labor, luck, or subterfuge. Envy became "legitimate," and all its destructive force was ready to be released.

Industrial Age workers found themselves in an entirely new environment. Its characteristics were as follows:

In the factory or in the office they could not produce anything by themselves and had to be a part of a work brigade. Within a brigade, each worker had a strictly defined function.

Workers could no longer see themselves as creators because each of them did only a small part of what was required to make the final product. Thus, they lost the sense of personal responsibility for the final product that a Pre-Industrial master had. The satisfaction that a true creator experiences was thus transferred to the brigade. This is very important. We talked about creator's rights and the creator's outlook having to "fight it out" with the outlook of the envious masses. But to have this fight, we need creators, i.e. human beings who actually have this outlook. But suddenly there were none. Individual creators were "no-shows", and thus the victory was awarded to the collective. A Ford factory made a lot of cars, but no worker could say, "I made this car", as all he ever did was to attach windshield wipers. A sense of personal responsibility is no less important. In the Nuremberg Trial, the judges asked who killed the Jews. And the answer was, "Nobody", as one of the accused was only signing papers, the other just guarding the camp, and the third just opening the door to the gas chamber. The accused felt that they were being treated unjustly: the calamity was caused by their work brigade, and this brigade was not on trial, even if some of its members were.

In production, workers were now dependent on one another, and the real producer was the work brigade: several workers, united in service to the machine tool. We will see shortly that this setup had tremendously important consequences.

The character of work was such that it was detrimental to the development of human personality: the tasks were repetitive, narrow, identical, predictable, and determined from the outside. A peasant wakes up at sunrise and goes into the fields to perform many different tasks, under the open sky, working together with his animals. And suddenly this peasant finds himself in a sooty factory building, in front of a machine tool that requires of him just one repetitive operation.

In their daily life, people now had to conform to a strict schedule; in the assembly line environment even their individual movements were pre-determined and controlled.

At work, if you thought or dreamed, you risked being injured or fired; you could no longer appear in any way different from the others and had to wear a uniform. Thus the worker lost his unique personality traits. His personal experience, his thoughts and knowledge were no longer relevant; and yet this is exactly what the vertical outlook is based on.

People's lives were separated from nature; their environment was urban, almost wholly artificial, that is to say, machine-made.

People had no time to talk or think, but this did not appear to be any great loss. Working in a thoughtless and artificial industrial environment, they found out all they needed to know from newspapers. Newspapers were written in a language of clichés. A pre-fabricated and industrially reproduced part of speech, a cliché reduces the range of human feelings to one, most often negative and destructive, emotion. Yet clichés are very convenient as they can "fit" every circumstance, thus freeing people from the need to think. Soon the opinion of one person was indistinguishable from the opinion of another. Language itself lost its sparkle as sentences were assembled out of clichés and were no longer able to transmit feelings adequately. As a result, people became emotionally detached, more alienated from their own hearts.

In the process of production the human being, once a proud creator, became the weakest link. Working with the machine tool, he did not move fast enough, he daydreamed, and he wanted to talk. How to make humans work better?

A NEW CANDIDATE FOR THE POSITION OF GOD: THE MACHINE TOOL

There once was a God who created the world, and created people in it. Each person had his place and his destiny: the nobles were destined to be nobles, and the peasants had to grow crops. But a peasant turned factory owner did not grow rich because of God, as this was clearly the consequence of his own ability. What was emerging was a society created by people, not by God.

Prior to the Industrial Age, human life took place in a setting created by God, among trees and animals, and under the sun and the stars. Now, returning from work, a man sees the roof of his car. Indeed, people live in a world that is entirely created by machine tools. When was the last time you saw a wild animal or walked the earth barefoot? Things were being created by the thousands, they were everywhere, and the machine tool was the creator of everything.

In a very short time, the Industrial Age created an explosion in productivity and immeasurably increased human power to influence the Earth. If before only Zeus could blow up a mountain, now, with the invention of dynamite, humans could easily do it. For thousands of years of human history, the only human who could fly was Icarus, but now humans can part the seas and make rivers flow backwards – though not by themselves, but thanks to the machine tool. Scientific knowledge was advancing so fast that people said, "We can understand, change, and control everything on Earth." And that meant that God of Raphael and Bach was no longer seen as Creator or Master of the Universe. There was now a different God. That which was created by the old God, the God of individual responsibility, was swiftly retreating before the machine tool: the Earth's surface was being covered up with asphalt.

It was not Man who was the new creator: in fact, the individual produced nothing. The new creator was the machine tool. And humans served the machine tool, adapted their lives to the machine tool and lived in the world that the machine tool created.

Now we realize that the machine tool not only resembles God, but appears to be even better! God did not make people the masters of nature. The machine tool accomplished that in an amazingly short time. God created many things, each different from the others. The machine tool produced the greatest miracle since Creation: a whole lot of things, each identical to the next. Some of the things created by God were alive, and thus hard to control. All of the things created by the machine tool were inanimate, predictable, controllable, and immediately useful.

God did not succeed in making people live according to His commandments; indeed, He could hardly get people to pray one hour a week, but now, for at least ten hours a day, the workers completely subordinated their lives to the dictates of the machine tool.

Religion has God, the Mystery of Creation, and a World created by God. For the worker, the Collective, assembled for the purpose of working with the machine tool, became a substitute for the World. Your ideal became that of Sameness and Unity, your chief desire – to become as indistinguishable from others as were the parts produced by the machine tool. The ideology of equality, indeed the ideology of human sameness, is a perverted "religion" that proclaims the Machine Tool as the new God.

Because of technology, society seemed to be undergoing too rapid a change. The workers could not deal with the complexities that suddenly became part of daily life, nor could they take advantage of the multitude of new opportunities. Yet they did not want to be left behind. The ideology proposed a fivefold solution. It promised:

1) to unify people so that they could face the complexities of life together, as one unit;

2) to simplify their lives by centralizing the decision-making process and controlling the flow of information;

3) to help people deal with envy by decreasing the range of opportunity;

4) for those frightened by the rapid change brought about by science and technology, to replace change with the certainty and stupor of the ideological society;

5) to allow each person, separated from his traditional community as he now was, to acquire a new sense of belonging, a clearly defined function, a new identity not within the rapidly changing and enormously complex world, but within the understandable, rigid, and permanent structure of the collective.

Pre-Industrial society seemed impossible to change. Thus, the only way to better your condition was to change yourself, and this has always been very difficult. But now technology was rapidly and drastically transforming the world, and soon people realized that the union of ideology and technology could help them to achieve happiness the easy way: without going through the daunting process of spiritually improving themselves.

People now thought that they did not have to work on turning themselves into moral, successful, and unique individuals. Instead they submitted themselves to society, to the collective, as raw material, asking, "Here am I, please assemble me, please make me into a Member, please tell me how to move and what to say". From now on, shaping the person was the job of society, and society began to perform this task in the assembly-line fashion to which it was accustomed.

Industrial technology permeated all areas of human life, and in every instance it pushed people towards choosing the horizontal outlook over the vertical one. But, in fact, the reinforcement was mutual: without the horizontal ideology, Industrial Age technology would have been difficult to introduce because people would have found the Industrial Age technological environment overly oppressive.

What was it that the horizontal outlook promised to people that made them forsake their individuality and start worshipping the new God? For the most part, it happened subconsciously. Industrial technology permeated all areas of life so quickly that the industrialized societies simply had no time to adapt psychologically to the changes.

A SCENE FROM A RUSSIAN MOVIE

In *Chapayev*, a classic Russian movie about the Russian Civil War, there is a scene that, in my view, explains why the civil war was won by the

Communists. Hundreds of White Army (Tsarist or Republican, but anti-Communist) officers, march in a tight formation to attack the Reds (the Communists). The Whites march fully upright, with drummers up front, in neat, freshly ironed black (and that is a color of death) uniforms with all their medals attached to their chests. Some Reds panic and run away, as the tight formation marching in straight rows with their bayonets out is very scary, indeed. But one peasant girl, in a kerchief, just learned to use a machine gun the other night. She opens fire, and in the five terrifying seconds of a machine gun firing non-stop, we see the field littered with corpses, all the White officers dead.

Why did the Whites attack in straight rows, marching to a drumbeat? The tight, straight row formation was good for Napoleon, because at that time firearms had to be fired in salvos to be effective and machine guns did not exist. But in the age of the machine gun, what could possibly be the rationale for such a suicidal attack?

I think that in a world of machines, the Whites may have unconsciously wanted to impersonate one, to show that this was not a simple attack by a thousand individual human beings. Straight rows of attackers marching to the drumbeat made the soldiers look as if they were made by a machine, and that made them look as if they were inanimate, immune to bullets. That is what made the attack so scary, and that worked, for a short while.

But the girl had gotten hold of the real God, the Machine Gun, and in five seconds she killed all those people. White officers wore Christian crosses, meaning that their God was not the Machine Gun, and their attempt to adapt to the new industrial reality, to attack in straight rows as a sort of "make-believe human machine gun" was squashed by the real Machine Gun and those in service directly to It.

As a historical footnote, we might add that attacks of large masses of infantry, often marching to a drumbeat, against machine guns and artillery, were not just in the movies: tens of thousands of soldiers died in such attacks in World War I.

Nobody consciously thought of the Machine Tool as the new God, and nobody called people to worship the Machine Tool and the world it had created. But it was not necessary to do so openly. There is the obvious reality, and then there are the undercurrents, as every advertising person knows. If a man asks a woman to come up for a cup of coffee, a good historian will not ask what brand of coffee they ended up drinking, particularly if the woman gets pregnant that day. The Communists and the Fascists won popular support because in their particular countries at that particular point in time they used the keywords and the symbols that mattered. The woman doesn't accept the man's invitation because she likes the brand of coffee he's offering. The Communists and the Fascists didn't know that they were worshipping the Machine Tool, but they consistently acted as if they did.

It could be said that there are two types of discoverers, Einstein and Hitler. Einstein discovered what nobody knew, while Hitler discovered what most people in his country craved but could not formulate, a political undercurrent that everyone sensed, but that only Hitler could embody and represent.

CIVILIZATION'S PYRAMID

Feudal society had a simple structure. Slaves were almost like animals and therefore their opinion did not matter. All peasants were seen as stupid and had to be controlled by the whip and by arbitrary taxes. All nobles were seen as smart, and held administrative positions, often in rather strict accordance with their respective titles. The king was presented as omniscient and beyond reproach. Of course, everybody knew that the system did not correspond to reality and thus was very inefficient. In terms of natural talent, there could easily have been a simple soldier more qualified to lead an army than a prince. But that never happened because the military of the day was so low-tech that most every prince could lead an army more or less well. On the other hand, soldiers were mostly illiterate and uneducated, and so their natural talents were not usually apparent.

But the more difficult the task, the fewer the people who are able to accomplish it (unless there is a significant conscious effort to reverse or diminish this trend). With the development of technology, some tasks became so sophisticated and so important that not everyone could perform them well. In the early Middle Ages, your wealth was pretty much determined by your title, the size of your landholdings, and your closeness to the throne. But with the invention of such things as double-entry bookkeeping, fast seafaring ships and improved manufacturing technologies, to name just a few, your personal qualities such as intelligence, education, skill and courage started to matter much more.

Everyone can walk, and so the invention of shoes directly benefits everyone. To drive a car, you need to pass the hurdle of getting a license, and so there are some who fail to directly benefit from the opportunity to drive one. Only a tiny fraction of people are capable of piloting a jet, and fewer still can became astronauts. This could be called the "problem of civilization's pyramid": technology creates new, unheard-of opportunities, but the number of people who can take advantage of them grows progressively smaller. With the advent of the Industrial Age, the growth of new technologies was so explosive that it sharply separated people into more capable and less capable.

Consider the psychological pressure on a person born in 1900, when a motorcar was a miracle and speeds of 30 miles per hour were considered physiologically incompatible with human life: by the age of 60 this person witnessed a space flight and by the age of 69 saw astronauts walking on the moon.

The 19th century European society was slow to change, and those who wanted to effect change could only try to change themselves, change their perceptions of reality, improve the understanding of their own inner world. That is why 19th century literature started to seriously examine the psychology and the character of the people it described.

But with the advent of the industrial technology that was rapidly changing the world, society no longer seemed stable. And then there came an idea that seemed perfectly logical: "Why should we try to improve ourselves, when we can simply improve the world around us?" This idea has very profound implications. Once there was a God, and God decreed that man should change himself for the better. But now this no longer seemed relevant.

Too many people were upset that life was passing them by: the benefits of the Industrial Age seemed to be distributed very unfairly. Ideology offered a ready solution to this problem: the weak should be unified into one huge and strong social organism that would destroy everything that the weak saw as inaccessible to them.

The weak wanted to worship a new God, one who would direct the change not of individual persons but of whole societies. For them, this solution had a great additional advantage: you no longer had to blame yourself for your own failures; instead, everyone gained the right to blame society for one's personal failures.

Why have a God who teaches us how to develop and change ourselves, if instead we now have technology that can change the society around us? To change yourself is a handicraft, an outdated mode of production, while changing an entire society is what modern technology is all about: mass production, huge scale, conveyor belts, a job for a brigade of workers.

This idea seemed very progressive, and it won out. Those who still thought that human beings should not kill or lie, those who thought that God was the one that was described in the Bible, now seemed hopelessly outdated. There now was another God and a different bible. Marx's *Capital* was very appropriately named, as capital is what gives birth to machine tools and the Machine Tool was the one who changed the world. Capital was the new Heavenly Father, the Machine Tool was the Son that came to change the World, and the Industrial Age ideology was the new Holy Spirit. Marx gave us the new Holy Scriptures, and it was very appropriate that he was supported by angels, or Engels as fate chose to spell it.

Communist doctrine was seen as a weapon in the hands of the disadvantaged and the backward, and yet at the same time it appeared as the most advanced, the most modern teaching of the day! A miracle! A dream come true! A fairy tale: the last one turns out to be the winner! Communist doctrine seemed custom-made for backward and downtrodden workers and peasants and yet seemed so advanced that it attracted British lords.

Many individuals, and soon entire societies, were converted, and the horizontal approach to evaluation of one's situation came to substitute itself for the vertical one. In the Pre-Industrial Age, the horizontal approach was always chosen individually, in a moment of desperation, and then only temporarily. According to the "old god", envy, covetousness and all forms of suicide were crimes. But now a license was granted, and this behavior was no longer criminal. The horizontal approach was a given, and henceforth you could think about your own individuality only in private, and often at great personal risk. The dispossessed no longer walked naked, but they did not wear clothes either: instead, everybody wore a uniform.

ABSOLUTE KNOWLEDGE

In the 20th century we witnessed another unique phenomenon: Stalin, Mao, Kim Il Sung and Hitler were political leaders who were seen as gods that came to Earth. Each of these four leaders caused his people far more harm than all the previous leaders of these countries (or indeed all foreign invaders!) put together, and yet was worshipped more fanatically than any God ever was. Indeed, there are people who still see these leaders as gods! Think of that: in the entire history of the modern world there were only four leaders who were worshipped as Gods, and all four were born almost at the same time and came to power in war-torn, devastated countries. This could not have been an accident.

Now we know why it was so. People gave up their individual personalities in favor of a collective personality, their own future in favor of a collective future. The personality of all people, the future aspirations of all people were now encapsulated in one human being, the Great Leader. Suleyman Stalsky, a poet of the Stalin era, wrote a poem where the sun actually asks Stalin's permission to rise.

Stalin was the only person in Russia who had certain knowledge of anything, and indeed, he had the most certain knowledge of everything. People did not know they were spies, but Stalin knew it for sure, and the spies agreed with him, supplied evidence, and accepted their horrible punishment as just. Stalin was Russia's best music, film, literature, and theater critic; the best architect, linguist, philosopher, military leader, economist, historian, biologist. He was also the best in everything else you could possibly think of, but he simply was too modest to reveal it. And that is important to emphasize: if you were to say that there may conceivably be a person who can make eggplant lasagna better than Stalin can, that would be genuine heresy, quite possibly punishable by death.

Why is Stalin's eggplant lasagna the best one? Because whatever Stalin calls "eggplant lasagna" is eggplant lasagna and nothing else is. Stalin can reassign: for example, he could say that Guiseppe is the one that makes the best eggplant lasagna, and then it would be so. It would not then be possible for Pietro or Carmine to make the best eggplant lasagna, no matter how hard they tried, because Guiseppe's lasagna was defined as the best. Remember, there is no discovery, no comparison, and no change, just *definitions.* Why is a stone called a stone and not a sausage or a mhirtykbr? The answer is, "Just because". And the same here: Stalin was the only reality, and if you wanted to learn about reality, you just asked Stalin. The only other way was to change your realm of existence, and then Stalin would appear as a bloodthirsty monster.

Thus, Stalin turned into a new High Priest, the one who alone could communicate with the new God directly. Stalin knew everything, and all the others were reduced to asking him questions. That signals the transition of the entire society into the horizontal octant, one of whose angles has to do with Universal Death. People no longer seek happiness through self-realization: their expectations are focused on the Leader. At the same time, the state makes sure that those who retain the capacity to doubt are removed from the scene.

Now we understand why the Germans screamed Hitler's name like mad, while at the same time the British greeted Churchill with polite half-smiles. Germans vested their entire future in Hitler, turned Hitler into their everything, while each British subject knew that his happiness still depended for the most part on himself.

And Hitler kept his promise. By the end of the war, millions of Germans were dead, and Hitler, even though he too was dead, was fulfilling all their aspirations. Again, I will keep repeating until you get it: the only way to fulfill a person's every wish is to kill him; first you kill, and then you start fulfilling.

The West used to claim that Soviet policies were not "peaceful". Wrong. Soviet policies were defined as "peaceful" and therefore they were peaceful. If they had been defined as "warlike" or "xyz", they would have been exactly that. It is not useful to claim that inciting violence all over the world is not exactly "peaceful": it is a matter of definition, and not of degree. You cannot alter the inanimate object's view of the world. The problem with Soviet policy was not that it was warlike or xyz: the problem was that it was the policy not of the people but of an inanimate object, an inanimate object we are about to describe.

TURNING INTO AN INANIMATE OBJECT

The Machine Tool was the new Creator and the new God, while human beings worshipped Machine Tools but were still the weak link in the process of assembly-line industrial production. Thus, the goal was to create the New Communist Man, human in appearance, but an industrial robot in the way he thought and acted.

If you give up your individuality, you no longer notice someone else's physical death. That is why under a totalitarian regime people are not upset with their bloodthirsty leader: inanimate objects have no conception of death. Soviet literature of the Stalinist period covered this aspect of totalitarianism very well. We know that Stalin called the people *vintiki* (little bolts). Vladimir Mayakovsky (1893 - 1930), a very talented poet, described the Communists in the following passage:

Nails should be made out of those people!
These would be the strongest nails in the world!

People in their millions, were put into labor camps, which actually were more like death camps, and it was called *perekovka* or "recasting", i.e. an operation that could ordinarily be done only with molten metal. But this recasting created the Soviet people, which provided an environment in which the only product of the Communist system – the Communist Man – could be born.

The main Russian novel about the creation of the Communist Man was entitled *How the Steel Was Tempered*. The protagonist of this novel goes through the process of accepting the Communist ideology, and concurrently with this process gets progressively more paralyzed, becoming less and less capable of physical movement. At the end, his communist beliefs become as strong as tempered steel, and that coincides with his hardly being able to move his lips. He is being spoon-fed like a baby, but he now knows everything there is to know about the world. And this is not a satire: the author of this novel, Nikolai Ostrovsky (1904 – 1936), was a staunch Communist. I do not know whether he felt that the task was to turn humans into inanimate objects, into products of the Machine, but this is what he wrote, and this novel, out of many others, was chosen for all Soviet tenth-graders to study at school. In the Soviet

Union, from 1935 to 1987, you could not get your high school diploma without having closely studied this novel and its "ideal" protagonist. Moreover, this was *the principal* portrait of the Communist presented to the Soviet people for emulation. Obviously, Ostrovsky gave a description that the Communists thought was right. Ostrovsky knew what he was writing about: in 1919 he was a member of a "Special Task Detachment", that is, an execution squad. In fact, the novel is autobiographical: Ostrovsky dictated it when he was blind and paralyzed. It is very symbolic that Ostrovsky's last novel, *Born by the Tempest,* was published the day he died: in one day, he achieved both of his ultimate goals, the novel apparently was so good that only a true inanimate object, as inanimate as can be, could bring it out.

The emblem of Hitler's SS troops was a human skull. The task was clear: to die as a human and to be reborn as a New Man. That was the time when a man was most often seen wearing a steel helmet, so that a plate of steel would cover his forehead and his brain.

It is very important to repeat that the SS troops did not discriminate: they gave the Jews, the gypsies, the Poles, the Russians, and the millions of others a chance to be reborn as well. I see this as a crucial point: Genghis Khan killed a lot of people, and often did so with great cruelty, knowing himself to be a power-hungry, evil man. But Genghis Khan had no designs on the people he killed. By contrast, totalitarian regimes do not kill people: they attempt to remake them according to the requirements of their ideology, the ideology that happens to prefer the inanimate over the animate.

Totalitarian regimes, while being limitlessly murderous, are kind, optimistic, and forward-looking. Again. Ostrovsky's last novel was called *Born of the Tempest*, born, not killed. By killing millions of Cambodians, Pol Pot was giving birth to a new people, whose characteristics he thought would be much more superior. And from that we can draw one conclusion: totalitarian regimes are not just "bad": with the best of intentions, without a shadow of a doubt or remorse, they aim to put an end to the human race and initiate a New Beginning. Please note that God did the same: He put an end to the dinosaurs and initiated humans. Indeed, where would we all be now but for the Noah's Ark?

THE VICTORY OF THE INDUSTRIAL AGE IDEOLOGY

Again, we recall that Religion has God, the Miracle of Creation, and the World created by God. The horizontal "religion" has all of that as well: the Holy Machine Tool, the miracle of machine production, and the world consisting almost entirely of things produced by the Machine Tool. The people, organized into a work brigade serving the Machine Tool or consuming the products made by it, play the role of faithful parishioners in the new god's temple, the industrial plant.

The God of the Bible made man to be the undisputed master of the world. Only a man or an act of God could kill a man, and killing of a human being tended to be a long ritual: first a loud conversation, then the introductions, then the swords are drawn, then a long fight, a tragic death, and a lengthy funeral. People mattered: they had their names, titles, and traditions. Suddenly, there were the tank and the plane, the Killer Machine Tools. A tank is a killing machine that seems to be acting on its own, independent of human will, as the human beings riding in it are totally hidden. When a tank crushes a human body under its tracks, this is very symbolic, as is a bomb that comes from the sky and demolishes a church in one huge explosion.

By the end of World War I, it became clear that the old way of life had been hopelessly lost. If more than ten million Europeans could die in a meaningless war within a short four-year period, then how could we continue saying that each human being is unique, that people are created in God's image, that Christianity carries a message of love? By 1917, with Europe in ruins and seemingly covered by soldiers' cemeteries, the old moral order seemed utterly irrelevant. Instead of a human being, there now was the tank, instead of love – the machine tool and its products.

For human beings, God wrote His words in the Bible. It was just a matter of a few years before the message that the Big Tank wanted to transmit to its human servants and/or targets was put into words. Thus, the totalitarian ideology made its appearance and came to substitute itself for religion.

When World War I was over, for the victors all the sacrifices were vindicated by their victory, senseless as it was. That is why England and France, though considerably weakened after the war, continued with their old way of life. But for the vanquished it was an entirely different story. Germany, Austria, Italy and Russia had nothing to show for the devastation that the war had inflicted on them. These countries were defeated, and that meant that their God had abandoned them. It was clear that the old way of life was dead, the old ideals no longer relevant. As these countries lay in ruins, people could not help wondering: maybe their God was too weak, maybe it was time to find another God?

Germany, Austria, Italy, and Russia were industrialized societies, and it was clear who their new God could be: the Machine Tool was actively shaping their environment and they were servicing it twelve hours a day. And so people came to the Machine Tool asking how they could best serve it and what the new rituals should be. For them, the time had come to remodel the old society to fit the commandments of the new God. People were not identical enough, were not all dressed in uniform, did not all march in step, and did not all think alike – all of that needed to be changed to serve the Machine Tool better. Strict discipline and a metal helmet were present as far back as Roman times, thousands of years ago, but uniformity of thought was a new feature, a way to worship the new inanimate God, the Machine Tool.

There was no conscious decision to "appoint" the Machine Tool as the new God, but for starters the high priests of the Machine Tool organized themselves into Workers' Parties. An industrial worker at that time led a truly horrific life, working long hours, in a dirty workshop, in constant physical danger, and often in mind-numbing boredom. Very often, his work required no education, no knowledge, no skills whatsoever: unlike a peasant or a craftsman, an industrial worker did not have to think: he only had to coordinate his movements with those of the machine tool. Yet the Worker was now seen as the possessor of higher knowledge; he was the new priest, a member of the new church called the Workers' Party.

What is a human being but a product of God? In hungry inter-war Germany thousands of people marched in step, in long finely aligned columns, in uniform, with steel helmets on their heads, and with stony faces. Why do that instead of working, dancing or drinking beer? What could possibly be accomplished by marching in step through the streets? There can be only one answer: people wanted to present themselves as bolts, they wanted to become bolts. And bolts are not just silent or obedient: they are inanimate, dead, and their desire to make humans to resemble them cannot possibly be limited by compassion.

Up to the early 19th century, marching did have military sense. Marching into battle in close and orderly formation was very effective for infantry armed with spears, and later for infantry armed with rifles that could not be aimed properly and had bayonets attached to them. But by the mid-20th century, with all these tanks, machine guns, and artillery, what could possibly be the reason for teaching soldiers to march in step? And yet this is what the Germans and the Russians were doing. There can be only one explanation for that: it was a ritual dance of sameness, a dance called "we are the nails made by one nail-making Machine Tool", a way to show that their society was truly industrialized because its products, human beings, were now as indistinguishable as nails.

And how do you achieve sameness in humans? You set up a perfect specimen (the Communist Worker or the Aryan), and you put all the faulty humans (such as the Jews or the non-communists) into a wastebasket, to be disposed of or recast. And you could easily put into the wastebasket millions upon millions of human beings because, just like any other product of the Machine Tool, humans should be inanimate.

If your God is the Machine Tool, you are not afraid that by killing humans you will lose any unique knowledge that an individual may possess. If your humans are mortal, it means they are not made in God's image, because they are animate while the Machine Tool is not. And humans are supposed to be made in God's image, that is, they must be made inanimate. If your God is the Machine Tool, you never kill humans: you use them, throw they away, recast, recycle, reprogram and control, exactly like you do with your computer disk, your towel or your toothpick. Ideology is about humans that cannot die, such as Lenin or Mao.

One constant feature of the Soviet parade in the thirties was a representation of a plane or some other machine made out of human bodies. This was a magical representation of the ideal society and of the role that human beings were to play in it: humans were to be united into a Machine, and the engine of this Machine was the Party. In such a society, human beings are evaluated only in terms of their usefulness to the Machine; they have no intrinsic, inalienable, inborn value, and can easily be destroyed or recast. They are no longer seen as live individuals; instead, they are a kind of intelligent bolts that can easily be rendered immobile and silent with the help of a bullet.

God is a spiritual being, and humans have souls as well. That is why it is possible to bring human beings together with their God. But how do you create a union between people and an inanimate Machine Tool?

We have shown that when a person accepts the horizontal method of evaluation of his situation he acquires certain inanimate characteristics. When you reject your uniqueness, sacrifice personal development, lose your historical memory, you turn into an inanimate organism that has moving parts, an ideal complement to the Machine Tool.

Just as the vertical method was based on the morality and the laws established by God, the horizontal method and the world it created was founded on the morality and the laws dictated by the Machine Tool. Once there were Ten Commandments given to people by God, but now there were very different Commandments dictated by the Machine Tool. It is easy to say what they were: self-denial, stoppage of time, lack of attachment, sameness, obedience, envy, hatred, and self-righteousness.

Please note that this list does not include certain character traits often wrongly assigned to totalitarian leaders, such as cruelty and propensity to lie. Stalin and Hitler were not cruel at all, and were always absolutely truthful. This is a very important point. With respect to these leaders, you cannot define killing millions of innocent people as "cruelty", which is a feature of psychologically disturbed human beings. These leaders were trying to build a structure for the efficient functioning of an Industrial Age Machine Tool, and they tried to build this structure out of human beings. If you paint a red brick black, you do not kill it, even though your red brick is no more. If you throw out the bricks that seem damaged, that is also not murder. What happens here is not "cruelty" (which after all could be cured with kindness, therapy, or medicine): here we are faced with a situation where people are genuinely seen as bricks. This distinction is very important, because at some point in history about half of the world's population thought that either Hitler or Stalin was absolutely right. Let us not forget that at the time people thought that the form of the human skull or the color of human skin had much to do with any given human being's worthiness.

Neither Hitler nor Stalin ever physically killed anyone, but they had millions of enthusiastic supporters extremely eager to do that for them. Hitler and Stalin were the two most madly adored persons in all of human history, and not because they had certain adorable human qualities, but because they made it perfectly clear that the crowds they were dealing with did not consist of people, but of bricks, on which every emotion could be laid as easily as a coat of paint.

There is a dangerous tendency to represent totalitarian leaders as evil, bloodthirsty, vengeful, or paranoid. This trivializes the situation and is very misleading. To kill one or two people you have to be evil. But to kill millions you have to love humanity and want to make it better. A totalitarian leader who has killed millions may well be much kinder and far less paranoid than a democratic leader; in fact, a totalitarian leader may well be serene and saintly. The only problem that a totalitarian leader has is that he thinks that humanity urgently needs to be scientifically improved, and does what needs to be done out of kindness of his heart.

The American pilots that dropped the atomic bomb on Hiroshima probably found it inconceivable to be impolite while talking to a lady, and certainly did not have a record of juvenile delinquency. They thought that their deed would improve life on Earth, and they were probably right, provided you do not take into account the lives of 140 thousand innocent civilians.

Returning to our discussion of the two methods, we can conclude that each of these methods leads to the idea of God, formulates the moral principles dictated by this God, and creates its social laws on the basis of these moral principles. One principle is that each particular human being has the right to live, to create, and to develop freely. The other principle is that humanity must be improved, and that you happen to know exactly how it should be done and think that if there is a price to pay for this improvement, humanity must be prepared to pay it. These moral principles are located in opposite octants, and have nothing in common.

RUSSIA FINDS A NEW GOD

In the Pre-Industrial Age human life in large measure depended on nature, illnesses, accidents, harvests. Religion was seen as the cornerstone of the technology of survival. But then people reached a higher level of proficiency in agriculture, health care, and control over their environment. The role of religion in the arsenal of survival techniques became less important, while the role of agricultural and industrial technology and the role of science very much gained in importance. Thus the technological progress of the Industrial Age considerably weakened and undermined traditional religion. That created the vacuum that was filled by the new religion, the one based on deification of the Machine Tool and the world it created.

By 1917 the Russian state, devastated as it was by World War I, was far from being weak, dysfunctional, ineffective, dishonest, unpopular, or outdated. It was based on a long tradition and was fundamentally sound, both economically and ideologically. Its economic performance during the decade prior to the war was excellent. But the Russian state was rejected by a great majority of its citizens, and its few remaining supporters were soundly defeated during the Russian Civil War. What could be the reason for that? The reason was that tsarist society was based on the Orthodox Christian religion, which proved unable to save the country from the devastation of the war, and thus was no longer seen as adequate.

And so one day there was a bloodless coup that completely changed the political regime in Russia. For a thousand years prior to that coup, Russian life was based on the Orthodox religion, with the church being the undisputed foundation of life. Now the parishioners were destroying and defacing their own churches, killing the priests, burning the holy images, and turning church buildings into barns. What could cause this anger, this lack of reverence, this lack of fear of God's retribution? It must have been a religious war: only those who fervently believe in a different God can viciously desecrate a church.

Having blown up the churches, the Russians went into building their new temples with equal fervor, and these were the temples to the Machine Tool: automobile factories, steel plants and the like. The tractor is an efficient machine, and tractors were being built in most European countries, but only in Russia was the appearance of the first tractor turned into a nation-wide celebration with speeches, blessings, banners, and the like. Western economists wonder: why did the Soviet Union build in the seventies ten times more tanks than could possibly be used in any war? And the answer is now obvious: it is not a tank but an offering to God, a prayer, and the priest that prays the most is the best. The tank, an Industrial Age killing machine that keeps the human unseen and confined, is a symbol of the Soviet system: both appeared roughly simultaneously, and as soon as the computer-guided antitank missile was developed, the Soviet system melted away.

The new religion came to substitute itself for the old one, and it brought with it an entirely new morality, entirely new goals and ideals, an entirely different type of social organization. If we are to understand the Soviet system and the reasons for its collapse, if we are to understand the post-communist transition – we need to understand this new religion and the reality it brought with it.

THE SOCIAL MACHINE

The factory is an ideal environment for machine tools, but now the entire country was remaking itself to serve the Machine Tool. To serve the Machine Tool, human beings had to be united into a collective.

We defined a collective as a group of people assembled for the purpose of ideological remodeling of each of its members. That makes a collective very different from a group of people or from a work brigade working together on a certain task. A collective does not simply perform a task: its primary goal is to modify all its members. A brigade of plumbers does the plumbing, but a collective of plumbers works on the behavior and thoughts of plumbers themselves, and not necessarily in the context of doing the plumbing. Political indoctrination sessions are a must, while the plumbing often remains undone. And of course the best "plumber" is not the one who does the best plumbing, but the one who occupies the highest ideological position, the one who is appointed by the Machine to be the best. The task of plumbing is simply an excuse for ideological remodeling. Similarly, the boss of a Mafia family is much more concerned with enforcing a code of behavior on the members than with the outcome of a particular robbery or extortion.

When we consider the collective, we should never confuse the goal (ideological remodeling) and the context in which this ideological remodeling is taking place, such as plumbing (or, as the case may be, marching, murdering someone, or discussing Pasternak's poetry).

Hitler's goal was the ideological remodeling of the Germans, and since the Germans did become obedient, and millions of them were turned into inanimate objects (with the help of the Russians and the Western allies), the goal of the death-worshipper, as far as these dead Germans were concerned, was achieved. Of course, Hitler himself embraced death a very disappointed man, because he had wanted to transfer all the Germans to another dimension, as live Germans represented intolerable dissent and the possibility of recovery of humanity. Babies born in Hitler's time turned out to be democrats, and that is proof that the whole grand design of creating the nation of the living dead was not achievable in his time. Hitler died childless and poisoned his wife, while Goebbels and his wife poisoned their eight children before committing suicide.

The Industrial Age saw the appearance of powerful ideologies that worship the Machine Tool. The collective based on such an ideology can be called the Social Machine.

The Social Machine is a collective organized as if it were a human Machine Tool, made out of speechless, unquestionably obedient, and expendable human "nuts and bolts". The goal of the Social Machine is to fight the human nature of its members, and that of all human beings that surround it. The ultimate goal of the Social Machine is to fight life itself.

The Social Machine consists of human beings, but acts as if it were inanimate, and aims to turn its members and all those around it into inanimate objects. The Social Machine is a Machine Tool whose parts and whose products are (appropriately modified) human beings.

We need to understand the workings of the Social Machine, because in a totalitarian state, such as a Communist or a Fascist one, the Social Machine becomes the only social actor.

What is the Social Machine and how was it created? We know that the Social Machine consists of people, but has inanimate characteristics. How is it possible?

The Social Machine is located in the realm influenced by horizontal ideology, and that is why it is necessary that we approach every social phenomenon both from the point of view of the individual and from the social point of view, i.e., from the point of view of the collective of which this individual is a part.

Let us consider a particular human being. This person has his character, habits, knowledge, attitudes, beliefs, and a personal history. His character can be said to be located in the Individual octant, otherwise known as LIFE. But then the Communists come to power in his country and force everyone to change the realm of their existence. One opportunity is to transfer to the octant called DEATH, but most people prefer to avoid it. To physically survive, they have to become part of an ideological collective.

Thus, the character of every human being separates into two parts: the Individual Self, which is based on the vertical outlook, and the Social Self, which he contributes to the ideological collective of which he now has to be a part. The Social Self is located in the octant called COLLECTIVE.

Thus, in response to the advent of ideological dictatorship, a person transfers to the realm called COLLECTIVE and presents to the world his Social Self as his true character. His Individual Self, considerably reduced in size, does remain hidden in the octant called LIFE, and remains there at great risk to this person. Ideological dictatorship punishes failure to totally destroy the Individual Self.

Here is an example. A person wants to sleep till 8 a.m., but the factory schedule is such that he must be at work at 7 a.m. Here the desire to sleep till 8 a.m. is a manifestation of one's Individual Self, but the schedule is the dictate of the Social Machine. Of course this example is trivial, as the Social Machine usually does not limit its dictate to a wake-up call. Suppose this person actually likes to wake up at 7 a.m., meaning that his individual preferences happen to exactly correspond to the requirements of the Social Machine. Will there be a dictate then? Of course there will be. Individual preferences can change as time goes by, in accordance with this person's individual circumstances. The Machine requires that people should always conform, rain or shine. Even though the Social Self is simply a outer part of a person's two-part character, just a role that he is playing, the Social Self does not "belong" to the individual and is not controlled by him. The factory may one day announce that work starts at 6 a.m., and the workers will arrive on time regardless of their individual preferences or personal circumstances.

The Individual Self exists within every human being and makes every person unique, unpredictable, and capable of change. That is why it is impossible to use Individual Selves to create a collective. But the Social Selves can take cues only from one another. This means that all of them are cast in the same mold and are united in a network. Thus, the Social Selves of all the people in a particular ideological realm in fact constitute one "object", the Social Machine.

Why were totalitarian states so fixated on unanimous voting? Why make a fuss when 250 million people vote "for" and only one, Andrei Sakharov, votes "against"? What difference could it possibly make? Why was it a top national preoccupation for years? No other theory attempting to explain totalitarian regimes can give a rational explanation of this phenomenon. But the answer is actually very simple. If you take an Industrial Age machine tool that makes nails, nails are all it makes. If you put your hand in a box full of newly made nails, and fish out a hook, that would signal a catastrophic breakdown of the nail-making machine tool. The existence of just one dissident signified a malfunction of the entire system: the Individual Selves cannot show and the Social Selves cannot dissent.

On the other hand, the existence of dissent means that the struggle is not over, that the transformation of society to another realm has not been completed, and thus it has a mobilizing effect on the Social Machine. One dissenting vote may signify that there are a million humans who could benefit from spending time in jail.

In the realm controlled by a certain horizontal ideology we can observe the Social Machine at work. We know that all those present in this realm have developed a Social Self in order to know what to say and how to behave in certain situations, or else we would not have seen them there. In this realm one is able to express only officially sanctioned opinions, which means that if one's own opinions are different, they must be carefully hidden. We also need at least two people as the Social Self can manifest itself only when it can establish a connection with other Social Selves (that is, when it can become part of the Social Machine).

Now if one of these people mentions a forbidden topic, another person, fearing provocation, will express the official point of view even though his own (Individual) point of view may be quite different. In fact, the more this person has to hide the more orthodox he will want to appear. And this will scare the first person, so that he also will attempt to appear orthodox. Thus, none of the participants in this conversation is able to express their true feelings; on the contrary, they will probably scare each other into even greater conformity.

We see that in an ideological environment, private behavior is absolutely different from public behavior. As dialogue between individuals who do not know each other belongs to the public realm, the Individual Selves of these people do not participate in it: the Individual Selves remain silent and are carefully hidden behind the shield of the Social Selves. The Individual Selves are separated and do not attempt to establish a connection with one another because they fear detection, which would result in expulsion, increased control by the collective, or death. At the same time, the Social Selves, being on the outside, are all connected with each other, creating the Social Machine.

A totalitarian state resembles a pile of white eggs, all glued together. The totality of eggshells represents the organizational structure created by horizontal ideology, reinforced by industrial technology - propaganda being one such technology. Each egg white represents a Social Self, created by every particular individual in order to conform to the ruling ideology and indispensable for survival and social advance. The totality of egg shells and egg whites is the Social Machine, while each egg yolk represents an Individual Self. Thus, even though the "egg yolks" do exist, you would not know it by looking from the outside. The surface is totally white. But within each particular shell, the whites and the yolks continuously battle with one another in an effort to occupy more space within the shell. The proportions of white and yolk may be radically skewed within each individual egg. But from the outside each egg still appears white, as every egg with a cracked shell - to say nothing of the one with a visible yolk - is immediately discarded.

To show your Individual Self can be mortally dangerous, but still almost everyone understands that the total loss of the Individual Self turns a person into a walking cadaver. Thus, almost every citizen of a totalitarian state balances between physical and a spiritual death, and people have to find an outlet of free expression through music, science, sport, or chess.

This is yet another fundamental difference between the two realms: in every totalitarian state on the Social level we see stability, but on the Individual level there is a continuous struggle.

The process of building the Social Machine consists of strengthening and enlarging the Social Selves in their struggle with the Individual Selves. And each Social Self constantly uses the argument of physical survival in its effort to diminish the influence of the Individual Self on the host's ideas and behavior.

In its struggle with the Individual Self of each particular person, the Social Self has the enormous advantage of being united with other Social Selves, while the Individual Self exists completely on its own. Individual Selves can manifest themselves only in private, as an Individual Self usually has no way of knowing what roles the Individual Selves play in the lives of other members of the Collective. Moreover, even if the Individual Selves were to connect, there is no guarantee that they would support one another: unlike the Social Selves, all the Individual Selves are different. In any case, no Individual Self can count on overt help from other Individual Selves within the Collective.

If we look at any totalitarian state, we see that every citizen does everything he can to become an enthusiastic supporter of the regime, or at least to look like one. But if we were to x-ray the same people from the Individual point of view, we would see a lot of struggling Individual Selves, each of them thinking, "Am I the last one remaining alive?" That is why radio broadcasts from abroad can be very effective in undermining a totalitarian system.

The greatest weakness of a totalitarian system is its inability to recognize the citizens that dislike the system. On the other hand, such citizens also have no way of gradually influencing the system. What happens if the system, unbeknownst to it, loses popular support, as happened in Russia? One fine day, the system just evaporates. Can you imagine America drastically changing its economic system in one day? This is impossible to imagine because America is always changing its system, so that in each particular moment, it is more or less adequate to the requirements of its citizens. In a totalitarian state the number of citizens is exactly one, the Social Machine as personified by the Supreme Leader.

Even though the Social Machine is made up of the Social Selves provided by human beings, its goals are no longer human: they are the goals of an organism whose relevant characteristics are those of an inanimate object. (For example, the Social Machine simply does not understand that death is irreversible: witness its tendency to posthumously rehabilitate its victims and think that justice has been fully restored.) And yet, people are powerless to oppose the Social Machine as their Individual Selves are hidden and disenfranchised.

Soviet society seemed to contradict what we said about the faceless Social Machine, as there were many outstanding Soviet personalities: artists, writers, scientists, musicians, sportsmen, cosmonauts. These people certainly had their distinct individuality, they were not part of the gray mass. We need to say three things about this:

The Soviet Union was not a "pure" totalitarian state because it chose to compete for world domination. You cannot invent a rocket engine at a political meeting. If you choose to have economic development, you must permit at least some individual initiative, even if under control. In the Collective octant you can only release the energies of envy, so that you can build tanks, march under banners, put everyone into indistinguishable gray housing. But if you want to compete with America, you must have a Zoo of Creators that consists of people who are allowed to create in exchange for agreeing to live in a metal cage. We can ask every accomplished Soviet individual who seemed to have the world at his feet, be it a famous scientist, a great sportsman, or a ballerina from the Bolshoy Theater, and each of them will tell you that the bars of the cage were thick indeed.

These outstanding personalities were all appointed and controlled, they were not independent of the will of the Collective and were subservient to it. The Social Machine developed and promoted many sportsmen as they seemed to further its glory, but it permitted no businessmen as economics was off-limits. As a consequence, in the Soviet Union there were millions of people who could play chess and none, not one, who could run his own coffee shop or sell a sandwich. In a Machine Tool, some parts are hidden inside and thus seem insignificant, while other parts are more visible and thus seem relatively more important. But in fact, all of them are the same: just parts of the machine. There are significant differences between becoming and being appointed, even if you objectively deserve the appointment.

In an "ideal" totalitarian state, such as during the Cultural Revolution in China, Cambodia during the Pol Pot regime, or in North Korea today, such displays of individuality are not permitted.

THE DEVELOPMENT OF THE SOCIAL MACHINE

The horizontal ideology allows you to cease being a person. You no longer have to deal with the complexities of life on your own, as you are now part of a powerful new organism: the Social Machine.

The Social Machine is physically non-existent, yet once you start to depend on it for guidance and survival you see (with horror or with pleasure) the Social Machine enter into an irreconcilable conflict with your living soul. Soon you realize that the reason for this conflict is the Social Machine's (or ideology's) inanimate qualities, but by that time you usually are already under the Machine's total control. The Social Machine is inanimate, but it is now the complete master of the human beings that created it.

Everyone fears that the Machine will notice that even though on the outside he does appear inanimate (that is, ideological), he actually remains alive. Will he be turned into an inanimate object for good?

It is now impossible to live outside of the Social Machine, but what should you do to escape physical destruction? The requirements of the Social Machine are largely unknown, but when a person desperately tries to conform to what he imagines them to be, he defines and creates them, at the same time achieving his own spiritual destruction.

It is the individual's own contribution that turns the Social Machine (which he is more likely to hate than to love) from imaginary to real.

ORWELL'S 1984

George Orwell gives a description of the Social Machine in his novel *1984*, but his description is flawed. Orwell describes the Social Machine as something that forces a person to behave according to its orders. It is as if people do not want to conform, and resist as much as possible, but the Social Machine simply proves much stronger. At the very beginning, that may be so for some people, but as a general description of how the Social Machine imposes itself on people this is absolutely wrong.

If a Master tells a Slave what to do, then the relations between the Master and the Slave are authoritarian. But if the Master tells the Slave nothing, and yet the Slave somehow knows that if he fails to please the Master he will be destroyed, if the Slave is thus forced to anticipate and to create the Master's assumed desires (the Master may well be asleep at the time), then the relations between the two are totalitarian.

Fearing for their lives or trying to give meaning to their existence in the ideological realm, people feel the need not just to conform to the stated orders of the Social Machine, but to formulate for themselves what the Machine may want.

To anticipate the unspoken desires of another – this is why totalitarian relationships so closely resemble real love.

A totalitarian regime is not one where you follow orders: it is one where you formulate what you should be ordered to do next. Passive submission is not enough: what is required is active submission and self-reshaping, that is, doing everything to better formulate an order for yourself and to carry it out better. By doing so, the parts of the Social Machine create the Machine themselves even if at the same time they are in mortal fear of it, hate it, or despise it.

The most important indoctrination is the one that you conduct alone with yourself, knowing that conformity is necessary to safeguard your physical existence. Orwell would have us believe that people would rather not attend indoctrination sessions, and in that he was profoundly wrong: the real merciless controller is one that lives inside and tries to take over your personality, tries to become what you are. Hitler's SS guards did not just wear their skull and crossbones emblem on their caps: they wore it on their minds and made sure that it fully determined their behavior.

It is only at the very beginning that the ideologically desirable behavior is ensured by coercion and intimidation: soon the citizen himself realizes that in order to survive, he must not only maintain his ideological conformity, but develop it to the point of being able to formulate or to anticipate an order.

Thus, the Social Machine moves in its development from a dictatorship to a "democracy": no one can be expressly blamed for people being enslaved, as the people (often enthusiastically) enslave themselves.

In the totalitarian state enslavement is used only to start the process of self-enslavement, and it is not on enslavement but on self-enslavement that the totalitarian state is based. Because of this, the influence of the totalitarian society can be felt many years after the totalitarian society itself disappears, as people fondly recall the features that they taught themselves – even if they did so out of fear - to see as life-saving and often as positive.

As each and every citizen contributes a part of himself to the Social Machine, the Machine is able to control, through each particular Social Self, all socially significant actions within the collective and eventually within the state. This is what makes the state totalitarian.

As the Social Machine presents itself as a substitute for God, the stringent restrictions on personal freedom that it imposes start to be seen as God-given, so that any individualized behavior becomes a genuine heresy.

Now it becomes totally irrelevant what any of the citizens of the totalitarian state feels in private. What matters are the conditions and the requirements of the Social Machine. The Social Machine, with its language and morality, becomes the only reality, while human beings, of which the Machine consists, turn into abstractions, together with the world around them.

Orwell never lived under a totalitarian system, and so he thought that people put on a totalitarian mask in order to survive, while all the time awaiting the first opportunity to take this hated mask off. Following this logic, Soviet experts thought that the day the Soviet Secret Police fell apart, Soviet citizens would become as freedom-loving and as democratic as Americans. In fact, a totalitarian system creates deep psychological recasting, and people carry totalitarianism inside themselves for decades, without any coercion from the Social Machine. Moreover, and I cannot repeat it often enough, *totalitarianism is attractive, and failure may well be seen as more desirable than success.* If you do not believe me just look out the window or, better, re-examine your own life. My life is certainly full of unconscious desire to fail, to assign the responsibility for my own life to others.

The important thing is that everyone is made aware that showing the Individual Self means certain death: this gives you a great incentive to destroy your Individual Self. It is not those who believe in ideology who are the most bloodthirsty: the best executioners are those who have their doubts, and will therefore do everything to hide them, to avoid their own death. A citizen of a totalitarian state who happens to believe in ideology tends to get lax as he has nothing to hide, while those who are justifiably afraid of being unmasked as doubters show great fervor and cruelty.

An Individual Self exists within each person, and it consists of this person's character, experiences, preferences, and background, whereas the Social Self, even though it functions within each human being and to a great extent determines his behavior, was created outside of this person and is not controlled by him. An Individual Self is like human legs, and the Social Self is the pants that cover them up. As far as pants, the choice is arbitrarily determined by someone on the outside. At one time, everyone had to wear Levi's, today it is a different label, and it is the pants you wear that determine who you are.

You may decide to write poetry, and this poetry will be fully determined by who you are. You may decide to buy a pair of pants, but you will not fully determine what these pants are, as they can only be either Levi's or Calvins. Everyone is well advised to criticize the dissident, otherwise you will be next in line to be executed – and this total loss of control over your own behavior should be contrasted with the absolute freedom you get when you are writing poetry.

The best definition of a totalitarian state was given by Lenin, who said that "Communism is Soviet power plus electrification of the entire country". Indeed, the totalitarian state is the ideology that came to impose Industrial Age technology on every aspect of human life. That is why Lenin's definition is both correct and complete.

The art of the thirties reflected the transition of humans into an inanimate state very well. The French artist Fernand Leger painted portraits of workers as if the workers consisted entirely of squares and triangles, i.e., geometric figures that do not exist in nature and could be made only by the Machine Tool. "Realistic" portraits become depersonalized as well: consider the famous sculpture "Worker and Collective Farmer" by Yelena Mukhina, a huge metal structure depicting generic male and female whose faces are utterly featureless, yet show great determination.

STALINIST PURGES

In the 30-ies and 40-ies millions of people were arrested, indicted on charges that were often wildly improbable, tortured, and sentenced to death or long terms of imprisonment after a theatrical trial where a defense attorney would also claim that the defendant is certainly guilty. Then the family of the convict would be indicted for being "the family of an enemy of the people", imprisoned or shot, and their apartment vacated. Soon after, the next in line to get an apartment invites his friends to a joyous housewarming party.

These horrible purges are usually described as Stalin's way to get at his enemies. But they are more than that. These trials reveal the very essence of the totalitarian legal system; they are perfectly logical and legitimate.

Let's give an example. Mr. Ivanov is courteous, quiet, wears glasses, and has a Japanese silkscreen. Obviously (this is a very important word), he is a Japanese spy. We have this hypothesis now. Now we check with the relevant Party functionaries: we seem to have discovered that Mr. Ivanov is a Japanese spy, is it alright or would it interfere with some other considerations or circumstances? If the answer is that it is fine with everybody (though of course we all are now filled with righteous indignation regarding Ivanov's treachery), then he is a spy, indeed. It is now a formality to convict him, and the facts are utterly irrelevant. This is perfectly legal, and it is important for us to understand why it is so.

In the West, a crime can be defined as commission of a physical action found to be against the law. A human is free to act, and some actions may be illegal, so the law must punish those who perpetrate such actions. The key here is that humans are seen as being free to act, and the law as used to control physical actions.

But the Social Machine consisting of humans does not see them as free to act: it sees them as inanimate, mechanical parts. Do you expect a headlight of your car to go hide behind the backseat? No, you do not expect a headlight to commit this, or any other, physical action. But you do fear that inside your headlight there may be some flaw that would cause it to break. You are not concerned about your headlight's independent physical actions, but suspect that a headlight may have a hidden character flaw that could cause it to fail. That is why you read the attached labels, thinking that a brand name headlight is unlikely to have a "character flaw" while a no-brand headlight may have it. Here the function of the law is to discover, or to assume a possible existence of, hidden character flaws. You end up not buying a no-brand headlight because it conceivably could break, though outwardly it looks just fine. You reject the headlight just because you made an assumption about its future state, just because you suspect a hidden flaw that may or may not be there. The Social Machine does exactly the same: once it formulates a hypothesis, there is no place for doubt: you say, "it may break" and reject it. Did you disassemble the headlight right in the store to find and reveal the suspected hidden flaw?" No, you "convict" the headlight without looking at the evidence.

Here is the difference between the democratic law and the totalitarian law. The democratic law regulates physical actions of free individuals. Totalitarian law searches for inner character flaws in inanimate objects, assumed to be incapable of independent physical actions. In a democratic state, you develop your own purpose and manifest yourself to society through your physical actions. In a totalitarian state, the Social Machine is the only one that knows your purpose, and it conducts checks on you in an effort to figure out whether you are adequate to that purpose. If it assumes that you may have an inner flaw, you are immediately discarded. Your own actions or character are utterly irrelevant here: it does not matter where did Mr. Ivanov get the Japanese silkscreen or indeed whether or not it was his.

THE INFORMATION AGE SOCIAL MACHINE

Totalitarian ideology of the type we observed in the Soviet Union or Nazi Germany is a manifestation of psychological maladjustment born specifically as a response to the realities of the Industrial Age. Once the Industrial Age gives way to the Information Age, with its entirely different requirements, the Industrial Age totalitarian ideology reveals itself as absolutely outdated and collapses. But there could easily be a totalitarian state created on the basis of an Information Age ideology. People must stay in touch with themselves, consume information that is relevant to them, control their own behavior on the basis of moral principles born out of respect for the rights and freedoms of others. If people are subjected to a barrage of information that is irrelevant to them, if they can no longer tell the virtual from the real, if the information noise prevents them from hearing the voice of their own conscience, they become ripe for ideological exploitation.

When you watch TV, the TV makes you switch your attention from one object shown on the TV screen to the next. You sit on the couch, motionless. You're not really living: all your emotions are inside the TV box, completely controlled by it. You do not discover relevant knowledge in response to your needs, but get what is given to you by the box. Thus, we again see the same Social Machine: millions of people suddenly acquire inanimate characteristics: they gave up their emotions and personality, forgetting their individual needs as they sit motionless in front of the TV. We also see that the TV network assumes the role of a modern-day Stalin: it suddenly is the only entity that knows everything, that tells everyone what to think, and can control the thoughts and actions of everyone. There was a whole slew of recent Hollywood movies about one theme: a human being somehow loses his personality: gets a new face, gets cloned and replicated, forgets all he knew, etc. This is a sign of the times.

Fifteen years ago, young Russians could not express their political views because of censorship; now, since they spend every waking moment listening to music, they have no views to express.

Human beings should not permanently attach themselves to the Social Machine: they should not lose self-control and freedom of choice by permanently lending their senses, their eyes and ears, and very soon, their brains, to outside influences. These outside influences are increasingly more sophisticated, manipulative, self-perpetuating, addictive, and evil. Their natural tendency is to degrade and control human personality. When we rent our eyes out to the TV and our ears to the CD player, we give ourselves up to outside management.

The means of delivering information to an individual are improving very fast, but the quality of information itself is declining, and our ability to select and evaluate information properly is declining as well. Our calculators are now extremely sophisticated, and we use them a lot, because we are no longer able to do even the simplest addition. We risk becoming zombies that are so overloaded with useless information that we completely lose touch with ourselves. Yet the whole point of the book is that people need to be alive, and not all of those who walk and talk are. If we were to turn into parts of the Information Age Social Machine, we could be easily manipulated and even directed to self-destruct. Like astronauts in outer space, we are becoming 100% gadget-dependent.

In the Industrial Age, the Social Machine could not get inside a person, and if a person behaved in a certain way, it was assumed that he actually was what he pretended to be. Now we have increasingly sophisticated lie detectors, surveillance cameras on every street, traceable credit cards instead of untraceable cash, and even unmanned remote-controlled killing robots that have already been used in Afghanistan and Iraq.

Since a totalitarian society of the Information Age is very possible, we must make sure that each individual gets the information he needs, that he is able to evaluate, access, and use information correctly, and that he is protected from the barrage of information that interferes with his personal judgment.

THE SOCIAL MACHINE TURNS FROM AN ABSTRACTION INTO THE ONLY REALITY

Here is a real-life example of how virtual our life has become. There are millions of men in Latin America. On one fine Sunday, they could have played with their kids, read a book, hiked in the forest, helped their wives do the laundry. But they spent the day differently: they watched a soccer game. Soccer is a part of virtual reality: twenty two men running after a ball as if it were important or relevant to anything in real life. But of course the great majority of men did not even attend the actual game: they were watching it on TV. This is a virtual reality of the second order. A TV cameraman showed a particular episode of the game at such an angle that it appeared that a goal was scored incorrectly. This is a virtual reality of the third order. But the result was a real war between two Latin American countries, and many people lost their lives.

Let us trace the development of the Social Machine. At first, the Social Machine appeared to help people deal with the realities of the Industrial Age, and this initially made it attractive. The Social Machine did not physically exist, but people started to depend on its imaginary presence and thus tried to do whatever they thought the Social Machine wanted. Since the Social Machine desires to turn everything it touches into an inanimate object, human beings found themselves in conflict with it. They tried to resolve this conflict by impersonating inanimate objects the best they could. Every living person was afraid as either moral or physical destruction appeared inevitable. Now the inanimate and virtual Social Machine, a simple product of human imagination, stood in complete control of human life - the lives of those who had created the Social Machine and now pretended to be featureless parts of it. These parts no longer could exist without their Guide, Savior, Hope, Horror, or Murderer, all rolled into one and appearing in the person of the ideological leader. The Social Machine became the absolute ruler of every aspect of their life, and then suddenly disappeared as if it were just a dream. Could these nice Germans really have been members of extermination squads?

Saddam Hussein asks the Iraqis, "Do you love me?" "Yes, we do." Then he makes their lives even worse. "Do you love me?" "Yes, we do love you so very much!" He tries very hard and makes their lives twice as bad still. "Do you love me now?" "We adore you, you are the best that has ever been!" He makes their lives worse still. "Do you love me now?" There is only silence, as all of the people are dead. Saddam is satisfied, as he has achieved his mission.

Clinton asks the Americans, "Do you love me, just one tiny bit?" "We do not mind having you, but if you misbehave we'll throw you out." Clinton makes their lives much better and asks the Americans, "Do you love me now, just one tiny bit?" "We do not mind having you, but if you misbehave we'll throw you out." Clinton ends his Presidency all in debt and with his honor tarnished, even though he presided over an enormous economic expansion. In the Social octant people are always satisfied as things could have been even worse; in the Individual octant people are always dissatisfied as things could have been even better.

It is natural for human beings to have a vertical orientation, to develop and grow. But when the avenues of development seem blocked, when development appears impossible, it is also natural – in fact, it is inevitable – to transfer from the vertical octant to the horizontal octant, which seems to offer a magical solution. This magical solution is a pseudoreligion where the individual good is replaced by the common good and instead of God there is the Social Machine. There was a person who could not develop himself, but now personal development is simply no longer necessary, so he is no worse off than the others. Yesterday I was just a janitor, but today, precisely because I am a janitor, I am standing on a podium criticizing a Nobel Prize winning poet! It's magic!

The horizontal orientation kills the impulse to develop yourself, to become somebody, but it releases the energy of envy. This energy is destructive as far as the individual is concerned, but it is creative from the point of view of the collective. The horizontal orientation, envy, and the pseudoreligion unite to create ideology. One of the features of ideology is that it is an expression of an inanimate object. This is a consequence of the self-denial of the person who chooses the horizontal orientation. Another feature of ideology is that it is magical, and magic was born because when the avenues of personal development appeared to be blocked a magical solution was suddenly made available.

Self-denial and lack of opportunity are two sides of the same coin: when they are found together, they unite to propose an ideological "solution". A lack of opportunity, real or perceived, may cause self-denial, flight into envy. For self-denial, in order not to appear self-defeating, it is very helpful to have a real or perceived lack of opportunity.

The difference between envy and ideology is that ideology is envy practiced in an organized fashion. It is not the envy of one person towards another, but envy as a worldview of a group of people who see themselves as deprived. Ideology is envy presented as a magical solution for all people. Since ideology appears both magical and universal, ideology can substitute itself for religion, and, having become the new "religion" of a particular society, present itself as a foundation for the new world order.

To a certain extent, every Industrial Age society abandoned religion in favor of ideology. People are trying to achieve salvation (in the traditional religious sense of this word) not by "collecting" good deeds, but by collecting and worshipping Machine-made products. If I have the right kind of jeans, I am a good person; if I do not have them –I am bad. My behavior, my character, my opinions – all become irrelevant if I do not have a pair of Levi's.

A totalitarian regime is not so much the deification of the Social Machine as it is the deification of self-rejection through envy. That is why a totalitarian regime can be limited to a small sect, it can be based on a peasant society (as in China, Albania, or Cambodia), it can exist in a society that has no industry (as in Cuba). Every envious person is a totalitarian state of his own: just reject yourself and you will be aggressively dead.

Let us introduce the term "close quarters living", or CQL, meaning the absence of the wall of individual rights surrounding every individual. CQL turns envy and unhealthy dependence on others into prominent features of social life. Communist society starts by enforcing CQL. CQL leads to envy. Envy leads to destruction. Destruction leads to despair. Despair leads to magic. Magic leads to ideology. Ideology leads to the Social Machine. The Social Machine turns the envy-based ideology into the foundation of society. The Social Machine, reinforced by ideology, now controls all aspects of society. This society starts to turn people into inanimate objects: the more alive a particular individual is, the sooner he gets transformed. The Machine develops and expands. Individuals, having become parts of the Machine, are destroyed. The goal of the Machine, which was to destroy whatever causes envy, is thus accomplished. The Machine is increasingly left without a mission, and it starts to collapse or adapt to a changing reality.

A human being can exist as a part of a Social Machine, as an Individual, or in a Virtual State.

TABLE 3. THREE STATES OF HUMAN EXISTENCE

SOCIAL MACHINE	HUMAN BEING	VIRTUAL HUMAN BEING
The individual human being is not a social actor: all decisions are taken collectively and unanimously. All North Koreans are either silent or screaming with joy.	The human being has a physical body, a particular physical location, a voice that can be heard by his interlocutors.	The image of a particular human being can be seen all over the globe, his voice can be transmitted everywhere without him being aware of it. The geographical location of a person is no longer important.
A symbol: the human being is hidden inside a tank, inside an ideological Social Machine.	A symbol: the human being is seen as a part of nature or in communication with other people.	A symbol: the human being is reduced to a TV image or to an Internet nickname.
The human being is nowhere to be seen.	The human being is here.	The image of a human being is everywhere, but the actual human being may not even exist.
The human being is technically alive, but since his individuality cannot manifest itself, he appears dead.	The human being lives out his life, and then dies.	The human being may be long dead, but he appears alive thanks to the picture.

CHAPTER FIVE. TRANSITION TO ANOTHER DIMENSION, OR HOW ONE CAN DIE WHILE REMAINING PHYSICALLY ALIVE

FOUR SPEEDS OF TIME

In our discussion, we encounter four different speeds of time.

When we discuss Soviet history we speak about seventy-three years of the Soviet regime. In this case, time passes with its **normal speed**, as if a person is describing his life day-by-day. When we discuss the Russian national character and the Russian attitude towards laws, it appears that **time goes very slowly**, as we can discern no perceptible changes over the centuries. Russian laws are not much fairer today than they were a thousand years ago.

But if we are talking about the last decade, time goes **very fast, both forwards and backwards**. Capitalism took root very fast, and the Information Age also arrived almost instantaneously. But if in 1990 Russia was a reasonably strong industrialized state, today half of the population survives by practicing primitive 19th century agriculture, raising vegetables for their own consumption on plots of land that are barely larger than the average Western apartment. The political system can only be described as feudal. Today Russia is a country where someone who spends his days working on a powerful computer has to supplement his income by raising vegetables on the weekends, and to do so exactly the way it was done centuries ago: with a rake and a spade.

Russia seems closer to the year 1000 than to the year 2000. The Russians again need to accept Christianity (which they first accepted in the year of 988), they are currently fighting the slave-holding Chechens, and it is high time for the Russians to discover the concept of universal law, to write their own Magna Carta.

Yet whatever is the true calendar year in Russia, today's reality is much better than Russia's very recent past, the period when the Communists were simply **destroying time**, falsifying history, reinventing culture, murdering the best people. The Communists wanted people to forget their traditions and their personal history, and one of their slogans was "Time, go faster!"

There are many Russians for whom time has stopped: ten years after the fact, they still pretend to live in the Soviet Union.

Social Selves have a common goal, which is to build an ideological state that will last forever. And this eternity is being built by Social Selves that are based on immediate, momentary obedience.

In Russia, people are fond of asking why people in the West are living, while people in Russia are mostly dreaming. Because the horizontal orientation comes in conflict with growth, development, and the time perspective that goes with it: whatever is static, like a stone, has no time. Instead, one can hope for a miracle where everything appears suddenly, in an instant.

But the most important human skill may be understanding the concept of "now". "Now" is a unique category as far as time is concerned. Whatever was taking place in the past is not taking place right now; whatever will be taking place in the future is not taking place right now. But whatever is happening now is your life. When you read this text, you should be aware that reading it is the most important thing you could be doing in this moment of your life. If the focus of life is shifted either to the past or to the future, your life becomes virtual and can no longer be controlled and properly managed.

Which of the two methods gets you in touch with "now"? At first, it appears that it is the horizontal method as this is the method that stops time, seemingly arresting the movement of time in the "now". But the horizontal method makes an individual look not at himself but at others, thereby completely losing touch with himself. This individual does not have his own "now": he only has the "now" of the collective. That is why it is so natural for every horizontally-oriented person, not knowing whether he is dead or alive, to falsify the past and idealize the future.

The vertical method helps the present to grow out of the past and thus gives us the opportunity to evaluate the present, to compare it with the past, and in so doing to really get in touch with the present. The present is nothing without a future that you can control and direct, and that again is something that is possible only for those who choose the vertical method. The present moment is all that is important, but at the same time it is meaningless if it is not connected with the future and the past.

The successful use of the vertical method depends on how well the individual can get in touch with his present situation, as only then can a comparison with his past or future be meaningful. The key words of the vertical method are "here and now", while the horizontal method reduces a person to using "there and now" and "here, but not now".

Often people use the vertical method and yet are afraid to accept their lives as they are or to make them what they should be. The correct use of the vertical method presupposes respect for the past but not submission to it. However uncertain the future may be, you should not resign yourself to it, but should be able to shape it, because it is your own.

TRUTH AND TIME

Western newspapers use words like "The Times" or "The News" in their names. By contrast, the ideal name for a newspaper in a totalitarian state is *The Truth* (or *Pravda* in Russian). Those who oppose the totalitarian regime and think in the vertically-oriented language often try to catch *The Truth* in lies that it prints on its pages. They say that yesterday *The Truth* was saying one thing, while today it says the exact opposite. That argument shows a total lack of understanding of the language in which *The Truth* is written. In fact, *The Truth* is a full and complete expression of the entire reality that stands before the collective at this moment, and since there is no movement of time, the reality of one particular second does not have to be connected to the reality of any other second. Indeed, if you are moving through an art gallery, one moment you see a painting by Raphael and the next moment you see a Jackson Pollock. It's no use trying to see in Jackson Pollock the interpretation of Raphael's beautiful madonnas: it is simply a different thing. Today's issue of *The Truth* encompasses the entire history of humanity, and the very same thing could be said about tomorrow's issue, however different it might be. Today Stalin was the Greatest and the Kindest, and tomorrow he is the Devil that came straight from Hell. To see a contradiction in that, you have to have a personal memory, and your Social Self simply does not have one, while your Individual Self cannot afford to show it.

The collective speaks a language that denies everything unique, multifaceted, and sensitive to time. In this realm, objects acquire mythical dimensions. If you have money, it means you are bad and have to be hated. If you wear the wrong uniform it is reason enough to shoot at you. It is left up to the individual to wonder what could possibly be the connection between a living person and these arbitrary things.

A person can change, he can be evaluated from a multitude of points of view, but as far as the collective is concerned, it has just one second and just one measuring scale to attach a label on a person, a label that pretends to fully and completely evaluate him, and often to determine whether he lives or dies.

SCIENCE AND ART IN THE HORIZONTAL REALM

In the horizontal realm, science and art continue to exist, but they acquire very interesting characteristics. We have already noted that under the vertical method the basis for development of science is the principle of uncertainty, the incompleteness of human knowledge. As time passes, people may learn more, or they may discover that some of their earlier assumptions were wrong. By contrast, the horizontal method is firmly founded on the principle of absolute certainty. There is simply nothing in the world that can ever contradict the writings of Lenin, Stalin, Mao, Hitler, or any other totalitarian leader you may name. And that means that the result of every investigation is known before the investigation has started: the procedure is thus reduced to finding those who may disagree with the preordained result so that they can be eliminated.

The situation in art was essentially similar. The collective gave the recommendation as to what goal had to be achieved, what needed to be said or shown (this was called a "fulfilling a societal requirement") and the resulting product, whose social impact was meant to be much greater than its artistic qualities, was said to have been produced by the method of "socialist realism".

At first glance, socialist realism is the same as realism, that is, it depicts people exactly the way they are. But this is so only at first glance. Suppose you need to draw a portrait of someone. What is a portrait? It is the way one human being, the artist, sees another human being. We have talked about the collective long enough to see where the problem with this definition lies as far as the ideological realm is concerned. First, there is no artist who happens to "see": instead, there is a member of the collective, skilled at painting, who has been ordered to depict a certain human object in the way the collective would like this human object to appear. And the same can be said about the human object that is to be painted. Can there be a portrait of a person? Of course not: the collective sees no individuals unless they are about to be executed. This is a living symbol: the way the collective wants this human object to appear. Now take Stalin's time. There were thousands of paintings claiming to depict Stalin. But was there a portrait of the actual Stalin, the way an artist would see the real human being that was Stalin? No, such a portrait could not have been made within the confines of social realism. Stalin was always depicted as tall, handsome, wise, and kind, much younger than he was. Stalin's bad skin, just like Gorbachev's birthmark, had no place on an official portrait. Gorbachev's example is very apt: people saw on TV that Gorbachev had a huge birthmark on his forehead. But it didn't show up on his official portraits. No longer a depiction of a real life person, i.e. something that can be described as "alive", the portrait is now a symbol of a person, unchangeable, and therefore inanimate. Socialist realism does depict people, but only in a way that turns them into symbols, transfers them into the inanimate realm of the Social Machine, makes them perceptible and useful to the collective.

Again. There could be a talented artist who happened to adore Stalin. He might have wanted to depict Stalin looking much better than Stalin actually looked. There could be twenty red banners in the background. And yet this portrait will not be a part of the socialist realist tradition unless the collective approves it, accepts it as a symbol, and in so doing "pasteurizes" it, certifies that it is devoid of the emotions of one particular individual.

Or take Hitler. The Germans depicted him as a handsome knight in shining armor, while the Russians depicted him as an ugly worm-like dwarf. Both depictions were equally unrealistic, and thus both were made in the mainstream of the socialist realist tradition. If you were to draw a portrait of Hitler as he actually looked, both the Germans and the Russians would have you shot. Desymbolization and humanization are capital offenses under any totalitarian regime.

A painting done in the socialist realist manner is calculated to produce a collective emotion, an emotion of the collective of viewers. This art does not show reality as it is, as it is seen by the artist. Instead, the reality is transformed into the artist's conception of whatever the collective could best use to blind its members to reality, to lead them away from it. That is why socialist realism is something that is very much the opposite of realism.

Again there is a scale that goes through zero. An artist who sees Lenin can depict Lenin, a blind person cannot depict Lenin, and socialist realism depicts a Lenin that never was, thus leading its viewers even further from reality than a blank picture drawn by the blind.

The post-war movie *The Cossacks of Kuban* is a good illustration of this. This is a film supposedly depicting village life in post-World War II Russia. If it were realistic, it would have depicted starving people, women without men, people eating potato shavings and tree bark. But the film depicts well-fed peasants and fields filled with grain. Moreover, these peasants are constantly singing; they all wear medals from the war, yet no one appears to have been wounded. And this makes it much further from reality than an abstract painting, as the abstract painting honestly proclaims that it has nothing to do with reality.

Why does socialist realism turn out so unrealistic? To understand that, we need to return to our description of the two methods. The vertical method allows you to compare your situation today with that of yesterday or tomorrow. You live in real time, here and now. As there is time, you can see reality as it is, express your feelings as they are. The horizontal method calls for comparing your situation with the situation of others. This comparison is determined by the situation of others, and the protagonist is suddenly not in the picture.

Take the totalitarian novel as an example. The totalitarian novel is a novel without a hero, a novel where the main protagonist is the mysterious "them". Suppose there is a novel in which Johnny saves a girl. If he saves the girl because he is a brave person, then this is not a socialist realist novel. But if he saves her because the Party taught him how to be brave, because he wanted to become worthy of joining, then this is socialist realism. The Party does not need to be mentioned, but it has to be the reality, the thing without which this bravery would not have been possible.

A person is determined by others and thus ceases to exist. Since you cannot become just like someone else, there is no personal time, no personal place, no personal past or future. In the world the way it should have been, hungry peasants gorge on food and sing happy songs. The result is socialist realism – the form of art that is the furthest from reality, and from art.

ANIMATE AND INANIMATE IDEAS

A person lives in the world not by himself, but in contact with others; in fact, most of a person's world is his contacts with other humans. Without these contacts a human baby simply does not become a human being. People exchange thoughts and ideas, but these ideas should only serve as material for subsequent rethinking, contemplation, and adaptation, and this is something that cannot be overemphasized.

The goal should be not just to get information from the outside world (every animal that has a brain has this skill) but to interpret and incorporate this information, make it your own, a part of your personal world, a topic of your inner dialogue. Only then will this information be alive, will it in some form become a part of a living being.

There is another way of incorporating an idea into your life, and this way is truly dangerous. The idea can be incorporated "as is", without rethinking, without personal commentary, without the necessary change and adaptation. If an idea is incorporated in such a manner, it will turn into a bullet inside a live human body, it will become an inanimate part of a living being, a building block of an inanimate Social Self. It should be noted that in this case it would be absolutely unimportant whether this is a "right" idea or not.

Human beings need food, but if a sandwich gets into a human stomach in precisely the same state as it was on the plate, it will kill you: a sandwich must get to the stomach in small pieces, well chewed-up, and moistened with saliva. Ideas must enter human minds in a similar fashion.

There is nothing bad in reading Lenin if we can critically study the text, agreeing with some ideas and rejecting others. But when an ideology requires that we accept Lenin's writings uncritically as the ultimate and complete truth, if it requires that we reject and modify our own thoughts and views, then the writings of Lenin, who never doubted that he was right, turn into the functional equivalent of a bullet entering our bodies.

We should not take in any idea without critically examining it; moreover, we should resolve that the process of critical examination of an idea will never "officially" end, that is, there will never be a proclamation of this idea's absolute veracity and its unconditional acceptance. The idea must become a natural part of our internal dialogue, and must develop, grow, and change together with us.

Doubt is what every idea, every thought feeds on. Once a thought is written on paper, it is endangered because paper is far too permanent for a thought and a written text is not easily susceptible to change. This means that a written thought needs to be revived by being read critically. If that is not done, every thought turns into a slogan or cliché, becomes inanimate.

Literacy and print were highly beneficial advances. But in the sixties and seventies our entire planet was on the brink of an ideological war that could have destroyed all life on Earth. It took humankind enormous human and financial resources to defeat horrible ideologies utterly incompatible with human life. At a certain point in time, first the fascist and then the communist ideology appeared to be winning the struggle for world domination. And that may mean that we have become a bit too good in turning people into self-destructing zombies with the help of words and images. Since we are now entering an age where words and images account for most of our reality, this lesson must be learned well.

We had a period of rapid industrialization which we thought at the time was very good. Then we came to see its drawbacks and became concerned with ecology. Now we realize that the factories we built can damage our health or even kill us. We taught everyone to read, but now it is time to realize that we failed to teach everyone to understand the text or to subject it to doubt. Literacy can kill, and indeed the Russian Communists used it as a weapon. We must teach every user of information (just as we do with every user of machinery) to use it responsibly and safely.

If I say "two plus two makes four" would this statement be true? If I say so because I have accepted this statement uncritically, it will turn into an inanimate stumbling block in my learning. Now, even the statement "two plus two makes five" would be preferable, provided it is a step towards discovering the truth. A statement can be true only if it expresses my own conclusion. If I say "two plus two makes four" uncritically, I will not be able to understand more complicated formulas, and my mathematics will be reduced to the formula "two plus two makes four, and this is all one needs to know". As the next step, my mathematics would degenerate into a fight with more accomplished mathematicians.

A Stone Age man had hands, eyes, ears. He was alive. If you were to prick him with a needle, it would hurt him regardless of where you were to prick. A modern grandfather is different from that: layers of clothing, glasses, mobile telephone, dentures, an artificial hip, and in his hands he holds a newspaper, which he seems to have learned by heart. Not a grandfather, but a cyborg wearing slippers. Because of the bad food he eats, this grandfather has kidney stones, but he's got many more stones in his brain, as a result of the information that he is being force-fed.

There are statements that are clearly false ("an elephant has forty legs"). But it would be useful to assume that there are no statements that express the truth. Instead, we should just say that the falsity of certain statements has not been established, and so they should be considered as not false, and thus temporarily and conditionally useful.

The point here is that we cannot stop the process of examination and change. The moment we declare a statement to be absolutely true under all possible conditions an alarm should go off, and we should become aware that someone or something is trying to stop or distort the process of learning.

For Russia, this is especially important. Russians saw as absolute truth the ideas of Lenin and Stalin, the clean hands of the secret police, the existence of enemies of the people, the short and victorious war with the Nazis, unshakable friendship with Chairman Mao, the eventual victory of communist ideology all over the world, Communism in Russia by 1980, Gorbachev's perestroika, Yeltsin's honesty, Gaidar's economic reforms, Putin's genius. Russians badly need to stop believing and start doubting.

We see that individual truth and social truth are often directly opposite to one another. In the social octant, we had a newspaper called *Pravda* that in each one of its issues claimed to have assembled all the truth that there was in the world, but from the point of view of any live human being, every word of *Pravda* was utterly false. And this is not surprising, as an absolute truth and an absolute lie are one and the same. The Russian poet Inna Lisnyanskaya put it this way: "Whoever is always right is never right". When you assume yourself to be right, you formulate your conclusions in a way that excludes doubt, and if so, you would be best served to assume yourself to be wrong. When there is certainty, no statement can be described as true, because "true" means "passed the examination" and certainty means "no examination allowed".

For those who do not believe that an absolute truth and an absolute lie are one and the same, we can give a historical example. Under Stalin, it was made abundantly clear that *Pravda* said nothing but the absolute truth. The editor-in-chief of *Pravda* at the time was Nikolai Bukharin. One fine day Bukharin was "unmasked" as a spy, a terrorist, and an ideological foe. This seems to be a contradiction: one day a person is writing the ultimate truth, and the next day he is being presented as the most horrible enemy and a treacherous liar. But there is no contradiction, and in fact, nobody was surprised. It is not that people knew that *Pravda* was printing lies: it was simply that people sensed that an absolute truth, a truth that precludes and actively resists any doubt, cannot be a real personal truth. The newspaper was called *Pravda*, or *The Truth*, but it was not called *Your Truth*, or *What Appears To Be The Truth*. The name of *Pravda* and every word it ever wrote was absolutely honest, but it was not human, individual honesty.

An F-16 has the ability to see humans accurately with its infrared sensors. But humans are more than heat-emitting objects you aim guns at. *The Truth* faithfully reflected the view of the Social Machine that separated humans into "useful" or "enemies", and this view is not a complete depiction of reality.

An ideological statement, a statement that precludes doubt and forbids reexamination, is always the functional equivalent of its opposite: both are equally dead wrong. Bukharin was an all-knowing genius exactly to the same degree that he was a spy, personally recruited by a Egyptian pharaoh.

If *The Truth* is the ideal name for an ideological newspaper, the ideal name for a newspaper that exists in the Individual octant is *Time,* as only time can tell what is truthful and what is not. If time has not been stopped, there will always be time to check the information and to subject it to examination and reevaluation.

Certain things, especially those that appeared in the Information Age, have, on top of their usual characteristics, another dimension, one that has to do with information they carry and their mode of use. These jeans are blue pants made of cotton cloth, size 32; yet since they carry no brand name, they do not convey the necessary image (something like "one of the boys" or "young and strong"), they are no good regardless of how well they may have been made. For a pizza place, the price and quality of the actual product may be not as important as the speed of delivery or a phone number that is easy to remember. Ideas also have these characteristics: not only is the intrinsic quality of an idea important, but also how and in what context it will be used. For example, my book contains many ideas that may well be false, but they are sufficiently thought-provoking to be useful in a search for truth. On the other hand, I have tried to avoid ideas that seem correct but lead nowhere. I fear that readers may accept such ideas without thinking, and they would clog their minds.

Suppose that in a full movie theater, someone suddenly screams "Fire!" Those who believe it will start a stampede for the exits, not noticing that they are running over children. As soon as these people accepted the cry of "fire" as an unquestionable truth, the only truth of the moment, they lost their humanity. Now, what would have happened had this person screamed, "There seems to be a fire here"? Then people would have thought, ""Is there really a fire? I must see it for myself." There would have been no panic. Why was there a panic? It happened because people thought "I did not see a fire, but others did." In other words, they said, "My eyes are bad, I should trust the eyes of other people". This self-rejection gets us right back to the description of the horizontal method, and we know that this method causes a person to lose his humanity, makes his inner morality irrelevant. Panic destroys time as people think that they do not have a second to look around, to create a personal, rational, moral plan of action. In fact, we can define humanity as self-consciousness and time. Both of them exist in the vertical method, but not in the horizontal one.

Matthew Maly

"BRAVELY WE SHALL FIGHT FOR SOVIET POWER, AND EVERY SINGLE ONE OF US WILL DIE STRUGGLING FOR THIS"

These are the words of the most popular song of the Russian Civil War period. People sang it time and again, but what did its words mean? Why fight for something if everyone will die? The key to this is the words "every single one of us" Imagine a division of ten thousand men, former plumbers or engineers, married, single, childless or responsible for a large family – and all of them are prepared to die for "this". Could some of them not care for the cause, or simply be afraid? There certainly will be at least a few such people. In the individual realm, the song does not seem believable. Now, can we imagine these ten thousand people dead? Sure we can, and that means that in the ideological realm the words of this song do not contradict reality. Thus, the song does not say, "Most of us are willing to risk death in this struggle" (as a reasonable individual would assume); instead, it actually says "we will all be dead". The words "every single one of us" immediately translate into death for everyone.

All right, we will all die, but for what? The song makes it abundantly clear: "for Soviet Power" or for "this". "Soviet Power" did not exist for a single day, it certainly did not exist when the song was popular. So "every single one of us" was ready to die for an empty promise, for nothing. And indeed, the very next line tells us that we were all supposed to be ready to die for "this".

Most of us are ready to die for our freedom, for our loved ones, or in defense of our good name. But once we say "every single one of us" we are already, that very second, assumed to all be dead. And the dead are not the ones who would die for anything definable, honorable, or dear: the inanimate ones can only die for "this".

People are not proclaiming that they, as individuals, will die. Rather, they are proclaiming that as members of the collective, they are already dead as individuals. They are in a different dimension, dead as far as their individual history and morality is concerned, but they are still marching, fighting, and singing. For a time, these zombies were even winning their war with humankind.

Words that can hardly be grasped by an individual are absolutely natural for a member of a collective. Is not it a marvel that the author of this song knew exactly what needed to be said, even though there was nothing like the theory that I propose here? Universal death was something absolutely natural, and it was correctly referred to, every time. The motto of the Spanish falangists was "*Viva la muerte!*", or "Long live death!" What a marvelous slogan! The Spanish fascists were also all dying for "this"! Now we know that this slogan, which seems utterly self-contradictory in the language of humans and certainly appears to promise total devastation, actually means "Our commitment to ideology is unshakable (that is why we appear dead), and we will convert to this ideology all the others (by teaching them to think like us or by physically killing them)". This translation explains how people fighting under such a mad slogan could take over a country and rule it for forty years.

This realization allows us to solve another long-standing mystery. A totalitarian regime declares war on the outside world and proclaims that it will be the victor in this war. Fine. But the totalitarian regime also says that this war will be permanent. Now, there seems to be a contradiction, as once victory is declared the war should end. But now we know that there is no contradiction as the discussion here is not of one, but of two wars. Hitler's Germany fought with the outside world, and Hitler's propaganda predicted that Germany would be victorious, i.e. would defeat England, Russia, France – whatever country you care to name. That is possible, there could have been such a victory, and in fact, France was defeated. But what about the war that would be permanent? Here we are talking about the war waged by the Social Machine, personified by Hitler, with the Individual Selves of all humans on Earth. This war could only end with the death of all living humans (this is where "*Viva la muerte!*" comes from!), and as at this moment there will be no one to proclaim the end of this war, this war will indeed be permanent as far as human history is concerned, though the cockroaches will live through it.

In the aftermath of the September 11th terrorist attack, the Taliban was faced with the question of whether to take on America and NATO, and the answer was obvious. A rational person would never take on a force that is thousands of times stronger. A death-worshipper welcomes this opportunity and in so doing reveals his true nature.

TRANSITION TO ANOTHER DIMENSION

In our drawing the Individual one and Collective octants diametrically oppose one another, and the transition is described exactly as in a geometry textbook. Here are the words of the *Internationale*, the Communist anthem and, for a time, the anthem of the Soviet Union. "We shall completely destroy all the world of violence, and then we shall build our own world, the new world, so that whoever was nothing will be everything." A plane that is perpendicular to another plane is projected to it as a line. A line has no area, while the area of the plane is limitless. Just a turn, and whoever was nothing turns into everything.

Transition to another dimension is the same: once you compare yourself to others you die and then act as if you were dead. Throughout their long history the Chinese venerated their elders, and then there came a day when the Red Guards insulted them and tried to kill them all.

TURNING INTO AN INANIMATE OBJECT

We noted that once a person accepts the horizontal ideology he turns into an inanimate object. We have already discussed the classic Soviet novel *How the Steel was Tempered.* In it, the protagonist becomes increasingly less capable of moving his limbs, concurrently with his growing acceptance of the Communist ideology. But those who read *How the Steel was Tempered* will note that the paralyzed protagonist of the novel never compares himself with others, is not envious at all, disregards material possessions, indeed, freely gives them away. How does he fit the picture of the envious claimant that inhabits the Collective octant?

Transfer to another dimension takes place as a consequence of a claim against others. The protagonist of *How the Steel was Tempered* insisted that he knew how we all should live, in effect claimed for himself our freedom of choice, our future. He did not need our material possessions, but he was ready to usurp our freedom of choice and our destiny. Once he knew for sure just how we all should live, he lost the ability to move even his fingers. There are many such people around, and often I am one of them. Once I am certain I know how some other person should live, I die a little.

At the Nuremberg trial the Nazis did not admit their guilt. And they were right. They did carry out all the orders they were given, and thus, from the social point of view, they were to be commended. It is those who failed to carry out the orders that were guilty. From the Individual point of view, we can only say that those who function in the realm of such an ideology as the fascist one cannot be considered alive even if they appear to be. That is why the Nuremberg trial simply transferred the Nazi leaders, with the help of a noose, into a state of existence that from the Individual point of view, was appropriate for them. That was not execution: you cannot kill a person who has already committed suicide by accepting a hate-filled ideology.

Here we are touching on a very fundamental question: "When can a human being be considered alive?" We can now have a human heart beat forever; indeed, we can have a human being with an artificial heart, artificial limbs and a remote-controlled brain. We can have a human being with a nose job, new breasts, and green hair. We can have a human being change its sex. We can have a human being cloned, or with genes from Dolly the sheep. We can have a human being recorded on tape and operated by computer, so that the computer gives this person's opinion and show this person's face, appropriate to any possible situation, so that this person will live on the screen (which is now possible in three dimensions) long after the real human being is dead. My answer is. " A being is alive only when it is conscious of its own situation, thinks about itself and the world around it, and does not formulate claims regarding the behavior of other beings".

When the dead play the role of the living they tend to have a symbol, that of an Unburied Corpse, otherwise known as the Eternally Alive One. Lenin, Mao, Kim Il Sung, Ho Chi Minh – all of them must be buried before the Communist ideology can be considered a thing of the past.

Choosing the vertical orientation allows you to grow and develop, but it does not guarantee success or happiness. You can be like the Beatles, recognized and adored when they were still very young, or you can be like Van Gogh or Modigliani, who did not see any recognition when they were alive. The opportunity to succeed should not be equated with achieving success. There may be many more "satisfied" people in the ideological realm than in the individual one. Choosing the horizontal orientation means the death of your personality, but you can still feel happiness and satisfaction. In fact, humanity will never invent greater happiness than to scream "Hail Hitler", nor will there be greater calm than to lie in a coffin. That is why you should choose the vertical orientation not in order to achieve success, satisfaction, or happiness, as these are not assured. One simply chooses the vertical orientation in order to be, and chooses the horizontal orientation so as not to be.

CHAPTER SIX. THE LOGIC OF IDEOLOGICAL DEVELOPMENT

CHANGE AND CONSTANCY IN FASHION

Let's ask ourselves, "Will a woman dressed in the fashion of 1973 be fashionable in the year 2003?" Of course not: she will look very outmoded. But this is unfair: she read all the fashion magazines, bought all the right labels, and yet now she is a laughingstock simply because this is a different year.

Fashion is one of the most widespread ideologies. Someone "discovers" how people should be dressed, and everybody changes their clothes to conform. Such a change is possible only if clothing is being industrially produced, in millions of identical copies. An ideological language that connects all people, an ideological preparedness to appear identical to others – both of those must also be in place. People should be ready to attach labels, to judge each other according to the clothes they wear.

Failure to conform with the ideology carries severe sanctions. For example, if a job applicant appears at an interview without a tie, he will lose his chance to get a job even though he is seeking the position of lawyer, not of a tie-wearer.

Fashions change very quickly, and this is not dictated by any objective necessity. It is not just that a lot of usable clothing gets thrown away: a lot of financial and emotional resources are sacrificed just in order to conform. We will soon see that resource waste is a major hallmark of ideology.

In an ideological realm it is important to be a part of the collective, to be attached to an ideological dogma, but not to its expression at a certain point in time. In fashion, the ideology is "you will be judged by your dress, which must be up to date", and that is why allegiance to the fashions of 1973 appears so counter-ideological today.

The foundation of ideology is extremely stable, but its manifestations are extremely changeable, unconnected to one another, contradictory. In fashion, you can actually do anything at all, but you cannot reject the ideology of fashion, cannot stop dressing exactly as you are expected to dress.

CHANGE AND CONSTANCY OF THE COMMUNIST IDEOLOGY IN RUSSIA

Now let us see whether the communist ideology in Russia is on its way out or if it simply modified itself to adapt to changing circumstances.

In 1917 the workers of Russia felt that the system under which they were living was unable to provide them with enough opportunity. It was no longer "their" system, and they abandoned it as soon as they were told that they could build a new society that would be geared to "their" needs. But they were also told that to build it they would have to start looking at the world from another point of view, to unite, and to follow orders of their leaders. In other words, they were asked to accept the ideology of the new society they were about to build.

At that time, their outlook was absolute, and they were guided by a morality that was vertically oriented due to its religious base. Of course, if the people had not believed the promises of ideology they would not have undergone the required ideological transformation. Thus, in the beginning, belief in this ideology was very important. But the whole point of the transformation to the ideological realm was to make them imitate the behavior of others rather than to act according to their own ideas. Once your outlook is relative, all your actions are determined by the ideological collective. From that point on, belief is no longer needed; in fact, it becomes detrimental for further ideological development because when you believe, you cannot adapt to ideological change quickly enough.

To survive, you had to be communist, but not against Lenin (right after the Revolution), then a communist, but not a follower of Lenin or Trotsky (late twenties), not an associate of the Old Bolsheviks (the thirties), not an associate of the Nazis (early forties), not an associate of the British or Americans (late forties), a Stalinist (early fifties), not a Stalinist (late fifties), et cetera, et cetera. Once you are in the ideological realm, having personal opinions or beliefs is considered an act of rebellion.

Any belief, even a belief in ideology, is part of the individual outlook, and ideology attempts to destroy all individual manifestations. Thus, there must come a time when showing belief in an ideology means that it has not really been accepted. As a result, those who continue to believe in ideology eventually come to be seen as enemies of it.

We have just shown that a woman who strictly adheres to the fashions of 1973 would not be considered fashionable in 2003. That is why at some point there must be a Purge, as a result of which those who still believe in ideology - that is, those who tried but failed to transform to the Social realm - find themselves in the same concentration camp with those who never attempted such a transformation.

Ideological belief allows you to behave as if your soul never existed (as you are in the process of creating a new "soul" for yourself – the Social Self). This makes such belief indispensable, but only as long as the soul continues to exert its influence. Belief is needed "only" to bring about the transformation from the absolute to the relative outlook.

For ideology to be used correctly, the object of its influence must lose his belief in it after the ideological transformation has been accomplished and the relative outlook has been adopted. From that moment on, the object will continue to unconsciously (mechanically, unquestionably, and unfailingly) adhere to the ideological principles, following them in all socially significant situations.

The Russians have a term, *sovok,* which designates a person who continues to be Soviet long after the Soviet Union is gone, and many Russians would agree that the term still applies to them, as they continue to be influenced by ideology.

A communist or a fascist can easily pretend to be a democrat by learning and mouthing all the necessary clichés, but a true democrat respects people and assumes that each of them has a memory. This is something that no totalitarian personality can imitate: an ideologically-influenced person always treats people as objects and assigns no value to them. There is a danger that the democratic institutions in Russia are just an ideological veneer, and that could make the Russian political system very unstable and unable to cope with the country's pressing problems.

CHANGE AND CONSTANCY IN SYSTEM MANAGEMENT

We say that to make a person ideological, his personal belief in this ideology must be destroyed. Is there a contradiction here, have we made a mistake?

System management often involves actions that appear contradictory. To make soup, water must first be boiled, then the soup must simmer. After we eat some of the soup, we put the rest of it into the fridge, again changing the soup's temperature. The next day, we heat it up again. If we were to conclude that to make soup we must continuously boil it, we will simply burn the pot. Soup is not about boiling, but about feeding the family.

When the underlying goal is being achieved there is a continuation of policy. If the underlying goal is not being achieved, there is a break in policy. The continuation of policy may involve contradictory action, and a decisive break in policy may involve the continuation of previous action. In fact, we know that in all living systems life can be maintained only by the continuous interplay of contradictory actions, such as going to sleep and waking up. If this is so, then in order to continue with a policy, the action may change. A good example would be that of Stalin and Trotsky. Trotsky faithfully followed Marxism, being rather rigid in his beliefs, and he was correctly accused of being anti-Marxist. Stalin juggled Marxism every which way and his policy was very flexible, often going in exactly the opposite direction from just a few months ago. Throughout such changes in actions, the overriding goal of preservation of the communist state was maintained and indeed the communist state expanded and prospered. This tells us that Stalin was a faithful Marxist even though he contradicted every major tenet of Marxism. To bring the idea closer to our day, in 1990 the Communists and the KGB in the former Soviet Union appeared to be in danger of losing power; now they are being freely elected and enjoy enthusiastic support. Did the Soviet leaders abandon communist ideology, or did they just use it correctly?

Democracy is not when leaders find it politically expedient to mouth democratic slogans, but when ordinary people feel themselves strong enough to become independent political and social actors, when they demand, receive, and responsibly use their political and social rights. Russia is still populated by inhabitants and not by citizens; rights are not demanded, and when they are given, they are not used. A truly democratic leader is thus out of place in Russia and appears alien and unwise. The political system that is being built does not aim to empower the population, and there is no dialogue between the people and the state.

TOTALITARIAN SOCIETY AND CENSORSHIP

A totalitarian state is habitually associated with strict censorship. But there comes a time when this censorship weakens or disappears altogether. Is this a sign of democratization? Not necessarily. The question here is: what do the people feel like saying?

Censorship is necessary at first to weaken the Individual Selves of citizens, to prevent the Individual Selves from communicating with one another, which would make the creation of the Social Machine difficult or even impossible. But once the Individual Selves are weak and have nothing to say, while the Social Selves have grown strong and verbal, why have censorship? In a totalitarian state each citizen is absolutely free to say how much he adores the leader. Today in Russia we have thousands of newspapers, almost all of them privately owned and uncensored, but what do they tend to say, what set of values, which of the two outlooks do they tend to advocate? When we examine these questions, we will see that sheer lack of censorship is not a perfect indicator of democracy.

CHAPTER SEVEN. THE TOTALITARIAN ECONOMY AND ITS AFTERMATH

THE GOAL OF THE TOTALITARIAN ECONOMY

Labor can be used to benefit human beings, or it can be used to enslave and control them. The Communists encouraged labor, but they never encouraged betterment of the human condition and prosperity as such: they rewarded submission and self-destruction. At first glance, it appears irrational to exterminate millions of peasants and then fill the pages of the newspapers with appeals for a greater grain harvest. But the harvest itself did not interest the Communists: their goals were never purely economic.

The goal of the totalitarian economy is the creation of the Social Machine, from which the communist ideology expects miracles. The Social Machine is made up of human parts. Consequently, the overriding goal of the totalitarian economy is the creation of a New Man, a ready-made part of the Social Machine, and this could be said to be the only finished product of the ideological economy. That is a striking assertion, but I would insist that it is true. What was the product of the Khmer Rouge economy? You would not be able to name anything, as all the specialists and all the infrastructure was destroyed. But there were a lot of human-like robots frightened out of their wits, and a lot of corpses. And that proves my point. The same could be said about Hitler, about Stalin, about several contemporary cults. We should abandon the pretense that the ideological revolution is made to build a better car or to feed the hungry: it is made to re-engineer human beings into obedient slaves.

The Communists insisted on total employment, because there was not supposed to be any labor that would serve someone's personal goals: all labor was to serve the Social Machine. The Social Machine seeks to control all labor because it sees it as a fundamental educational and developmental tool. Labor can teach you to be yourself, but a person whose labor is confiscated by society becomes a part of this society and cannot break free. Ideology demands that each person be "recast" into a part of the Social Machine, into a part of the collective, and confiscating his labor makes this task much easier.

The goal of the totalitarian society is the radical psychological transformation of each human being. The means of this transformation is the total control of information and of economic life. Under such a system, a person gets material and psychological rewards only in exchange for psychological transformation, only in exchange for self-betrayal and self-limitation. The goal is to make you pay with a piece of your soul for each slice of bread you get.

Material goods are distributed in strict accordance with your social input (that is, that which is destructive from the individual point of view) as opposed to your productive input (as would be the case under a free market system). If you chose to be independent and/or creative, prohibitive costs are attached. Still, since everybody is working, this labor threatens to produce whatever the people may need to become independent. Thus, the Social Machine makes sure that everyone works, but at the same time redirects labor towards unproductive, destructive activities. Production of tanks, initiation of wars, construction of monuments, organization of rallies, political indoctrination sessions – these are the products of the Social economy, and the highest paid person in it is the slave driver.

RUSSIAN SOCIETY AS AN OUTCOME OF THE TOTALITARIAN EXPERIMENT

The Soviet economy was not designed to produce consumer goods, cars, or even missiles. All of these were the means, not the goal- not the finished product. The finished product was one: the Soviet Man, a part of the so-called "new historical community of people, the Soviet people". And the population of today's Russia consists of Soviet people, living under new conditions and by new rules, but still Soviet people. The Russians are much different today, much better, much freer than ten years ago. This is yet another testimony to how inhuman and unnatural the communist regime was. But there is still a long way to go before these Soviet people become the people Russia needs to join the family of civilized nations.

The Soviet people are a result of the harshest possible process of unnatural selection. Also, people themselves tried very hard to adapt to the requirements of the Social Machine, and passed the necessary traits down to their children. If in the West we can say that democracy is naturally assumed to be in everybody's interest, in Russia such an assumption cannot be made. In a drug rehabilitation center, the doctors do everything to get the patients off drugs, the patients are there because drugs have destroyed their lives, and yet all the patients can think of is how to get more drugs. The rehabilitation center is not a democracy: many people are there against their free will and are there against their inclinations and natural tendencies. If there were no bars on the windows, the place would be empty.

Today the people of Russia have clearly shown that they prefer an authoritarian government, and that they are suspicious towards those who treat them with respect. Corruption and criminality are not just tolerated, but expected and condoned, while honesty is never assumed and is always seen as the clever ploy of a dangerous criminal.

HOW DO THE PRODUCTS OF THE TOTALITARIAN ECONOMY DIFFER FROM WHAT IS PRODUCED TODAY?

First, what is the product of the totalitarian economy? It is one that is produced in the Social realm. And what does that mean? It means that together with its "basic qualities" it must have an ideological dimension. Since one is no longer an individual, but a member of the collective, ideally, all the products one uses must be so transformed. Let us show it in the following table:

TABLE 4. PRODUCTS AND THEIR IDEOLOGICAL DIMENSIONS

PRODUCT	IDEOLOGICAL DIMENSION
Bread	A person gets two pounds a day in exchange for working for the Social Machine and being an ideologically acceptable part of it. A prisoner gets ten ounces a day, a party functionary gets his bread fresh, good tasting, and with butter
Radios	A worker should always listen to the government news and must be able to recite it by heart; nobody should ever tune in to the Voice of America
Ladies' shoes	A worker never wears fashionable shoes, as fashions emanate from the West; a party functionary can wear French shoes because she is ideologically sound and will not be corrupted by them
Books	Soviet people must read officially sanctioned books; for reading books that are not officially sanctioned you can get a jail term
Nuclear missiles	Safeguard the peace (Soviet missiles), threaten the very survival of humanity (American ones)

Looking at Table 4, we can define the product of the totalitarian economy as that which serves the goal of creating the New Man.

Since there was always a shortage of necessary goods (and an enormous oversupply of ideological goods, such as tanks and patriotic songs), the quality of goods was not important. Again, quality is an individual characteristic, not a label or a social task. That is why there were no brands, but simply a designation, such as "milk".

What is "milk"? It is not something that is white, tastes good, comes from a cow, is liquid, and has 3.2% fat content. Milk is whatever is designated by the Party as such; its purpose is to be consumed internally, by pre-selected deserving persons, for the purposes of raising the productivity of their socially-useful labor and/or as a reward for their satisfactory ideological standing. Milk participates in the ideological struggle with the opposing system and thus is better than Western milk. Please note, that from this description it does not follow that milk needs to be white, that it needs to come from a cow, or any of that. Moreover, those who claim that it needs to be so may well be designated as milk counterrevolutionaries, and may well be deprived of milk, bread, freedom, or life itself. Ideological milk is well protected.

Today Russia lives in a free market environment, and the definition of the product has drastically changed. In the last ten years, there appeared many branded products in Russia, there is market research, quality control, advertising, and even delivery. The ideological definition of the product is dead, and this is a great advance.

But huge problems remain nonetheless, as Russian infrastructure simply does not support production of many modern finished goods. Take pizza as an example. Pizza is not just cheese, dough, and tomato sauce: it is also delivery. To organize delivery, you need phones that work, roads that are not clogged, and charge cards to pay the bills. In America, you can get a pizza pie delivered to your home within half an hour almost anywhere. In Russia, a multi-trillion dollar investment in roads and in telecommunications is required to achieve that.

WAS LIFE UNDER THE TOTALITARIAN SYSTEM GOOD ENOUGH?

The Soviet system was often criticized because the standard of living was lower than in America. But this accusation totally misses the point, because a totalitarian system simply is not about providing wealth -or anything else, for that matter - to individuals. A comparison between the lives of individuals in a certain country and a system where no individuals can be found is like comparing the proverbial apples and oranges.

Here is an example. Let us take a wild boar. Here he finds a tasty root, there he finds some berries. Some days he goes hungry, and one day he may be attacked by a wolf. Whatever happens, he is a wild boar living a wild boar's life.

Now let us consider life in a pig farm. You stay in a clean shed, you eat balanced meals, you listen to light music, you take showers, you have no sex, your skin is protected from cuts, and at the end you are killed painlessly. Sounds better than a boar's life - or should we assume that what we have described cannot be called life in the true sense of this word? Indeed, the weight of the hind legs goes up, while the brain grows smaller with each generation, simply because people like ham better than pig brains.

We, the people, need to make a choice: whether to have a hide that is scarred but our own or to have a hide suitable for making designer belts. Under a totalitarian system, individuals cannot be described as living: they are being used for a purpose that is outside their control and is in fact directly opposed to their interests as persons.

The Soviet people made tanks, betrayed their friends to the secret police, glorified Stalin. And we should not compare their incomes with the incomes of those Canadians or Haitians who cultivated corn, drew paintings, or worked as firefighters, because these pursuits were entirely different, individual as opposed to social.

What is a person's character? It is the way a person treats himself: what he has built himself to be, how he sees himself, what he knows, and what he cares about. But the Communists told each person what he must become, how he should see himself, what he should know, and what he should care about. It was no longer important for a person to treat himself as one: it was important to become whatever the Communists wanted him to become, be it a person or not a person. Character was no longer important: what mattered was to carry an acceptable label, to conform, to pretend to be a part of the Machine even when you were, and wanted to be, a live human being.

If under Stalin they could execute someone who only yesterday was a member of the highest political leadership, it is not his character that changed but his label. The crime of the Communists is not that they killed people: they never once did that, as they simply did not function in the octant called "Life". They committed their crime when they transferred people from the octant called "Life" to the octant called "The Collective": some human beings arrived at this octant physically alive, others – as victims of an execution.

The Communists and the Fascists can be accused only of an attempt to murder all the people of their country without exception. When we say "murder" we have in mind "deprivation of the right to have one's own future, one's own opinion, one's private property". The only catch here is that some of these murdered ones continued to physically exist and to resemble human beings in their appearance. Many people only pretended to be zombies and were able to shake off the spell once the pressure was no longer applied, but others were not so lucky.

THE PYRAMID OF EQUAL DISTRIBUTION

The horizontal method promises to redistribute material possessions equally among everyone, thereby removing any cause for envy. But as the only social actor is the Social Machine, which simply does not notice individuals (except, we repeat, at the moment of execution) all material possessions go to the Social Machine. There is no envy as there are no individuals to express it.

Within the Social Machine, material goods are redistributed among its parts according to the tasks they perform. In your car, all the fuel goes into the engine, and none into the back seat. The back seat is covered in real leather, but the engine is not, and this is fair and natural. Accordingly, if the General Secretary of the Communist Party gets in salary and perks about a thousand times more than an ordinary worker, this is a fair distribution as it ensures the smooth functioning of the Social Machine, whose stated goal is equality.

As we will discuss later in greater detail, the desire to redistribute goods equally automatically leads to distribution that is fundamentally unequal, and this inequality is now protected by an all-powerful ideological political system. Moreover, one is rewarded according to the place one occupies in the Machine, not according to the value of the product of one's labor.

As a result, a society ostensibly built on equality (the mask that envy wears to hide its ugly face) institutionalizes unequal and unjust distribution while making people absolutely powerless. But everyone's outlook remains horizontal and you don't look upward, at how the well-to-do live, but right at your neighbor. Now, if one of the neighbors has an ounce of bread more, there is a fistfight, so that the deprived can never unite and are very easy to control. This creates a multilevel pyramid where everyone is his neighbor's worst enemy. No level of this pyramid is cohesive, and all are easy to control. This allows the one person occupying the topmost position to control the entire system easily as long as there is enough fear, hatred, and despair within it. Thus, a society built on the principle of equality becomes the most unequal and the most unjust, yet very stable.

Food, clothing, an apartment – all give people a certain level of independence. If a person is hard to control, then his independence must be taken away, and so the food, the clothing, and the apartment must go. If a person is not independent, he can be given more goods in exchange for his services. The more deaf you are the louder can be your music, just as long as it is below your threshold of hearing. Soon the poet is in jail while the Party leader lives in a palace. The society is based on equality: it tries to make each of its citizens equally dependent.

A society based on equality is indeed a just one from the horizontal point of view, but from the vertical point of view it is a society of equal dependence, a meritocracy in reverse, a hierarchy that aims to enslave everyone equally, regardless of the hierarchical level.

HOW DO I GET AN EXTRA RATION?

What if you are not satisfied with your ration and want to get more? Then you could steal for your own benefit, i.e. not as a revolutionary trying to build a paradise on Earth. The system does not condone this behavior. Thieves recognize one another and have grudging respect for one another, but when it comes to splitting the loot they all have their knives out.

But there's another way. You can buy your jeans on the black market, and you can make a handwritten copy of the poems you like but can't get. But this behavior turns you into a criminal.

And so, who were those who tried to avoid the police? It was those who were carrying either stolen goods or a volume of poetry, either the worst or the best people in the country. Even though their behavior was fundamentally different, neither of them wanted to eat what the state was dishing out to them: they wanted to make their own food. To eat prison food, or to spend stolen money at a restaurant was more human, more honorable, than to get your chow at a Soviet canteen, be it the cabbage soup of the worker or the sturgeon soup of the Kremlin. Thus, the poet and the pickpocket often ended up in the same cell.

The greatest taboo of the totalitarian morality is independent action. Since business is always such an action, it is always criminal. The totalitarian morality cannot distinguish business from theft, and Russian thieves took to business as fish to water. Other people make the opposite mistake: they think that business is whatever poets are forced to do to make a living, so a business should not make a profit or materially benefit its owners. At any rate, everybody knows the address of the Russian business school: it is a jail cell. Almost no Russian will tell you that since business can be defined as organizing the process of creation, it is the most honorable and necessary human activity of them all. Wealth, success, profit, achievement of business goals: all of them continue to be seen as shameful, immodest, irritating – in a word, immoral.

Pause for a moment before reading the following sentence: Russia is still a country where it is immoral to succeed and moral to fail.

THE GOOD

Today I went to the farmer's market and bought a bunch of carrots from an old lady. She gave me several fine carrots, and I gave her the money she wanted for them. At that, we parted satisfied with one another. How is that? She had been growing these carrots for a long time, and I just gave her some coins. Yet she felt it was fair. She gave me the good, and I paid her with something: money. From that, I draw a definition: money is a unit of human kindness. If a person does something kind, if she produces a good, she can be repaid with money to her satisfaction.

If money is a unit of human kindness, who would a person who has a lot of money be? It would be someone who either inherited it from his parents, or was instrumental in the creation of a lot of kindness, of something for which people were willing to pay.

And who is the poor man? He is someone who is unwilling or unable to do good for others: that is why he has no money, the units, for which he exchanged his kindness. Or, as is often the case, he is simply a victim of such people, unable to develop his creative potential. Poverty hinders professional and spiritual growth, lessens choices, destroys opportunities. That is why poverty is immoral, unfair to oneself, to one's family, and to others. Moreover, some poor people become envious and try to destroy the good that has been created by others, and the creators themselves. That is why everyone must try to get out of poverty, and society must do all it can to help.

Poverty is almost never a result of adverse natural conditions (as Japan, South Korea, Taiwan, and post-war Europe proved beyond the shadow of a doubt), but a consequence of envy, destruction of resources, barriers to personal development, envy, and hatred. People are poor because they are unkind to one another, because they interfere with growth, because they are envious. Since morality is kind and kindness is repaid with money, it follows that the country with little money may be deficient in terms of the morality of its citizens.

CHAPTER EIGHT. CRIMINALITY AND BUSINESS IN RUSSIA

ON CRIME

When we discuss crime in Russia, we first need to define what a crime is: after all, we are discussing a country where only recently, listening to a Voice of America broadcast or having fifty U.S. dollars were crimes that could be punished by a prison sentence. Thus, in the case of Russia, we cannot simply say that a criminal is one who breaks the law. Instead, we need to define what a real crime is.

Crime is when a person is deprived of his personal possessions, be it life, material property, the right to enjoy nature, freedom of choice and action, his good name, the opportunity to acquire knowledge, etc. Crime is thus very closely connected to the idea of personal possession. We immediately note that once the concept of personal possession itself is outlawed, it becomes "perfectly legal" to exterminate millions.

But we have also discovered that the thought of possessing the property of one's neighbor, controlling your neighbor's freedoms, opportunities, and choices, formulating a claim against your neighbor – all of this is a crime against yourself, a spiritual suicide. Such a thought is a crime against yourself, but an action inspired by such a thought is a crime against the entire society. Of course, if your rights have been violated by your neighbor, your claim to restore your rights becomes legitimate. Thus, a criminal is one who acts upon illegitimate claims against the property of others.

The Russian communists took all private property away, and then redistributed back to the people rations that left all of them forever dependent on the regime, and forced to support the regime just to survive. As the communists took away all property, of all kinds, according to the above definition the communists committed the gravest crime of all, fully justifying even armed struggle against their regime. That is why their political opponents were as willing to habitually violate the communist law as common criminals were, even if they were violating different articles of the Criminal Code. Both groups thought that it was life in accordance with communist law that was criminal, or at least unbearably shameful.

FOUR TYPES OF PEOPLE

Let us consider the four broad types of people that populated the Soviet Union.

The first type were the communists. The communist ideology is horizontal, it is based on envy, and therefore it is criminal. Often the communists were led to commit real crimes, such as denunciation, confiscation, brainwashing, etc. We must be mindful that the horrible nature of the communist ideology was unmasked and understood only very recently, and for several decades it had been considered the pinnacle of hope and social justice by millions of people all over the world. There were many communists whose intentions were very pure. Some of these people eventually experienced a conflict between their lofty ideals and the criminal and envious nature of communist ideology. Some of them repented and turned into dissidents, but others killed millions in the name of the "fairness and justice" that the communist ideology promised to bring about.

The second type of people were those who tried to gain at least some independence from the communist system of distribution. Some of them were common criminals, thieves and swindlers, and of course they had a criminal outlook that was based on an envious claim against the property of others. Granted, many of them became criminals because they lacked moral guidance, especially internal moral guidance, but there also were those who turned to common crimes in response to the monstrous, all-embracing criminality of the system itself. Unlike in the West, many Russian criminals are victims of the regime; you could even say they wanted to adapt by mimicking the regime's inhuman face. It is no accident that the Communists called common criminals "socially close", thereby admitting that the desire to redistribute property made criminals appear as if they were following the communist ideology. As far as the communists were concerned, the only crime of those convicted of theft and robbery was that they committed their crime without an official ideological sanction - in a disorderly manner, as it were. And of course, stealing from the state was punished much harder than stealing from individuals, proving conclusively that the problem was not theft itself, but a simple lack of state sanction to steal.

Finally, crime is often a suicide attempt in disguise, a manifestation of a desire to become institutionalized, powerless, convicted, officially guilty. Many people try very hard, go to incredible lengths, and show considerable skill and inventiveness, even talent, to prove to themselves and to others that they are failures. Other people conscientiously plan for the moment when they will lose the need to make further plans. Humans are excellent at self-destruction at the best of times and circumstances, but here the extreme cruelty and injustice of the communist system triggered this defensive response in very many people.

The third type of people were those who tried to exist outside of the communist system of spiritual enslavement (and here we should not take into account the "freedoms" that the system bestowed on its most talented helpers and on a few storefront mannequins, as privileges are very different from freedoms). Refusal to proceed along the road of spiritual self-enslavement was harshly punished, and such people had to learn to hide as if they were big-time criminals on the run. These were the very best people, the true elite of the nation, but their problem was that they were outside the system, quietly working as elevator operators, librarians, or any other profession that could make them socially invisible. Some of these people committed petty crimes just to avoid to be "spoon-fed by the system". When the ideology crumbled, and there was freedom of action, many of these people remained passive, and many were professionally unprepared to take charge. Some of these people continued to be antagonistic towards their country and chose to emigrate.

The fourth type of person represents the vast majority of the population. They are absolutely separated from power and do not understand that the function of government under a democracy is to serve the people. These people simply do not believe that they deserve any consideration from the government, and limit their aspirations to the desire to be left alone. They are easy to manage, they are gullible, and they want all their problems miraculously solved by the government. Russian citizens do not control their government, they want nothing to do with the government, and yet they wait for the government to solve all their problems. These people are afraid to take the initiative, await external guidance, and are reluctant to accept responsibility for their own lives. Many are simply not functional enough: they lack computer skills and foreign language skills, have no experience traveling, do not drive. Many are not in good health and/or are addicted to alcohol or drugs. Liberation from slavery means little if it is not accompanied by psychological and occupational liberation. Many Russians do not think they deserve to live any better: it is a miracle of sorts, as these are the people who were promised the world.

For most of their lives, the Russians were under great psychological pressure, first from the communist state and then from the traumatic post-communist period. To the extent that they did not succeed in preserving themselves as functional and independent individuals, they can be said to have committed (or been forced to commit) a crime against themselves. If being unable to live as an independent and free individual is a crime against oneself, then we can say that all citizens of the former Soviet Union were criminals. The communist regime turns all of its citizens into criminals – and that makes this regime a truly criminal one.

INFORMAL PERSONAL RELATIONSHIPS

If people cannot (and never could) rely on the government, what could they rely on for support? The answer is the informal personal relationships from which the entire fabric of Russian society is woven. What are these relationships like? In the West, people go to a party where often most people do not know each other, and there they mostly engage in small talk. In Russia, people socialize differently. They get together in a small circle of friends, where no one is present without a "recommendation", and almost immediately they start talking about something deeply meaningful to them. The Russians know that they have a friend when someone tells them, "You idiot, I hated the way you behaved last night, I did the same thing myself about a month ago and only recently did I realize how stupid I was to do something like that". It seems that a Russian cannot become your friend until he calls you an idiot: but he calls you an idiot not because he wants to hurt you (he knows you can take this and more) but because he wants you to get better. Here, it is not the offensive language that is the problem (in using it, your friend simply underscores that the relationship between you and him is already informal, that is, strong and meaningful), but the fact that you can never be good enough.

Again. What is the message hidden in an act of calling someone an idiot, while giving him deeply thought-out and heartfelt advice? It points to the depth of a relationship that can withstand offense, sincerity, and self-exposure. In other words, there exists not an official relationship, but an informal one. Here is one of the reasons why Westerners do not get along with Russians as well as they could. Drinking coffee around a coffee table creates an official atmosphere, drinking vodka or going to a steam bath together creates an unofficial one. But neither of these two ways to meet should be mistaken for an informal personal relationship, and business still remains practically impossible to conduct. To deal with Russians, you have to talk to them, "really talk", as many Westerners now call this process. And this might be hard for you, as it seems that some Westerners do that very rarely. In Russia, however, it is an absolute requirement: you must show yourself as a person, not as someone acting in an official capacity.

Once the conversation is going, you may - cautiously at first, lest your counterpart be startled - mention something personal. If there is a response, then you will soon find yourself talking about your desires, problems, family, listening to your counterpart doing likewise, giving and soliciting advice, and when you find yourself not looking at your watch, then you might have something that can start a relationship. Only then does it pay to really start talking business. And it is not the environment that matters: vodka and baths help, but the coffee table is also possible, as long as the parties forget about coffee and take their jackets off, as long as they stop behaving like strangers and start talking as friends.

Note that while in the West there exists a principle of abstract professionalism whereby a physician treats you to the best of his ability no matter who you are, to be treated well in Russia you have to be "a good person": instead of a professional approach, there is a personal one.

Russians think that they cannot be your friend unless they think that you want to achieve greatness and are strong enough to take criticism to reach this lofty goal. That is why Russians actually consider harsh criticism to be friendly.

And how do you sign a formal contract with the one whom you want to have as a friend, how do you negotiate price with such a person? The answer is that you don't. Most deals are done on the basis of a vague verbal agreement, where both sides appear actually to be embarrassed to bring any formalities into the process. And that means that a failure to pay becomes not a business occurrence, but a personal insult. And many Russians feel that personal insults justify murder.

We started this topic by discussing something that appears to be wonderful – informal personal relationships – and ended this discussion with the word “murder”. Now we are ready to discuss the formal manifestation of an informal personal relationship, the *krysha*, that is, a way to circumvent the law and gain an unfair advantage.

THE KRYSHA

When Russian entrepreneurs start their businesses they quickly discover that, as sure as the sun going down, they will break some law, regulation or instruction, often unknown to them, unpublished or unpublicized, serving no purpose but that of separating the Gods from mere humans, and yet carrying severe punishment.

Thus, the first thing a Russian entrepreneur thinks about is a *krysha*, which means "roof" in Russian. (In the West it is the law that is supposed to play the role of the roof, but in Russia, where there is no law, you have to look elsewhere). A *krysha* is a person or an organization that can protect you from trouble as you do business. For that, your *krysha* usually demands a share of the profit, and often exercises at least some control over the business. In the West, the role of *krysha* is played by your in-house legal counsel, by your law firm, and by the body of law under which you do business, by the civil society in which you live. As you will see, a Russian *krysha* is quite a bit different from your average Western law firm.

A *krysha* is supposed to be able to protect you from assault and rackets, take care of your personal security, negotiate on your behalf, pay bribes, or exchange favors. There are two types of *kryshas*:

First, there are *kryshas* connected to the state, and their purpose is to bend laws in your favor. This *krysha* might be a policeman or government official who can intervene should an investigation be started against you, that is, a policeman or government official acting illegally in an unofficial capacity.

There also is a criminal *krysha*, one that protects you by sheer force: a mafia grouping or gang of criminals whose weapon is intimidation.

Opinions vary as to which of the two kinds of *krysha* is better, and most people try to have both. But there is one question on which everyone is unanimous: your *krysha* is by far the most important aspect of your business. Many Russian businessmen proudly tell you "under whom" they do business or to whom the "belong" in the first few minutes of conversation. And not just small or medium businessmen: the largest ones, too.

If you do not have a *krysha*, you cannot do anything and are totally exposed: even the law can get you, to say nothing of those who can really get you. But if you do have a *krysha*, you are breaking the law, placing yourself outside of it, either hiding underground below it, or flying above it. This places you firmly in the realm of the informal and vague, the realm that is extra-legal, and yet the only realm in which business can be conducted. *There just ain't no tradin' in Russia unless it's insider*. And then, *you ain't got no krysha against your own krysha*, and that matters very much, especially if your *krysha* is a bandit who has killed before and is ready to do so again. Your relationship with your *krysha* is very important to you, but at the same time it makes you a part of the criminal network.

You need a *krysha* not just when you have a problem with the law: your *krysha* is indispensable in your routine, day-to-day business activities. It is according to your *krysha* that your partners decide whether or not to fulfill the contracts that they have with you, it is according to your *krysha* that the other mafias decide whether or not you should be subjected to extortion, and it is your *krysha* that, in a court of law, plays a major role in determining your guilt or innocence, as well as your sentence. If you have a business dispute, it is not just you, but a representative of your *krysha* that attends the negotiations with you. In fact, more often than not you and your business adversary both wait in the lobby while representatives of your *krysha* and his talk your situation over!

Laws and regulations are often created solely to restrain, to control business activities and to extort. Thus, you need a *krysha* to place you in the extra-legal environment, the only environment where you can act. But the extra-legal environment (in which you both hide from the law and fend off the assaults of criminals) is troublesome and undefined, and no *krysha* can ensure consistent protection.

The relationship between you and your *krysha* is always extra-legal and cannot be formalized. Thus, having a *krysha* leads to dependency, from which there is no escape.

If someone owes you money and refuses to pay it back, you cannot go to the State Arbitration Court and wait for more than a year for your case to be resolved. So either you do not get the money, or you go to your *krysha* or to freelancers specialized in "settling accounts" (these guys will then be entitled to something like 50% of the take). That is how you get your *krysha* to talk to the debtor's *krysha*. If a decision is not reached, both *kryshas* appeal to higher criminal authorities. If that does not help, sometimes they shoot at each other. But usually a decision is reached.

The official legal system is slow, vague, and incompetent; it has no performance incentive, is readily corruptible, guarantees nothing, and exposes you to the tax authorities. By contrast, mafia justice tries to sell itself as fast, well-defined, relatively more professional, actually able to collect debts, and able to hide the proceeds from the taxman. Thus, it is not surprising that the overwhelming majority of businessmen started to work under the mafia.

Today the former mafia bosses are legitimate business owners, “upstanding citizens”, politicians. But the outlook that brought them their wealth and success did not change, and this is very important: a thief cannot successfully act as a creator, owner, and service provider.

WHY KRYSHAS?

Kryshas came about because under the communist system doing business was a criminal activity, because Russia lacks a system of law in the Western sense of the word, because there is a great reliance on informal personal relationships, and because of the need for protection from envy, both interpersonal and institutionalized.

In post-communist Russia it became indispensable to have a *krysha* because the state did not offer any protection or justification for capitalism, either moral or legal. In fact, by and large the Russian state still actively opposes private business, especially those businesses that fail to provide sufficient profit to the bureaucrats who graciously permit these businesses to exist.

In Russia, business in effect remains only semi-legal, as full legalization of business would entail the loss of administrative control by the state bureaucracy. The underlying problem here is that the state wants to control, not to serve, the population. From that comes "telephone law", by which bureaucrats call judges to tell them how to rule – a system that flourishes in an environment where state laws are intentionally vague, contradictory, intrusive, and make no economic sense.

On the other hand, the system is simple and not confusing at all: if you are a friend of the powerful, you are fine whatever you do; if you are not, you are defenseless. In Russia, it is not enough for business to lobby or to bribe the administration: it is the administration that appoints those who succeed.

Under normal conditions, if three old ladies sell meat pies on a street corner the one that gives the highest quality for the price wins. But in Russia, the winner is the old lady that gives the biggest bribe to the policeman, who then chases the other two sellers away. As a result, the money she should have spent to buy better meat goes into the policeman's pocket. If the business is good, it is the policeman's mother that gets to sell the pies there. And then – damn the quality.

In the West, illegal businesses also must hide from the state and enter into various protective relationships with corrupt officials, but in Russia all businesses without exception must do so, and that is a huge difference. Those who want to do honest business find themselves at a huge disadvantage. To survive, they are forced to enter into extra-legal relationships, and now they have really broken the law. Since every businessman is sure to be a lawbreaker, he is easy to control, both for the government and for the bandits. Thus, the laws continue to serve those who live by redistribution and are motivated by envy.

THE THREE LEVELS OF RUSSIAN LAW

In Russia, the law exists as if on three different levels, which – in ascending order – mean the following:

1. To defend the right party in a dispute, to defend individual citizens (in the West, the law begins and ends here);
2. To allow those in power to control, and, if need be, to discontinue almost every activity that takes place in the country;
3. To make sure that the best-connected always wins.

The first level is legal. There are laws, and violators are punished. For example, for a traffic violation you may have to pay a fine. But in fact, the law is rarely allowed to take its course. In this instance, you just pay a bribe to the traffic policeman. Moreover, you may have to pay a bribe even if you are guilty of nothing. After all, this is Russian law, and the strongest wins.

The second level is pseudolegal. The policeman accuses you of a traffic violation, citing the law that you supposedly violated. This is done exclusively to extort a bribe, traffic safety being just a pretext, and everybody knows that. Here the law is simply a weapon of a uniformed criminal. That is why the Russian traffic police lobby for laws that are impossible to follow, obscure in interpretation, contradictory, assign harsh punishment, and are all-encompassing.

The third level is anti-legal, a simple rule that "might makes right". A policeman need not reduce himself to making you pay a bribe: he can simply beat you up, or put illegal drugs or weapons in your pocket and then find them. On the other hand, powerful Russians like to violate traffic laws on purpose, for the simple pleasure of seeing the fear in the policeman's eyes once he gets a whiff of the violator's powerful connections.

In Russia, the first level of law very quickly transforms into the second one, but the case is often decided on the third level: the point is that the law books need never be consulted. Laws are relevant in Russia, but in an indirect fashion. For example, if for drug possession you can get five years in jail, then a policeman who plants drugs on you during an illegal search can count on a bigger bribe than if the punishment were only two years. However, if you can make a call to some powerful person, you have nothing to worry about, as it will then be the policeman's turn to be concerned.

Just law must have three origins. First, a sound theory of justice, and I know of only one such theory: protection of the creative rights of individuals. Second, laws must be written and implemented by representatives of the people. Third, the separation of powers. In Russia, we have none of the three.

In America, there are tax laws, and 1% of those doing business may be violating them. In Russia, there are such tax laws that 100% of businessmen do everything possible to violate them, because compliance is objectively impossible. And the state loves the situation, as fearful businessmen are obedient and subservient. The functions of American and Russian tax laws are diametrically opposed: in America the goal of government is to provide citizens with necessary social services, to facilitate and nurture business. In Russia the goal is to subjugate business and keep the bureaucrats rich and powerful, making sure that those who redistribute are stronger than those who try to create.

In the early nineties, many Russian businesses fell under the control of people who were thieves, not creators. For them, the important thing was to strip the company off assets, to steal the loans that the company could help them to get. These people could not manage a successful and sustainable business simply because they had a different mindset.

Moreover, such "entrepreneurs" discredited the whole idea of business in Russia, so that most ordinary people now believe that business is necessarily a dishonest and destructive pursuit, that businessmen make people's lives worse. Instead of being run by successful businessmen who have fine products to show for their efforts, Russia continues to be run by bureaucrats whose only claim to fame is that they "keep in check the immorality of the businessmen", while profiting handsomely through bribery and corruption, profiting without producing anything of value, profiting by standing in the way of creativity, by actively promoting and causing destruction.

And the worst thing is that the bureaucrats are right: they have forced the businessmen to become immoral. A businessman who is forced to have a *krysha* thereby largely removes himself from the vertical realm. His business now depends not on his creative and organizational skills but on his informal (and extra-legal) personal relationships with criminals and corrupt bureaucrats, all of whom are clearly horizontally-oriented.

For example, someone wants to open a business making shirts. He buys cloth and buttons, but they are never delivered. In court, he cannot enforce his contract: it takes a lot of time and he cannot give a bribe large enough to win. Since the bandits have already come to him and expect their share of profit, they start by harassing him (claiming that now they are entitled to his apartment), or they might try to fight with the supplier of buttons. The outcome of this fight may be a murder, and the businessman would then be one of the guilty. So, here is how it all came out: you only wanted to make shirts, and now you are in jail for murder, and have lost your apartment in the process.

A RUSSIAN LEGAL CASE

Suppose there is a conflict that needs to be resolved in a court of law. In the West, each party would look at the circumstances the various parties' actions, and consider the applicable laws and precedents, carefully building a legal argument. In Russia, a party in legal trouble starts reaches for his net of relationships. The goal here is to find people in power who can make a phone call on your behalf. Finally you find the hairdresser of someone who knows a friend of a judge's wife, the phone call is made, "boxes of candy" of various shapes and sizes are presented, and the case can then be won. Unless, that is, the other party got the ear of the former girlfriend of the brother of the Mayor's personal driver. Of course, there are many people in Russia who have no one to call and cannot afford a box of candy. These are the unfortunates who are reduced to studying the law and arguing their cases on legal grounds, in front of a judge who can hardly contain his derisive laughter. In Russia, when a serious case is being deliberated and decided, the law is never consulted: it is utterly irrelevant, as are, in most cases, the actual circumstances of the case. If you are convicted, it does not necessarily mean you were guilty, but it certainly means you were matched against someone who had better connections than you. But the law cannot be totally disregarded either: if you have an overwhelming, towering, clear-cut legal case you do have some chance of winning the case on its legal merits; say, a ten percent chance. Five.

We should note that the system is efficient in one respect and inefficient it two respects. The system is efficient in building social cohesion, as if you are alone there is no law to protect you: you must always seek favors from those who are in power. But its inefficiencies are far greater. First, there is very considerable economic value to fairness and justice. Fairness and justice are crucially important as guides for human behavior because they strongly point people towards seeking win/win solutions as opposed to lose/lose solutions, and win/win solutions are immeasurably more efficient. The second reason is that the informal personal relationships that you have accumulated cannot outlive you, while the law has a much more permanent character, and can be built upon and developed. The law also applies to everyone, everywhere. That is why the rule "Thou shalt not steal" is better than "Ivan Ivanovich is a good guy no matter what he does because he is (the last we checked) well liked by Peter Petrovich himself, unless Viktor Viktorovich tells Peter Petrovich otherwise." Some places on Earth have stone houses and solid laws, others have fluid verbal agreements and, as a direct consequence of that, crumbling temporary shelters built on barren land.

"PAY YOUR TAXES AND SLEEP WELL"

In 1999, on Russian TV one could frequently see a commercial from the Tax Police: "Pay your taxes and sleep well". It showed an entrepreneur who had lost sleep, fearing arrest for failure to pay his taxes. And yet everybody knew that if a businessman, any businessman, honestly paid all taxes, his enterprise would be instantly bankrupt. You're made into a criminal just for wanting to preserve your business!

But this is not all. It is not simply that taxes are too high: it is that the state has nothing to show for the taxes it does manage to collect. Where are the roads, the pensions, the deposit insurance, the support for science and culture? There is none of that, and it is clear that tax money is simply being stolen and/or used to oppress and control even more.

Here we should recall the discussion we had on the very first pages of this book: just because something is called "law" does not mean it really is law. The same is true of "taxes". Western financial institutions demand that Russia collect taxes, presumably to enable the state to provide the necessary social services. But what we have in Russia is state racketeering. The state bureaucracy does not aim to spend the taxes it collects to provide social services: it aims to perpetuate its hold on power. Since taxes can be defined as an advance for services to be provided, there are no real taxes in Russia.

Taxes enable the state to serve its citizens better, to provide public goods, to serve as an impartial arbiter in disputes, to preserve the environment. But the Russian state is horizontally oriented, and as such it is unable to serve or to contribute to growth and development. That is why, no matter how much the Russian state collects in taxes, it will always remain poor: an entity motivated by envy can never hold on to property, as "possession of property" belongs to the vertical realm.

THE LAW AS A TORTOISE SHELL

Since informal personal relationships and connections mean so much in Russia, Russian law is personalized, and we can say that each Russian carries his law on his back the way a tortoise "carries his house". It is not whether or not you violated the law that is important, but whom you can call when you're in trouble.

The official law does not work, it cannot render a timely and fair decision that both sides will respect. And this is not just because of corruption and inefficiency: it is also because the law cannot decide whether it should side with an envious claimant (as did the communist law) or with an independent creator (as does Western law). The law does not see that these two "legal theories" are in an irreconcilable conflict and that it has to resolutely chose one or the other.

The official law does not work, but the criminals' law does: at least the criminals' law is not contradictory. Its principles are well known : "Thou shalt steal from thy neighbor", "Thou shalt kill", "There is no truth or justice on Earth", "The ends justify the means", Might makes right", and many more. There is in Russia a large number of experienced "judges", each having done about ten years for theft or murder. As it happens, and this is not a joke, these judges are called "thieves-in-law", and they are charged with enforcing the criminal law.

Today's Russian state is envy-based, yet it pretends to be pro-business. That is why the state lives a lie: it is duplicitous and certainly cannot be efficient. Criminals' law is utterly unfair, it is as wrong as can be, but it is non-contradictory, not at war with itself ideologically, and thus can afford to be honest, to declare openly what it is. Today the influence of the state and that of the criminal world are about equal, and it is likely to remain so, as the two work together in concert. Certainly, there is no ideological conflict between the two: a Russian taxman is not going to explain to a pickpocket why it is wrong to forcibly take someone else's property, to which you have no right at all.

When a bureaucrat is found stealing, he is not fired, but promoted. Indeed, now he is "one of us", as the threat of prison will always keep him under control. Criminals commit crimes together for the very same reason: they want all members of the gang to be bound by blood.

Between the state and the racketeers, a businessman has nowhere to go and always gets fleeced.

However, today the common criminals are starting to worry: the state is becoming much too powerful a criminal organization. Today, by far the strongest criminal *krysha* is the police. It is law enforcement (officially created to enforce the law and to protect all citizens equally) that offers the most protection for such activity as tax evasion, unfair competition, fraud, prostitution, and drug dealing. Indeed, law enforcement officers often run these businesses themselves. After all, law enforcement gets its guns legally and can put its opponents in jail.

Racket or security expenses in Russia amount to at least 20% of profit, and there also are official taxes and levies that add up to a lot. As a result, Russian entrepreneurs spend most of their time fending off thieves and settling their claims, and at the end of the day they have no money left for investment and no time to run their business. Russian industry has equipment that is 30 years old or more, its management practices are antiquated, its markets are shrinking, its workers are malnourished and ill. But a Russian director simply has no time to tackle these problems: he is at the bureaucrat's office begging the bureaucrat to accept a bribe!

Salaries in Russia continue to be very low, and that means that few Russians can buy anything. The internal market is small, and that hits the Russian producer very hard. Food products for internal consumption and raw materials for export – this is the structure of the Russian economy, and it means that the poverty and despair can only grow worse.

When the police openly collect bribes and payoffs, you would expect that people would protest. But there is deafening silence: Russians can only protest against injustice in Kosovo, because they do not know where it is. And that is the worst news about Russia, for no matter how bad the situation, if there is a will to change it, there is a way. But in Russia, there is almost no pressure to build a Western-style society.

THE CRIMINAL MENTALITY OVERTAKES SOCIETY

The revolution destroyed the class structure of traditional Russian society. The nobility was Russia's link to Europe, even if culturally it was not really a part of the European tradition. But the nobility was totally exterminated during the revolution and in subsequent purges. Traders and businessmen were exterminated as well, and with them went many crucial notions: personal initiative, business law, honesty, professional reputation, rights and duties of citizen, the idea of service, business innovation. Priests and churches were also totally destroyed. With the priests, away went morality and the sense of community. Individual peasants and farmers, the keepers of the soul of Russia, were exterminated in the millions, so that the harvests are still poor.

The revolution cut the roots out from under every Russian citizen. And soon after, many Russians found themselves in Stalinist camps. These camps were a truly unique place. Thieves and professors, Reds and Whites, Christians and Moslems, young and old, peasants and nobles – all those who would never ordinarily be in contact – found themselves in the same labor camp, and under the harshest of conditions. Peasants and princes were sleeping right next to each other, 300 people in a cell for 10, smelling each other's socks.

The camps had people of all kinds, but it was the thieves who were "socially close" to the communist guards, and that was why the thieves became the rulers of the camps. Even the best educated people of Russia, once in the camp, had to use the camp's lingua franca – the language of professional thieves. Once the doors of the camps swung open, this distinct and intentionally ugly language of thieves, and especially its aggressive and caddish intonation, went everywhere and became known to everyone.

This is very important, as your choice of words determines the topic you discuss, and that, in turn, determines what you can think about, determines your world. You cannot say, "Hey, motherfucker, how do you like the second movement of Mozart's Symphony #35?" If you address someone this way, you can only speak about fighting, a stolen spoon, or whose turn it is to clean the toilet, and that becomes your entire world.

Today in Russia many university professors are fluent in criminal slang. On the other hand, many Russian criminals now ply their trade abroad and are presumably learning foreign languages, but not democratic traditions.

TOTALITARIAN PLANNING

In the seventies the Industrial Age was nearing its end. The idea that the entire economic life of a huge and extremely diverse country could be centrally planned showed itself to be utter nonsense. Indeed, you can rigidly plan a simple sequence of events where little could go wrong. But if an event has thousands of diverse preconditions, there needs to be "fuzzy logic" for this event to take place. There simply had to be more than one decision maker to make sure that the lights were on in Siberia, the Uzbeks had all attended their political indoctrination sessions, and the Ukrainian cows were being fed properly.

Of course, the Soviet economy was never really planned: all that was possible was to achieve a few key objectives, at an enormous, truly unfathomable, hidden cost. To get imported machine tools in exchange for ten million Ukrainian peasants starved to death in 1932-33, to build a railroad that served as an unmarked grave of millions of inmates, to win the war with the Nazis by losing five times more soldiers than the Germans, to struggle for world domination only to fall behind many underdeveloped countries in terms of income per capita –totalitarian planning was capable of all of that, but it was not capable of functioning in a sophisticated economic environment.

Totalitarian planning was doomed to fail, and not because the planners were bad, but because totalitarian planning, from the vertical point of view, was a logical contradiction. What does it mean "to plan"? To plan is to find yourself in a situation where events can play out according to various scenarios, and to act in a certain sequence in order to increase the probability of a more desirable scenario or scenarios. Now, what is a "desirable scenario" if under an ideological system people are forced to hide their real desires? How can the economy fulfill consumer demands if they are hidden? How could it be that for thirty years the Soviet economy could not produce a pair of jeans while producing millions of pairs of trousers it could never sell? That is the first contradiction, but there is another one. Planning makes sense when the future can develop according to several materially different scenarios. But ideology wants us to believe that the future is known in advance. Khrushchev said that by 1980 the Soviet people will live under Communism. "Will live", not "might live". If the future is known for sure, what is the function of a plan?

The Soviet economy was not a planned economy, but an ideological economy. As such, it produced only one product – the Soviet people, and produced it with utter disregard for the cost. And once we have said that, we know what totalitarian planning is and why it is *not* a contradiction in terms. Social planning is the systematic destruction of all freedom of choice, removal of all alternatives. Only then can the future be at the same time planned and known. The cemetery is the one place that allows for a smoothly functioning plan and a completely predictable future. Communist ideology was not contradictory, ridiculous, or incomplete in any way. But if you think it through, whatever side you examine it from, you will see the words "universal death" as your clue.

CHAPTER NINE. IT'S ALL IN A NAME

STALIN, MOLOTOV, AND KAMENEV

At the height of communist rule the Soviet Union was run by three people, each of whom was known by an assumed name. They were Stalin ("steel"), Molotov ("hammer"), and Kamenev ("stone"). These were the names that they had chosen for themselves, the names of communist revolutionaries, of ideological leaders. Surely, these names were carefully chosen and meant to reflect that particular leader's understanding of the essence of the communist ideology. What was that understanding? How did it reflect on its bearer's subsequent fate?

We start by noting that each of the three chose an inanimate object for his assumed name. By contrast, Lenin's assumed name came from the name of a Siberian river, the Lena. Moreover, this was a continuation of Russian literary tradition, as the protagonist of Pushkin's famous novel was called Onegin, after a Siberian river, the Onega, while another Russian poet, Lermontov, called his most famous character Pechorin, after another Siberian river, the Pechora. In his assumed name, Lenin wanted to continue the tradition of great Russian 19th century poetry, and named himself after a river, but the communist leaders of the next generation knew that the object of veneration must be inanimate: clearly, they understood the nature of ideology better than Lenin did.

Let us start with Kamenev, the Man of Stone. Stone is inanimate and it sure is tough, but it is a part of nature, it is not man-made, and it has nothing to do with the Machine Tool.

Molotov the Hammer Man did a little better: the hammer is an emblem of the industrial worker, a servant to the Machine Tool. It is as if the ideology were about workers, but it is not, it is about the Machine Tool, and so the Hammer Man also made a mistake, though not as grave as that made by the Man of Stone. Also, a hammer usually has a wooden handle.

Stalin, the Man of Steel, hit the nail right on the head. Steel is not just inanimate, it does not exist in the world made by the God of the Bible as it is a product of the most sophisticated Industrial Age Machine Tool: the steel mill. Steel is not just the most crucial industrial product: it is what the Machine Tools are made of! At a Catholic Mass, you eat the

Body of Christ and drink the Blood of Christ. Stalin named himself after the material his god was made of. Steel is one of the toughest materials, but bore importantly, it is material that is used to kill humans, to turn them into inanimate objects. Again, an introduction of steel into a human being is likely to perform a miracle of religious conversion, to turn this human into an inanimate object, ready to accept ideology as his new religion.

I have been trying for fifteen years now to come up with a better assumed name for an Industrial Age totalitarian leader, and could find nothing remotely as good as the Man of Steel. Joseph Dzhugashvili really was a genius for having come up with such a name!

And of course, their understanding of the nature of totalitarian ideology reflected on these leaders' fate. The Man of Stone was shot, the Man of Steel was the paramount leader, and the Hammer Man was his faithful servant.

ME AND US

In the Individual realm there is time, change, growth, discovery and doubt. In the Social realm time has stopped and there is nothing but labels. There is a great chasm between the words ME and US. ME is what I know a great deal about, but I hardly know anything about US. The same chasm exists between YOU and THEM. I would like to know more about YOU, I am interested in YOU, but I am afraid of THEM, I see THEM as foreign and incomprehensible. Ideology tries to destroy ME and YOU and tries to start a war between US and THEM.

It is important to note that the British introduce themselves by saying, "My name is ...", the French say, "I call myself ...", but the Russians say , "They call me...". If you ask a Russian to describe himself, many would not give themselves a voice at all, saying, "People consider me honest, and some would say that I am rather accomplished." This is called "modesty", and using the word "I" is considered impolite. The Russian catastrophe shows that this self-denial is very ill-advised: the word "I" is humanity's greatest invention, bar none. The second greatest invention may be privacy. And here we should note that the British rejected "thee" as being too familiar and started to use "you" instead, and I think this was one of humanity's momentous decisions:

there may or may not be friendship between ME and THEE, but there will surely be law between ME and YOU.

CHAPTER TEN. THREE TYPES OF HUMAN INTERACTION

MUTUALLY BENEFICIAL INTERACTION

There are three types of human interaction:

1. win/lose
2. lose/lose
3. win/win

Actually, there also is a specifically Russian way to interact, loose/loose, where nobody knows what the hell is going to happen, but since neither do we, we will not discuss it further: suffice it to say that this type of interaction is most common in Russia and is its saving grace, of sorts.

We are reduced to studying the three types of interaction listed first, and so let us begin.

Basil had a shirt, but I took it. I am better off, and he is worse off.

Basil had a shirt, and we fought over it. We ripped up the shirt, I smashed up Basil's nose, and he broke my finger. I am worse off, and he is worse off.

I borrowed Basil's shirt in exchange for an ice cream. He is better off and I am better off.

Let us study these three types of interaction in a little more detail.

The first type is the simplest one. The shirt used to be Basil's, but now it is mine. What Basil will do now is an open question, but for now I am better off and he is worse off. As far as the shirt, it simply changed owners.

The second type of interaction is more fun. Basil had a nice shirt, and I envied him. As a result, the shirt is no more and both Basil and I are covered in blood. This type of interaction was by far the most prevalent one in 20th century Russia. Russia, the "shirt" of the Russians, is devastated, while the Russians fought with each other so hard there were millions of corpses.

But the third type of interaction is truly a magical one. I borrowed Basil's shirt and went to a party. How many shirts were there then? One that I wore to the party and one that belongs to Basil, and that makes two shirts. Also, Basil used to have just a shirt, but now he has an ice cream as well! The shirt has become a source of additional things for Basil! He is better off and I am better off: both of us got additional resources as if out of nowhere!

Why is Russia poor while America is rich? Some say that Russians are lazy, while Americans work hard. But this is not true: Russians work hard enough. The problem is that Russians are hard at work destroying, they tend to choose the lose/lose method of interaction, while Americans, almost exclusively, choose the win/win and are working to create. In Russia, tax inspectors, robbers, bureaucrats, thieves, proponents of hate and envy, hired killers – all of them put in an honest day's work. In America, it is mostly businessmen, elected representatives of the people, priests, workers, farmers, and civil rights activists that go to work every morning.

In America, resources are not being destroyed. Moreover, these resources are invested, used in a win/win sort of way. In Russia, if there is a resource, there are those who want to destroy it. If a resource is not hidden it is as good as lost. If you as much as preserve the resource, it's a feat. If you succeeded in using the resource to produce additional resources you are nothing short of a hero. In today's Russia, ordinary people have billions of dollars in cash, because Russians do not trust their own currency, their government, or their banking system. None of this money is invested: it is all hidden under the mattress. And this is not the worst there is, either: the talents of Russian people are also hidden under the mattress, and this is worse than to hide money.

Individual Russians, and especially the Russian state and Russian law, should stop actively searching out and implementing lose/lose solutions and instead discover the magic of win/win. This is the solution to all Russian problems, the key to understanding Russia, and a one-sentence summary of this book.

Of course, the reader will note that the lose/lose solution is a consequence of the horizontal orientation of at least one of the participants, whereas win/win comes naturally when both participants have a vertical outlook.

The horizontal outlook brings destruction of the spiritual and the material world, while the vertical outlook brings spiritual and material gains that are far greater than the simple sum of the efforts of all participants.

If two Russians have a hundred dollars, they will spend twenty dollars on booze, take thirty dollars each to buy booze later, and spend the remaining twenty dollars on business. Soon they will have a fight and spend the rest of their lives trying to kill each other. It should also be noted that the original hundred dollars was not earned, either: in the best case, the money came from selling oil.

If two Germans have a hundred dollars, they will bring three hundred more each, just to make sure that their business is a success, and will work around the clock to make it happen. And the money will not have come from oil: it will be the proceeds of a previous episode of successful cooperation.

Both in the West and in Russia human relationships are guided by kindness. In the West, kindness means cooperation, but Russians think that should they cooperate, the other party will lose an opportunity to grow spiritually by overcoming adversity.

THE DRAWBACKS OF WIN/WIN AND THE BENEFITS OF LOSE/LOSE

Suppose that two people found ten dollars and split the money three dollars to one and seven to the other. One of them is three dollars richer, he benefited from the find, but since the other person got more than he did, he may wish they never found the money.

Suppose that two people met a robber on the road, and he took ten dollars from them. If he took three dollars from one and seven from the other, the one who lost less, even though he is three dollars poorer, may in fact feel happy that the event occurred, since the other person lost more than he did.

We see that a tendency to compare our own situation with the situation of the other makes our judgment irrational: win/win is not always good, and lose/lose is not always bad.

Furthermore, we again see that an oppressive regime makes its citizens feel good by making the situation of selected individuals even worse than that of the rest of the population.

DEMOCRACY OR WIN/WIN?

American policy aims to promote democracy around the world, but democracy is a political system that any country has learned to imitate, with no tangible benefit for common people. Win/win, an envy-free moral, psychological, economic, and social system based on cooperation in promoting each other's growth and development – now, this is an entirely different matter.

What America is actually aiming to promote is a win/win system, with democracy being its natural political expression. But introducing win/win is profoundly different from promoting democracy.

Democracy is an old system invented by the ancient Greeks. It is a system where everyone (deemed worthy of it) was, from time to time, invited to cast a ballot. This was a system that assigned no value to the individual human being as such, and that is why it co-existed quite naturally with slavery or torture. If we were "promoting democracy" in Iraq in a way understandable to the ancient Greeks, we would be expected to enslave the Iraqis. Since we want the Iraqis to succeed and prosper, to derive all possible benefits from their interaction with us, it means that we are promoting not just democracy, but something much more far-reaching: a social system based on the win/win principle.

The Founding Fathers gave us democracy, a system of representative government. A democracy may have ten voters, a Congress of voters, or a universal right to vote. All it says is that decisions are taken by a vote, and that there is a system of checks and balances. That is why there is no contradiction between democracy and things like slave ownership, exclusion of women, inhuman cruelty, high taxes, or military aggression. A gang of bandits can take its decisions democratically: do we finish off the victim or just let him bleed to death?

The win/win system is very different from that. Since it is a system of mutually beneficial interaction, every type of exclusion, coercion, exploitation, and cruelty goes directly against this system and is repugnant to it. There is nothing "built-in" in a democracy that would protect individual rights of every citizen, but it is something that is built-in in a win/win system, a system that makes sure that everyone has an opportunity to succeed.

Democracy is an old system that exists in many countries of the world, win/win is a new system, invented, and most faithfully practiced, in North America. Ford invented it when he started to pay his workers enough that they could afford cars. Martin Luther King contributed mightily to inventing it and so did President Lyndon B. Johnson. President Carter advanced it with his emphasis on human rights around the world. President George W. Bush based on it his policies towards Iraq. And this is a very important point: by definition, democracy is a closed system, as its decisions apply only to those who vote and/or are represented by those who vote. By contrast, a win/win system is open to the world, as it is naturally opposed to every attempt to establish a lose/lose or a win/lose interaction. America's democracy, absent a clear and immediate threat from Iraq, had no right to authorize a foreign invasion. But a win/win system, fundamentally opposed to oppression no matter where it takes place, would authorize, if not actually require (!), the toppling of any cruel dictator, and certainly one who may threaten the world.

Democracy is a system of voting. It is irrelevant who the voters are or how many of them there are. Thus, democracy is easy to imitate, and in fact, most countries in the world practice democracy. No matter how underdeveloped, confused, or unkind a country, everyone is invited to cast a ballot. In almost all cases, the people are simply being asked whether they should be fooled and robbed or, in the alternative, misinformed and dispossessed. If "democracy" is already practiced all over the world, it is silly to proclaim that America is "promoting democracy". The win-win system, however, is another matter entirely as it requires a citizenry that is both professionally competitive and moral - a society that welcomes and promotes fair and open competition.

Democracy and win/win are not the same: Democracy is a political system, while win/win is certain level of a moral and professional preparedness of the population. Democracy is simply the social technology that a win/win system naturally chooses, sort of the outfit that a win/win population usually wears.

When a parent tells a child not to play with matches, this is win/win, but not democracy. The occupation of Japan after the WWII was win/win, but not a democracy, and the same goes for the war and for the occupation of Iraq. When the population is not ready for win/win, there is no time for democracy: in this case, win/win must be imposed by force.

The reverse is also true: if there is a democracy, it absolutely does not mean that there is win/win. Adolf Hitler came to power as the result of an election. Other leaders, such as Stalin, had a rating high enough to win any election. A group of humans were offered the chance to vote for something, pretended to vote for something, or actually did take a vote – but how can we assume that it was a “good” decision? It could be any decision, from the worst to the best. By contrast, a decision based on the two principles of win/win – thou shalt have no claim against the property of another and thou shalt help other people to succeed if such help does not imperil thine own progress – always gives the best possible solution.

Now, if America is promoting win/win rather than democracy, the task is much greater: it is the task of morally and professionally preparing a group of people to freely choose win/win. Until then, win/win should be imposed by force. If during this period we want to use the technique of democracy, it may be necessary to restrict the voting rights to those who are likely to choose win/win, such as property owners, accomplished professionals, businesspeople and civic activists.

There are many states where the leaders steal, intimidate, and murder. We come to these states asking them to be "more democratic". But the problem is that the great majority of citizens are not aware that any alternative way of exercising power exists. If they are put in a position of power instead of their oppressors, there is a good chance that they will also steal, intimidate, and murder.

Right now we are asking leaders to be "good", in many cases much better than the people they rule. Under the guise of promoting democracy we want the leadership to be unrepresentative of the population, i.e. undemocratic, but undemocratic in a good way. For example, in Afghanistan we have a western-educated, English-speaking President – that is, a president who is highly uncharacteristic of Afghanistan. But since his rule is undemocratic, the question is: can it be maintained democratically? And the answer is "no": uneducated shepherds would not vote for an American professor of Afghani extraction.

While there is debate about whether a murderous dictatorship could be a democracy, there is no debate whatsoever whether a murderous dictatorship could be a win/win system. Win/win is not a moral system: it is a rational system, and any murderer can participate in it if only he pursues his self-interest. While democracy may or may not result in a good system, while America may want benevolent dictatorship more often than it wants a genuine democracy, a win/win is a system we always want and a system that accepts everyone willing to live by its principles.

Suppose there is Mr. Badblood, who is a cruel dictator and his is a cruel regime. Well, we want Mr. Badblood to go, and we want the dissident, Mr. Goodkind, to be president. But Mr. Badblood does not want to go: he wants to keep on killing and stealing. This is an impasse or a civil war, with enormous human and economic sacrifices. Finally, Mr. Goodkind becomes the new President, but the people are the same and the social technology is the same. If win/win is unknown, the people cannot be described as "some citizens who are honest and others who are not": it can only be described as those who steal and those who do not have the opportunity. Thus, Mr. Goodkind turns into a dictator no less cruel than Mr. Badblood. In fact, Mr. Badblood is often fondly remembered. Robert Mugabe of Zimbabwe certainly fits this pattern.

Win/win is a system under which theft and cruelty cease to become the most economically efficient behaviors, as cooperation starts to bring better results. With win/win, no one needs to be excluded. Mr. Badblood can remain President, as long as he understands that win/win will make him wealthier and more powerful as he will be presiding over a prosperous and happy country, a darling of investors and tourists. Once win/win is established, it becomes clear that democracy – now true democracy, not just the process of using ballots – is the natural political technology for such a system. This is how we will reach our goal of "promoting democracy."

THE SPIRAL OF ENVY AND THE SPIRAL OF DEVELOPMENT

A producer can get two types of treatment from the state: envious or developmental one. A spiral of envy occurs when a producer is forced to give up so much profit that next year he can only pay less. This spiral ends with the producer's bankruptcy and zero tax revenue to the state.

Usually, a potential producer, seeing that the obstacles and worries are just too great to overcome, never even starts a business. Russia can certainly boast millions of businesses that were never started. The spiral of development is one where the tax bill is structured to allow businesses to expand and grow: the tax rate is low, but the producer is able to pay more every year without harming his business.

One of the manifestations of the spiral of development was when capitalists discovered that impoverished workers simply could not buy the products that the capitalists were trying to sell, so the solution was to pay workers more, not less. The capitalists pay greater salaries (with their profits going down in the short run) and yet sell more products and earn more in the long run. What is more, this spiral is sustainable and both workers and capitalists grow richer with every new turn.

Karl Marx claimed that the revolution was inevitable because workers would be reduced to absolute poverty, creating a systemic crisis of capitalism. He took for granted that there would be a lose/lose solution and never considered that people would search for a win/win! Why did Marx commit this mistake? Because he started with the horizontally-oriented word "redistribution", which is located in the same octant as lose/lose, instead of starting with the vertically-oriented word "creation" that comes from the same octant as win/win. For capitalists the word "creation" was not foreign, and that is why the win/win solution came to them quite naturally.

TO GIVE AND TO TAKE

The vertical orientation allows us to grow spiritually. This growth is internal, but its consequences are felt by society at large. An artist sees the world, contemplates the world, appreciates its beauty, but the outcome of these spiritual processes, his paintings, are enjoyed by all. He develops himself, which is an egotistical and spiritual action, but the material consequences are felt by all. And this is true not only with respect to art: all good and honest work is done for personal enjoyment, for yourself, and yet others reap benefits from it. A creator consumes a very small part of what he creates, yet he creates it all because of his personal spiritual need. That is why society can accept his creations as a gift: the relationship is not envy-based, there is no redistribution, and the transfer of the gift from the creator to society takes place within the framework of a win/win relationship.

We all live in places that have ample evidence of gifts left to us by previous generations. And yet there are places on Earth where previous generations left to their offspring very little, or nothing at all. Indeed, there are deserts in places where lush forests used to grow. And that may well be the proof that not all cultures are based on win/win.

And what are these unproductive cultures? These cultures are the ones that frown upon egoists, the cultures that demand that people share! What a wonderful "contradiction": if you create for yourself, you leave all your creations to all people, but if you are directed to leave everything to all people, you have nothing to leave.

The horizontally-oriented person is always unhappy, but unfortunately he cannot remain unhappy all by himself: his business is that of others. He has a theory, he sacrifices himself for the sake of our happiness, he wears a modest uniform, and he is concerned not with himself but with the entire society; indeed, with the whole of the world. In the 20th century these selfless servants of the common good brought the world to the brink of destruction.

In comparison with Western Europe, in Russia previous generations left relatively little: there was a tradition of sharing, individual rights were weak or non-existent, and people who were hell-bent on destruction could easily have their way. In terms of literature and music, previous generations of Russians left a great deal: poems are very hard to destroy once they are out, but houses and businesses are not so lucky.

In a vertically-oriented society people do nothing but consume, they take, and take, and take! They take paper, food, package tours – and all for their egoistical personal needs, without any regard for society. As a result, new poems, new buildings, new products are left behind. Each new generation is richer and happier.

But there is hope for the world! There are societies where each person will selflessly tell you how others should live. No one is permitted to take too much, there is absolute fairness in everything. The land becomes barren and empty, and should someone fail to hide so much as a piece of bread, there is an ugly and bloody fight. Once the offender is punished, the discussion of fairness and justice resumes.

In a vertically-oriented society, each citizen, each consumer, enriches society by producing (on average) very much more than he consumes. In a horizontally-oriented society, you always destroy more than you create, even if you consume very little. Under Stalin, the Soviet Union had thousands of wonderful scientists and artists, but they were all made to serve evil ends. Here is another description of Stalin: Stalin was the one who made Andrei Sakharov, the kindest person and a real humanist, produce a hydrogen bomb for the world's bloodiest and most cruel dictator.

SELF-SACRIFICE

The Communists claimed that only a member of a collective is capable of self-sacrifice. This is what they had in mind:

Having accepted the thoughts and actions of the collective as his own, each member of a collective dissolves in it and in so doing indeed sacrifices himself.

A member of a collective becomes indistinguishable from other members and, from the point of view of the collective, utterly unimportant. Should he die, his death will go unnoticed, and that is self-sacrifice.

It was fear and inability to manage one's own life that brings people into a collective. Having rejected themselves, they no longer fear death, but will fanatically defend the ideology that has now become their only connection to reality. There are many people for whom joining a collective was just a career move, but there were also those who feared reality so much they were ready to die for their ideological illusions.

And what can we say about real self-sacrifice, for example, about someone who died trying to save the life of a child? We said that vertical development is a process whereby spiritual existence becomes more important than material existence. A person equates himself with the spiritual world he has created, with that which creates harmony between him and God's world. The death of a child that he could have prevented would so disrupt this spiritual harmony that he prefers to risk his physical existence trying to save the child. His attempt signifies that he has reached the pinnacle of spiritual growth, that his egotism now tells him to value his spiritual world more highly than his physical existence.

As a vertically-oriented person develops himself, he realizes that all the vertically-oriented people are united in God and, since all people are one, the suffering of the child becomes his own. As horizontally-oriented people are unable to feel unity with God and with humanity, they are reduced to joining the collective, which proves a very poor substitute for God's world.

Soldiers who died so that we could live did not get anything from us, and we are said to owe them "a debt that can never be repaid". In fact, these soldiers have fulfilled their mission as individuals and their lives can be seen as a complete success, set as an example.

During World War II, there were German soldiers who fought very well and "died for Germany", and they were no less loved and no less deserving to live than the Russian or American soldiers who killed them. What can we say about these German soldiers? Were their lives a success as well? And the answer is that in order to have successful lives we must not only maintain our physical, but also our spiritual health. Ideology can blind us, it can paralyze us, and it can kill us: it can destroy our lives, make our lives lose their meaning and purpose. German soldiers were killed by their ideology, they were victims of it and should be mourned as such.

Human beings have lived on Earth for millions of years, but concerns about pollution, about our environment, arose only recently. It is time to be concerned about ideological pollution as well. We have biological, chemical, nuclear weapons – weapons that affect human beings in novel ways, without cutting into their bodies. But the worst such weapon of all, one that has claimed hundreds of millions of victims already, is the ideological weapon. We need to learn how to make humans immune to this disease.

A Japanese sect introduces nerve gas into a subway system; a destructive computer virus created in a couple of hours by a bored teenager causes billions of dollars in damage and destroys the work of millions of people around the world; a terrorist gang attacks the World Trade Center and starts a war. This tells us that a few terrorists may soon be capable of destroying the human race. And that means there should be a concerted effort to maintain ideological health on Earth. Envy and rejection of the unique worth of every individual – these deadly concepts must be searched out and eliminated just as if they were weapons of mass destruction.

To make other people happy, you must yourself be happy. Happiness is a non-contradictory joy, joy that is not at the expense of others. A happy person creates more than he needs and shares his creations with others. There is no difference between that sharing and giving up one's life in defense of others.

Now let us look at the horizontal octant, to see the opposite situation, the inversed mirror image of the vertical octant. Here sacrifice is defined as "selfless" giving up of one's resources, something that we would call self-denial or self-betrayal. Once the totalitarian ideology is accepted, the individual acquires the characteristics of an inanimate object. In a horizontally-oriented society a sacrifice turns into a poisoned gift. Parting with whatever is necessary for himself, the giver becomes unhappy. As far as the one who accepts the poisoned gift, he often ends up losing everything. Poor Russian peasants gladly accepted the communist gift in the form of the property of rich peasants and nobles. A decade later the recipients of this gift had no property at all and were dying from hunger.

Spiritual development is not a goal in itself, but a way to achieve a goal. The goal is to leave the product of your creativity to people. Since you consume much less than you leave behind, and since to create takes such a great effort, it is often mistakenly described as taking away from yourself, making a sacrifice. When a mother raises her child, an extremely difficult task, it seems as if it costs much more than the reward one can reasonably expect; yet raising a child is not a sacrifice but a fulfillment.

THE RUSSIAN CONCEPT OF UNIVERSAL HARMONY

The Russians seem to have a concept of "universal harmony" that they seek to achieve. They claim that if a person is happy, he must have taken more than his fair share, and in so doing damaged his spiritual connection to others. And that means that you have to run away from happiness, so as not to stand out, and instead try to become one with the people.

Russians also are subconsciously afraid that the West will destroy their "harmony" with tasty German strawberry yogurt and beautiful

Italian shoes, which can trivialize and misguide their search for greatness or interfere with their suffering.

This concept would seek to limit happiness, but would not seek to limit suffering. I see it as illogical: when a particular person suffers, it seems to destroy harmony as well. And that reveals the envious, destructive nature of this conception of modesty.

God created human beings in His image. He created human beings: not a party, a collective farm, an extermination squad, or a community of television viewers. God gave human beings their freedoms, the capacity to think for themselves, to act independently, to feel and to love. And He did not tell human beings to reduce themselves or to destroy themselves, so that the envious could momentarily experience less disgust with themselves. On the contrary, God told human beings to develop themselves, to create, so that they could make the world better and share their inner light with all living things, with all the universe.

CHAPTER ELEVEN. ON EQUALITY

EQUALITY

People's conditions are always different, because there is an infinite number of scales on which any two people can be compared. That is why attempts to put them into "equal" conditions are always a little artificial. If the judges treat two boxers equally, they do not take into account the difference in their height, age, and whether or not both had enough to eat before the fight. In life, you play the hand you're dealt – there are many cards, and no other person in the world has your precise hand. If one boxer is weak and the other is strong, their fight would not be really fair as the weaker boxer cannot use a knife, run away, or have his friends help him out.

When we place all runners on the starting line, it allows us to objectively measure their running speed, but seeks to classify them not as multifaceted and unique human beings but as runners. And this is dangerous as this reduces these people to a figure, representing their result. The starting line helps to determine the winner, but the desire to achieve equality does not stop with the idea of equal starting conditions: the outcome of an equal start proves once again that people are not equal. That is why the proponents of equality favor the concept of the equal finish.

An equal finish is an ideological ideal that totalitarian states seek to implement. An equal finish is what happened to the millions of victims of the Stalinist purges, to six million Jews, to about a third of all Cambodians. An equal finish takes less dramatic forms as well. For example, a 100% tax on profit makes all citizens equally successful in business, and censorship makes all people equally knowledgeable.

The equal finish was invented to defend the weak. A horizontally-oriented person thinks that if John is smart, rich, and healthy he is this way not because he made himself to be so, but solely to offend this horizontally-oriented person. If all John thinks about is how to offend, it means that John is bad and thus deserves destruction. John lived his life never knowing that this horizontally-oriented person existed, but the horizontally-oriented person thinks that he is justified in avenging himself.

A good poet is often accused of doing nothing more than trying embarrass other poets, who, let us say, are simply too modest to write so well. The poet replies that he was writing for himself and never knew about the hacks, but he is not believed: an envious person does not understand the expression "for himself". This looks like a paradox, but it is true: an envious person cannot steal for himself, all he does is to steal yet another piece of his life from himself, and keeps on doing so until he is left with nothing at all.

And that means that if you are good at something it means you are bad, immodest, heartless. The equal finish is proposed so that the cruel good ones will not be able to wound the pride of the weak.

Today I am running the hundred meters against the world-famous Carl Lewis. We have agreed that we will finish together, with a result of two hours, twenty nine minutes and seven seconds. The result is very fair as even a legless person could cover the distance at that time, crawling and resting frequently. And so Carl and I start to run. We run, and it appears that Carl could cover the distance in less time: he starts out covering half the distance in five seconds, as is usual for him, but then returns to his senses, stops, and now slowly walks back. But how can I finish at the same time with such a tall, athletic person? People are sure to blame me for running the hundred meters faster than three hours. I will fool Carl by not moving at all for four hours, at least… Oh, damn, Carl is pushing me forward, physically carrying me towards the finish line! He wants to make me finish first!

Many readers may feel that the preceding description is some sort of a silly joke: who ever saw people running backwards at a competition, doing everything possible not to finish first? Well, in Russia in 1917 maybe a million people spoke fluent French. How many people in Russia spoke French only three years later, in 1920? None. Why were so many people burning their diplomas and evening gowns, destroying their financial documents and ownership certificates? Was diamond jewelry really created to be hidden in a hole under a garbage dump? Why did the Chinese kill all their university professors in the course of one year? Why did the Khmer Rouge butcher all those who were literate? And why is the most historic place in Russia, China, and North Korea occupied by the "eternally alive" corpse of a mass murderer? Equality is never even an equal finish: it is a competition where the winner comes last, a situation where the most venerated person in the country turns out to be its worst citizen, ever.

If you are at a disadvantage – it means you should win. This rule is actually rather widespread. And it conflicts very much with the notion of making sure that everyone has a genuine opportunity to succeed, that everybody should be judged objectively, by the result of an impartial competition.

There is only one way to make eight runners show an absolutely equal result, so that there is no discrimination by winning, and that is to make sure that all the runners are inanimate. In this case, their running speed is constant and easy to calculate. We started out wanting nothing more than the fairness of an equal finish by eight runners, and now there are eight corpses.

The idea of an equal start causes enormous inefficiencies. If you want to know the fastest runner, measure the hundred meters, get a stopwatch, and let him run. But here everyone has to fly to one place, stand on the same line, there are three false starts, one of the runners stumbles, and we get the "winner". And who is that? The one who ran the fastest during that particular ten seconds. It takes three months to arrange for eight people to run a hundred meters, and that is a very, very slow speed. Just think of the economic costs of arranging for an equal start! The only good thing you can say about the equal start is that it is way better than the equal finish.

EQUAL DISTRIBUTION

Let us imagine that a wealthy person decides to distribute a million dollars among the guests attending his birthday party. At 9 pm he counted his friends (there were ten of them), and so each of them got one hundred thousand dollars. At 9:13, four more friends arrived, and so they got a pizza equally shared among them. And then yet another friend came out of the bathroom, and he got nothing at all. This is how equal distribution happens in reality, and this is a rigid hierarchy that is utterly unfair. Some would say that the birthday boy should ask for the money back and divide it equally among the fifteen friends now present. But what if another friend were to come in later? Also, what happens if the money that was originally distributed is no longer there? One of the friends bought herself a fur coat, and can only return seventy thousand dollars, a fur coat, and a gallon of tears. What should be done then?

The answer is clear. "Equal" distribution is either unequal, arbitrary, rigidly hierarchical, or does not really happen as none of the recipients is allowed to take possession of the money that is supposedly theirs, but should await the next redistribution according to a new set of rules.

An interesting thing has happened with the money. There used to be a million dollars that its owner could spend as he wished. But as soon as we heard the word "equally", the money died. It cannot be spent, it is unclear who the owner is, and it is stuck with the redistributors, who divide, collect, and re-divide the money until it is all spent on administrative expenses.

This example is directly relevant to the economy of the Soviet Union. That which seemed to belong to the state (playing the role of the administrator in the process of equal distribution), in reality did not belong to anyone. How else could you explain that the harvest from private plots was twenty times (!) greater than that of the collective farms (same land, same hands, same climate).

There is private housing in Russia, and of course its owners would never think of vandalizing it. There also is municipal housing in Russia, which belongs to no-one, and the entranceway tends to be covered with graffiti and garbage.

How can you share a pizza if the number of guests is unknown, but equality is an absolute precondition? There are two methods: one is to let the pizza get cold and throw it out, and then all the guests get an equal number of slices. Or the host can eat the pie himself, not as an individual, but as a representative of all the guests.

If the exact number of people is unknown, how can a pizza be equally divided? Here comes the great principle of equal distribution that the Russians call "the fewer the people, the more oxygen there is". The guests are all assembled around the pizza, but they are not sure if there will be any more guests. They are not eating pizza: they are looking with hatred at the entrance. Note this dramatic change: all they wanted to do was to eat pizza, but now they wish the host did not have any more living friends. The need to divide the pie equally has separated the world into "us" and "them". Look at that magic: all you did was to say "equality", and now three things happen: you hate all comers, you have the pizza you wanted to eat, but you do not eat it, your pizza gets cold and is thrown away and nobody has any of it. And what do you do while you wait, what do you do if you want more pizza than your equal share? You create theories to "prove" that someone or other is not entitled to have a piece. Racial, national, or other such theories come in very handy.

When you get a pizza, it is polite and fair to give an equal number of shares to everyone present. But this is equal opportunity, not equal distribution: if someone comes late, he loses his opportunity, and would get his slice next time, when he is not late.

Let us return to the people awaiting the distribution of a million dollars. What is the goal of the giver? He wants to distribute the money equally, not just arbitrarily give as many bills as his hand can grab until there is no more money. He wants to make sure that every recipient has an equal amount of money. But what if one of the guests already has eight dollars? Should he receive the same share as everybody else or his share minus eight dollars? In the latter case, what should be done with the eight dollars that would be left over? For everyone to get an equal share, all the intended recipients should first hand over all their money to the host, it should all be added up, and then distributed equally. And that is precisely what happened in the Soviet Union: all property was confiscated, and then propertyless people started to wait for the equal distribution that, as we now know, either never came, or came hierarchically, according to very arbitrary criteria. But for us it is important to note that once the guests became intended recipients in an equal distribution scheme, all that really happened is that they lose whatever money they had.

Well, now the recipients have no money. But can they earn some? Of course not, as this would utterly destroy the equilibrium. And could they just leave, just run away from the party? No, they cannot as this would screw up the calculation. People are awaiting equal distribution, and suddenly they are penniless, unable to earn money, immobilized, devoid of freedom – is it not a picture of the Soviet Union? In the eyes of redistributors the recipients resemble inanimate objects, statues standing with their hands outstretched.

The proceeds of equal distribution cannot be used: this property becomes virtual, and the attempt to distribute equally stops time and turns each participant into an inanimate object, by attaching to him an arbitrarily chosen hierarchical label.

But the desire to equally distribute a lowly pizza pie cannot be a goal in itself: people do not want pizza, they want talent, beauty, happiness, respect, luck, success. This is what they really want to distribute equally. And how can this be done? It can only be done in death, death being the only true equal distributor.

If creating a society based on equality turns out to be such a difficult and dangerous task, why does it attract so many people? When you stand immobilized and propertyless waiting for equal distribution to begin, you are in a very special state of being: you no longer have to be good or bad, you no longer have to act, you no longer have anything and have no one to envy, you are not alone but a part of a community of recipients, you are waiting for something to be bestowed upon you, and you have nothing to do but wait. Remember the Zen Point? It is exactly as if you have just died and are waiting for God's judgment to be pronounced upon you. Here is why it is so attractive: personal choice no longer matters, personal morality is no longer relevant – in other words, you are free from being a person.

The Commandment "thou shalt not steal", actually means "you die when you turn yourself into a claim against others, and instead you should live, create, and consume only the fruits of your labor". But now we see that in order to "die" you do not even have to do the stealing yourself: it is enough if you are simply labeled as a claimant, if you simply are involved in the process of equal distribution.

Religious teachings say that there will be a day when the dead will be revived, and that will be the day of humans' triumph as spiritual beings. In the horizontal octant, the equivalent of this is the idea of equal distribution of material resources, a paradise on Earth, a day when all human beings will still be alive, but will be as good as dead.

For most of human history, the greatest danger to humans came from hunger and disease, but now danger comes almost exclusively from other human beings. Ideologically modified humans have killed tens of millions of people, and it is time to learn to pluck them out before they strike. Next, genetically modified humans will come, and then intelligent machines, and we need to start learning how to program their brains so that there are no new Hitlers.

The idea of equality is one of the key ideas of our civilization. But the vertical interpretation of this idea is that of equal rights, while the horizontal interpretation is that of equal results. These two interpretations are opposite to one another, and the struggle between the two is fierce.

EQUALITY AND CREATIVITY

When you create something, you create inequality, as you now have something that others do not have. If you can create something, it means you must have rights to protect you, as otherwise you would have been afraid of envy of others. Since creators realize that others benefit from their creativity as well, they want others to create so that they can benefit from their creativity. Creators want to offer others immunity from envy, i.e. they wants everyone to have the same rights. Rights are not something we're born with: when people see each other as creators, they grant each other rights. Every creative act thus has a direct bearing on individual rights, convincing everyone to contain their envy so that everyone can benefit from the creativity of others.

Creativity does not create material equality, but it makes all creators equal, as they prove that they all have been created in God's image. Their creations stay with us for all eternity, while destructive acts are passing. The name of the poet is remembered much longer then the names of his murderers.

In the vertical octant, creative inequality leads to equal rights for all creators. In the horizontal octant, the attempt to distribute material possessions equally leads to a rigid and arbitrary hierarchy; as far as rights, there are equal rights for all the dead and/or incapacitated.

"LIBERTY, EQUALITY, FRATERNITY"

The French revolution put forth the slogan of "Liberty, Equality, Fraternity", and proceeded to show that it can be interpreted in two diametrically opposing ways.

From the point of view of the collective, liberty is interpreted as realization by each member of the collective of the need to submit completely to the collective's will. The appropriate definition here would be "liberty is whatever is perceived as a need". Equality is understood as ideological conformity (i.e., sameness of opinion) and equal distribution of material possessions. Fraternity is understood as the lack of the protection afforded by individual rights, as the opportunity to interfere with life of every person and institute total control over everyone and everything. We know that this interpretation of "Liberty, Equality, Fraternity" entails a transition to another dimension, the spiritual death of all the persons involved, a strict and arbitrary hierarchy, a lack of private property, and creation of the Social Machine that controls the social aspects of every person's behavior. It also translates into steady work for the guillotine, which chops off heads very humanely because it stands at the service of a lofty ideal.

From the vertical point of view, liberty is understood as the opportunity to act, coupled with personal responsibility for one's actions. The right and the opportunity to develop freely are necessarily based on private property, which serves as the foundation for independent spiritual and economic growth. Equality is seen as equality before law, that is, impartial, fair, and equitable treatment of each and every person by the state and by society at large. It is the task of the state to preserve the independence of each individual and to grant to each individual the maximum opportunity for unimpeded personal development. Fraternity is understood as the uniqueness of each person, but also the spiritual unity of all human souls in their belief in the Creator.

REDISTRIBUTION

What is redistribution of property? It entails the following:

All participants in the process of redistribution (willing or unwilling) give up all their property rights and make all their property available to the redistributor.

It is necessary to know what property each person owns. Nobody should be able to hide anything, and that means that individual privacy must be severely restricted.

As property may grow and thus interfere with the process of redistribution, all individual creativity must be outlawed and all productive capacity should be put directly in the service of the redistributor.

The first task of the redistributor thus becomes either to stop time (weapons are good at doing that to people) or to make everybody stop doing anything productive while redistribution takes place.

Now all property has to be collected and counted, and then redistributed. There needs to be a group of people who are responsible and empowered to do that.

These people, the redistributors, are working, while all the others are sitting on their hands in order not to screw up the calculation. The redistributors' work is hard. It is fair to pay for it, for otherwise we would have to declare that all labor shall henceforth be unpaid. Thus, everyone gets an equal share but the redistributors get more.

Leading the redistributors is even harder, and so these leaders should get more than the rank-and-file redistributors, unless we decide to declare that all intellectual input shall henceforth be unpaid. Thus, everyone gets an equal share, the redistributors get more, and their leaders – still more.

As a result of this equal distribution, we have ordinary citizens who starve and leaders who live better than royalty.

We started out protesting the inequality born out of diversity of talent and fate, and ended up with a society of glaring inequality, a very rigid hierarchy, and with society's productive capacity alienated from its people and no longer in service to them. Under such a system, property rights can only be conditional, partial, and temporary. Most property is concentrated not in the hands of producers, but in the hands of redistributors. Independent productive activities are suspect if not outright outlawed, and all those who as much as reveal their productive potential are under additional control. No one can increase the amount of property in his possession by producing; the only way to get more is to become one of the redistributors. The amount of property available to be redistributed tends to decrease very fast.

But why was it fair to confiscate the palace the tsar was living in, but not fair to confiscate the very same palace, just because now it is the General Secretary who lives there? Because the tsar owned the palace, while the General Secretary merely represents all those who "own" the palace; in fact, he represents the Social Machine that owns everyone and everything. Since property is alienated and transferred to a virtual owner, the Social Machine, people are taught to despise property, business as a profession, as well as all forms of independent creative activity, and encouraged to betray a friend for an additional crust of bread. Equality is one hell of a lofty ideal!

And why compromise? If you want equality, you should not pay for labor, you should not pay for intellectual input, and you should stop time to make sure you are stopping all individual creativity. This is a description of death, and that makes you eligible for the Pol Pot Award, the highest honor for a proponent of equality.

And this is absolutely logical. Indeed, those who thought about equality of material possessions could not have been thinking about live human beings. Human beings are not limited to dreaming of material possessions: they want beauty, health, talent, recognition. When one person is healthy and the other is sick, equal distribution of material resources would do little to equalize their conditions.

There is another contradiction. A society that aims to equalize people's material possessions calls itself materialistic. Let's count the cows: if you have more than two that makes you a rich peasant, and you should give up your property. But what do we see? In every Soviet movie, the rich peasant is necessarily an ugly, fat, and angry man, so that we are very relieved when, by the end of the movie, he is killed by a poor peasant, who always happens to be extremely handsome. Here is what having two cows can do to a man: an ugly nose and a fat belly. And this is anything but materialistic: these people assign to cows the magical power to make their owners ugly.

The redistributors stop time, and in doing so they lose perspective. For example, they think that if today they hit businessmen with a 90% tax, these businessmen will not respond by moving to tax havens. Another example of this loss of perspective is the accusation that the rich spend their money on luxuries. Well, at a certain time in history these luxuries included clothes and footwear, a bed of your own, baths, pepper, and sugar, and all the other things we have in our material culture, without exception.

All that we have today we have solely because at one time or another a rich person paid for it and obtained it in spite of the envy of others. "I want to wrap my feet in fur", said an extravagant rich man, and thereby invented shoes, and had enough power and strength to wear them in public. And this is important: a poor hunter could have made shoes for himself, but he would not have been able to walk in them without subjecting himself to ridicule and hate. Such a ridiculous thing as footwear could only have been introduced by those whom you would be afraid to subject to ridicule. There were many poor inventors, but unless they had powerful sponsors their inventions were likely to bring them considerable misfortune.

Our daily life is inconceivable without what used to be called the playthings of the rich. When the people of Russia revolted against the rich, the "revenge of the rich" was not long in coming: clothes and footwear, a bed of your own, baths, pepper, and sugar, and all the other things we have in our material culture, with a notable exception of guns and instruments of torture, disappeared.

Russian history has yet another example of poetic justice: in the thirties, the Russian peasantry was destroyed so that Stalin could buy machine tools for his factories, but today impoverished former factory workers return to the villages to grow food for their families, to become peasants.

SIX TIN SOLDIERS

This discussion may seem to be repeating our previous discussion about equal distribution, but we need to have it down pat, so here is a test question. Vic has two tin soldiers and Alex has four. How many should each of them have so that each will have an equal number of tin soldiers?

If you answer, "Alex should give one of his soldiers to Vic so that each will have three soldiers", you would benefit from following this discussion as this answer is utterly wrong.

The answer is wrong because Alex has a form that allows him to cast new tin soldiers, and this is probably why he has more soldiers than Vic does. Take one soldier away from Alex, and soon he may have not three, but thirty three of them. To make sure that the number of soldiers each of the boys has is truly equal, you should be certain that none of them could cast any new ones and does not have the resources to purchase them at the toy store. And these resources are not just money: a pen-knife, a stamp collection, a father in a good mood – all of these resources can get a boy more tin soldiers, and that means that all of these resources must now be tightly controlled.

Thus, you start out by destroying these additional resources, so finally there is no way to get more tin soldiers than these six. So, now, Vic and Alex, step forward and get your equal number of soldiers.

OK, reader, one more time. Vic and Alex have six soldiers in total. How many does each of them get? Right! You have the correct answer! Of course! Each of the boys gets zero tin soldiers and an admonition to never even want them ever again. And the six tin soldiers go to those lovers of equality who threw out the casting form, broke the pen knife, burned the stamp collection, and made damn sure that no father is ever in a mood good enough to buy his son a tin soldier.

Every attempt to establish equality transfers all the resources to the redistributors, while incapacitating those unfortunates who play the role of recipients without ever receiving anything. The inner world of the recipients is also destroyed, as they lose the ability to make do with what they have or to "cast their own tin soldiers".

The attempt to establish equality is the social equivalent of murder as it seeks to destroy both the material and the spiritual world of human beings.

And what if Vic did not want to have three soldiers, what if two soldiers was all that he wanted (or could carry)? His opinion was not solicited: he had to participate simply by virtue of being there. The desire to achieve equality is expansive and aggressive.

The topic of equality is hot: the poor South wants the rich North to feed it. But crocodiles are hungry, and these ancient animals deserve better. It is therefore fair to feed the proponents of the equality theory to the hungry crocodiles, and to state once and for all: there are no poor countries, but there are too many countries that are envy-ridden and cannot protect and nourish human creativity. The creative rights of individuals should be respected and protected, and the lack of such respect and protection has been mistakenly and tragically known as "poverty", while the correct word is "envy".

Redistributors want to "make the world a better place", but personally they are seldom kind, and consistently show incredible cruelty in their attempt to remake the world. Why? Kindness is when your desires correspond to those of someone else, when you are pleased to benefit another person. Redistribution is the desire to build a world where kindness would no longer be necessary. That is why the concept of redistribution is diametrically opposed to the concepts of helping, sharing, and creating. That is why the poor never benefited from redistribution: the resources do not get to the needy, but are transferred away from serving the people – to serve ideology and its bloodthirsty proponents.

Speaking of kindness and sharing the fruits of one's labor, we should note that charity has nothing to do with redistribution that the proponents of equality advocate, and of course charity, from which common people can directly benefit, should continue. Our previous discussion clearly showed that charity is a form of creativity.

When the state takes away a person's property and the opportunity to create, the state in effect says "you do not know what is good, and the state does; we do not need responsible citizens, but need to turn them into obedient robots."

The Information Age makes the idea of redistributing material possessions outdated, as the intellectual potential of human beings has become relatively much more valuable: a few lines of computer code or a hit song can get you a great deal of possessions.

Information is not a loaf of bread: it does not diminish when it is shared, it only gains in value. Information Age society freely shares its most valuable asset, information; and in that the Information Age, ironically, resembles Communism. But the Information Age also underscores the need of every individual to develop freely so the information can be understood and used properly. Only an experienced and competent user can benefit from information, and this is yet another thing that distinguishes information from a loaf of bread.

In the Information Age, envy is also under threat as other people's ability to obtain, interpret, and create information is hard to impede and impossible to steal. On the other hand, computer viruses always remind us that envy does not need to be personal, does not need to have a reason, and yet can be extremely destructive. Such crimes, motivated by sheer envy, should be reclassified as the most serious crimes possible.

THE MISTAKES OF THE RUSSIAN DEMOCRATIC REFORMERS

For most of its history Russian society was not based on creativity as such. The nobles did not work: they had a claim on the product of others. The material condition of slaves did not depend on how much they produced or how hard they worked: it depended primarily on the size of the claim against the results of their labor. The church collected alms, and the fruits of monks' labor were used in common. The freemen were few, and their position in the state structure was not well determined. As creators, the freemen existed in a different dimension from those whose life depended on processing a claim. Most people worked very hard and productively, but could not keep and enjoy the results of their own labor.

Capitalist society is the exact opposite. Investors get the results of their own investments; they may be wealthy, but they do not live on a claim or on an entitlement, they live on the result of the labor of their money. The rest of society is salaried employees or self-employed workers, and they live on the result of their labor. Those who live on entitlements are few, and they cannot influence a state run by creators.

The Russian reformers had a very hard task ahead of them. In August 1991, it seemed that the communist system had melted away. But as we discussed before, the Russian people did not have enough self-respect to create a truly democratic system of government. They were alienated from power, and totally disoriented. They did reject certain manifestations (but not the underlying philosophy) of the horizontal octant, but the vertical octant, with its personal responsibility and lack of envy, appeared very foreign to them. The number of Soviet citizens who in 1991 could be described as true democrats can be best estimated at zero. With such a narrow base, it is hard to blame Yeltsin for his failures.

Russia's democrats (for lack of a better word) gambled that people would sleep through the reforms, that they would calmly bear the difficulties, as was their time-honored custom. It may well be that politically this was the only possible course. On the other hand, one wants to believe that the Russian people deserve a bit more credit. If so, it would have been a good idea to initiate a dialogue with them, to try to explain to them what democracy is. In the 1993 parliamentary elections, Yegor Gaidar's party, Russia's Democratic Choice, talked to the voters as if they all suffered from severe mental retardation. Another democratic party, Grigory Yavlinsky's *Yabloko*, was a little more polite: it told its voters nothing at all.

Both the democratic leaders and the ordinary people were Soviets, and what they were trying to build was un-Soviet, because it appeared that everything Soviet had collapsed. Therefore, by definition, they were talking about something they knew very little about. I presume that many Americans would not appear very intelligent if they were suddenly forced to talk (and to think!) in Hungarian or Swahili.

With this in mind, we should discuss the mistakes and failures of the democrats, while reserving judgment on whether or not they could have been avoided.

The greatest mistake of the Russian democrats was that they apparently thought capitalism was simply a system where the means of production belong to private persons. But capitalism is an economic manifestation of the creative morality, and thus parceling property out to thieves and administrators did not bring about capitalism. Instead, there was a tremendous economic crisis, as envy-based people are incapable of truly owning property.

In Russia, privatization "appointed" as creators those who had never created. The head of the Russian equivalent of Microsoft would under this system be some former member of the Central Committee of the Communist Party who used to be responsible for library censorship and who may have had a computer on his desk to sort out the denunciations.

The democrats discovered that it was not enough to appoint a private director and to sell stock to make an enterprise private: the owners must have an outlook based on creativity, not on envy. Doing jail time for racketeering turned out to be poor preparation for the position of enterprise director.

Russia's reforms cannot be considered successful because they created a system with an extremely low creative potential, a system that subsists almost exclusively by exploiting natural resources.

IF THERE IS NO LEGAL SYSTEM, WHAT ARE RIGHTS FOR?

In Russian there is a condescending expression, "to be reduced to citing one's rights". By citing your rights you do not restore justice, but aim to get an unfair advantage and/or make a fool of yourself. To assert that you have rights is also dangerous, as it could offend your boss: the weak should offer their necks to the strong to make the killing easier.

If people are afraid to use their rights, granting any number of rights will not help. Until the legal system becomes independent, impartial, and based on equal treatment of all, the weak will be afraid to challenge the strong. But the law still serves those in power, and it is might that makes right, regardless of what the law books say.

THE MORAL SOCIETY

Capitalism or a market economy is the economic form of existence of a society based on the win/win principle, that is, a society that successfully contains envy, a society where the creative morality clearly prevails, a society where laws that ensure the unhindered development of every individual are more powerful than the state, and a society that consists of citizens who actively support such a system.

In Russia after the failed coup of August 1991, support for democratic reforms was very strong. That was the time to declare that the individual initiative that falls within the framework of win/win would be protected from envy. It was the time to enact the simplest system of basic laws that would securely guard society from envy in all its many forms and manifestations. It was also the time for a low, simple flat tax. And it was the time to limit voting rights to all owners of private property who did not have Communist connections. After seventy years of Communist "selection" which essentially was genocide, the population of Russia was not ready for a one man, one vote electoral system. These reforms were not enacted, and here is the result: free creative labor in Russia is not adequately defended. Consequently, the national economy cannot grow, and the people, with considerable justification, blame the democrats for their continuing misery.

Many of the Russian democrats' mistakes are attributable to the advice they received from their Western consultants – including advice based on the premise that every country, every people, is immediately ready for a full-blown democracy, democracy of form, rather than of substance, "democracy" that only looks good on a Project Report Form.

The Russian state continues to be envy based. An envy based state is a poor state, a poor state is an angry state, and an angry state is a bloody state, a state that cannot afford peace. An envious state is also a state that does not enjoy the support of creators and will not submit to their control. On the other hand, the envious state may be enthusiastically supported by the envious masses, and the main characteristic of these masses is that they happen to be suicidal.

ON MORALITY

Morality is simply a measure of how well a person treats himself. Indeed, if a person concentrates on developing his talents, pursuing available opportunities, his relationships with others will be free from envy.

In the West, individual morality is so entrenched, it is simply not credible to blame others for your own failures. As a consequence, there are many psychological disorders that simply provide an excuse for a slow pace of personal progress, creating outlets where fear and insecurity can "legitimately" manifest themselves. But fearing your own possible success is still better than fearing that of your neighbors.

A society is moral to the extent that it has a functioning market economy, and there are millions of Russians who actively participate in the market. But they are still a small minority; moreover, the rules of the game are very slow in becoming even half-way honest.

Today those Russians that are in power feel, with considerable justification, that ordinary Russians are not morally ready for democracy and a true market economy. The state has therefore embarked on building a sort of democratic feudalism. It is hoped that with time the Russian people will grow more self-sufficient and more responsive to democratic ideas. But a system of government in which people do not participate (not because they are forcibly excluded but because they simply want to be left alone) is inefficient. The challenges that Russia faces are too great for an inefficient government to handle: instead of breaking up and going up in flames, as was the case under Yeltsin, today Russia is more united and more tightly governed, but it is slowly sinking under the weight of the problems that remain unsolved.

THE PRINCIPLE OF THE COMMON GOOD

The Communists confiscated the property of the rich and pretended to give it to the poor. As a result, the poor got nothing and were soon dying from hunger next to those who used to be rich. But it is very easy to make a rich person share his wealth: all that needs to be done is to enact a law that protects private investment, so that money goes into the stock market, where it creates new jobs and contributes to the well-being of others.

Socialist ideas were born in Western Europe, and they remain popular. Since most of the property there was private and there were laws that defended it effectively, socialist ideas were understood vertically. The ideas of Karl Marx alerted the capitalist establishment that its relationship with the workers was not a win/win relationship, that society unnecessarily suffered from antagonistic relationships that were a holdover from another era. Thus, Marx became a respected Western economist. In Russia, his ideas were understood horizontally and created enormous destruction.

We noted that Russians think that kindness and spiritual growth come only as a result of personal suffering. In Russia, a kind person is one who would give you the shirt off his back. But the resulting suffering always creates uncomfortable dependency, anger, envy, hatred, and pain. In the West, a kind person has a shirt factory and sells a lot of shirts at a fair price, and as a result his wife can wear diamonds. The Russians thought that their suffering would produce the Second Coming of Christ, but instead there was just the first coming of Stalin.

CHAPTER TWELVE. THE LAW AND THE PEOPLE

THE RUSSIAN ATTITUDE TOWARDS LAW AS EXPRESSED BY PUSHKIN

Here is a poem by Alexander Pushkin, the greatest Russian poet of all time. Pushkin lived during the first half of the nineteenth century (1799-1837). I could not find this poem professionally translated and translated it myself. The rhyme is gone, but the meaning is as close to the original as I could make it. Here it is:

From Pindemonti

I have little use for those loudly proclaimed rights
That send many a head a'spinning.
And I do not regret that the gods have denied me
The precious opportunity to dispute over taxes
Or to interfere with the struggles of rulers.
I could not care less if the press is allowed to fool the idiots
Or if a censor limits the empty talk on the pages of newspapers.
All this talk of rights is but meaningless words.
I cherish very different rights, ones that are much better.
I sorely need another kind of freedom:
To depend on rulers or to depend on commoners –
What difference does it make? I do not care for either.
To report to no one, to serve and cater to no one but myself;
To never compromise my conscience, change my plans, or bend my neck
For the powers-that-be, or to get a position.
To roam here and there as I please, enjoying the beauty of nature,
Becoming ecstatic from seeing art, appreciating the fruits of inspiration –
Here is what I call happiness, here is what I call rights.

(1836)

Trans. by Matthew Maly

Most Russians agree that in his writings Pushkin succeeded in capturing and describing the Russian soul, writing about Russia as it has always been and is likely to remain. Quoting from Pushkin, especially from a poem as important as this one, is like quoting directly from the Russian soul. This poem precisely captures the prevailing Russian attitude towards rights, laws, state building, and state service. If we dare to assume that the expression "appreciating the fruits of inspiration" includes, but certainly is not limited to, the process of getting inebriated – then the poem seems to be a perfect one, indeed.

Of course, we are not saying that Pushkin should have called on his readers to challenge taxes or to apply to the School of Social Work, as this is a romantic poem about the importance of freedom, not a political statement. We also should not forget that Pushkin lived in a country where the great majority of the population were indentured servants, in effect, slaves.

Pushkin got an excellent education, spoke fluent French, was very knowledgeable about European culture, and was interested in politics. And yet, for the year of 1836, Pushkin's "definitions" of such concepts as freedom, law, rights, and the state seem strikingly naïve. Sixty years after the American Revolution, Pushkin did not even begin to understand what it was about. Pushkin's "solution" is a typically Russian one: why build a civil society, just run away where the envious can't get you. Just thirty four years after this poem was written, Vladimir Lenin was born, and forty eight years after his birth the envious were already putting all such free souls up against the wall: building a civil society, in retrospect, would probably have been a much better solution. It all happened more or less in one lifetime: if Pushkin had lived 120 years, he would have seen Lenin's firing squads himself.

In the nineteenth century Russia had the world's greatest literature, and yet Pushkin discounted freedom of the press, Tolstoy railed against courts of law as he thought that only the human heart could render a right judgment, Saltykov-Shchedrin laughed at bureaucracy, Dostoyevsky's characters interpreted rights as the right to kill, Gogol could not bring himself, hard though he tried, to respect the spirit of capitalism. These excellent writers could not be blamed, of course, as they were describing the bleak reality that surrounded them in Russia, but we should note nonetheless that they failed to put all these things in perspective: granted,

Russian law is unjust, but instead of dismissing it outright, a citizen must try to make it better.

In this poem, Pushkin appears totally alienated, unwilling to be a citizen of his country, longing to be left alone. Again, his position is perfectly understandable: he was censored, controlled, insulted, never allowed to travel abroad, and at the end was killed in a palace intrigue. But since that time, millions of Russians have read this poem as a manifesto, as the way to behave, as a justification for their rejection of their civic duty.

In Russia, nobody is willing to write good laws: you either violate the law or run away from it. Russians simply do not understand that laws can be written to defend the people, written for the benefit of all.

For a poet, not to defend rights is really unfair. First there was private property, something that a person could identify his being with. A baby first says "my mommy" and only then learns his name, so originally he is "one, whose mommy is this one". It is through property that human beings came to their greatest invention, the invention of the word "I". Once the word "I" was invented, its derivatives followed, and those were beauty, truth, honor, love, the future. And from that it follows that poetry could not have existed without private property and the law that protects it.

LAW IN THE WEST AND LAW IN RUSSIA, THE DICTATORSHIP OF LAW AND THE POWER OF THE PEOPLE

If we were to ask people on the street of a Western city for their definition of democracy, everyone would say that democracy is when people vote to elect their representatives. But then Hitler also was "democratically" elected, and so this definition fails.

Democracy is when every citizen is empowered, everyone has the unhindered opportunity for personal development and growth, and these achievements are protected. Democracy is a dictatorship of human achievements over human self-destructive tendencies, and this dictatorship should be strict.

Democracy is not "the will of the people", because the people may under certain conditions be overcome by suicidal, aggressive, or divisive ideas, and the role of democracy would then be not to carry them out but to check them.

In the West, democracy may be defined in a simplified fashion, because certain extremely important things are taken for granted, and these are the vertical orientation of the people and their ability to survive and prosper in a contemporary world. Indeed, if you cannot handle G-forces, you cannot fly a supersonic jet, and if you cannot drive, a car is of no use for you. Democracy implies that you are ready for the contemporary world, that you do not need to shut it out in order to be comfortable. If you ride a donkey, you wish there were no freeways: for you, they are just an irritant because a freeway does not let a donkey cross it or trot upon itself. That explains why America is the target of hatred and terrorism.

Western people, left alone, will choose democracy. Other people, left alone, will debate how best to destroy themselves and others. For them, democracy is certainly not a free expression of opinion, but a straightjacket, a dictatorship of respect for fellow humans – a respect they do not feel for others, or for themselves.

It is a crime to sacrifice humans solely to claim, against all evidence, that the entire world is as ready for democracy as the West is. This theory, like every ideology, stops time and denies history, stating that whatever the West spent two thousand years inventing, perfecting, and struggling for is obvious and available for the taking.

A group of kindergarten students cannot build a Space Shuttle, but let them grow up and they might. A democracy is no less technologically sophisticated than a Space Shuttle. Democracy is simply an advanced technology, and as such it requires mature and experienced users.

To build a true democracy in today's Russia requires all the necessary measures, including those involving force, control, and selection, to force people to live without dependency and envy. Only when Russia becomes a country of independent, self-sufficient, envy-free, and socially responsible citizens will there be a true Russian democracy.

Democracy has nothing to do with freedom of choice: in fact, democracy is a dictatorship, but we simply do not notice this because we have adapted. Democracy offers a very narrow and stifling choice between that which is good and that which is even better, and leaves practically no place for the wide spectrum of self-destruction, self-righteousness, chauvinism, and all the other ways to escape from the difficult task of self-development.

Democracy permits only half of the range of possible human action: it allows creativity while harshly outlawing destruction. In every interaction the citizens are forced to act according to the law, and this law is arbitrarily based on win/win as if it were the only possible principle of human interaction.

Here is a quick example. Suppose John throws a cup of coffee on Peter's shirt. The law calls for John to apologize and/or pay compensation. Why shouldn't they have a duel instead, one pistol shot each, at twelve paces? Pushkin was killed in such a duel, this solution being, evidently, good enough for him. Or John could pronounce Peter's entire family to be his family's mortal enemies. This solution was good enough for the Capulets and the Montagues. Those who live in a democracy should realize that they have simply adapted, agreed to voluntarily reduce the range of acceptable behaviors, and yet there are cultures or groups that arbitrarily outlaw win/win and are fondly devoted to lose/lose solutions. To blow yourself up and kill a few others in the process: what could possibly be better (or worse, whatever is the correct usage in such a person's language).

And where is freedom of speech? In America, if you are stopped for a traffic violation, there is nothing for you to say or do: you are a slave to the law, and the law is just, which in the minds of some people only adds to the boredom. In Russia, you talk to the officer: you can offer a bribe, threaten bodily harm, fight, or kill each other – now, that is freedom.

Laws are simply a technology of human co-existence, which in the West, but by no means everywhere, are based on a win/win principle. Russians do not accept a technological solution because they prefer to be guided by their hearts (read "their whims"), and prefer a loose/loose principle with a pronounced tendency towards lose/lose.

In the West, a suspect is considered innocent until proven guilty. Russians do not understand that: how could an innocent person be put on trial? Respected judges should not be asked to waste their time if the scoundrel (note the designation) were not guilty. He is guilty for sure, and the judges just need to make some phone calls (note that as well) to determine what to do with the guy.

In the West, if there was a technical mistake in the legal proceedings, if the jury is not certain, or if your "crime" is not on the books, you are let go. The Russians can't believe that the heart's desire for (harsh) justice can come second to some "technical mistake" or "lack of evidence": if the guy has no-one to defend him, then let him rot in jail!

American law is based on written precedent, and thus the law, just as any other technology, improves, develops, and becomes more user-friendly. Russian law is still mostly based on the human heart and on informal personal relationships. And the human heart does not submit to systematic improvement. The verdict depends on the power relationships of the accused, and these are always unique, so that the case is not an example or a precedent for similar cases in the future. And now the Russians start screaming, "Look, the Americans have outlawed their own heart, they do not believe in their heart's justice, they agreed to have a dusty law book instead of their hearts, they are abrogating their responsibility to carry justice within themselves." A different civilization.

ART AND MORAL LEADERSHIP

American movies concentrate on visual effects, a fast-moving plot, and adventure, and it is apparent that their goal is almost solely to entertain. By contrast, Soviet movies carried a strong moral message, and examined – often very deeply, lovingly, and successfully – human feelings and relationships. In Russia, an artist felt the need to become a moral guide for his nation as there was no church or other avenues to get moral guidance. Living in the Soviet Union meant facing a constant moral choice: there was the official viewpoint, which was usually immoral, and your personal one, which was usually confused. In America the law serves as a reliable arbiter and, in most situation, can serve as a moral guide as well. That is why American artists rarely choose to assume a role of moral leader. The artists are reduced to inventing evil creatures for their horror movies. This is what suburban America demands because in real life nothing bad or scary ever happens.

In Russia, words are more important than any law, because a word is spoken by a live person while the law is written on paper and can be read equally by everyone, regardless of his position or character. Human speech is changeable and can be interpreted differently, while the law is constant and does not allow for different interpretations. The word of an artist is a reaction to something, it happens after the fact, while the law aims to prevent something bad from happening, and is enacted before the undesirable event takes place. The Russian poet Pushkin was killed in a duel, and the Russian poet Lermontov wrote a great poem about it. In the West, the law forbids duels, and citizens are law-abiding. There is nothing as horrible as the death of a genius for the Western poet to write a passionate poem about, and so he is reduced to writing a limerick. If something bad does happen, a new Western law makes sure it never happens again, and it usually does not. For a poet, there goes the topic. A Western artist has nothing to fight for and nothing to depict: as soon as the fundamental moral questions were answered, art became abstract, and it even appeared that art had died. In fact, life in a law-abiding society quickly becomes so good that some citizens set out to do something bad just to widen the range of their experiences. In Russia, the law is irrelevant, but a poem has no direct bearing on social life, either: four years after Pushkin was killed in a duel, Lermontov was killed in a duel as well.

Each new generation is wiser than the previous one, and people's opinions and their laws change constantly. In America, your opinion is counted when you are right, and it stays in the body of law forever; in Russia, it is counted when you prove to be closer to power, and stays in force only until someone more powerful than you comes along. That is why in Russia suspects can be treated essentially as they were treated five hundred years ago: there has been no fundamental change in attitude, no learning process. A Russian judge of five hundred years ago is perfectly capable to preside over court proceedings today. All he needs is to learn to use the telephone. The Russian language, dress, diet, lifestyles, education levels – all changed tremendously in these five hundred years, but the attitudes are still the same.

In Russia, the only real law is the moral authority of the artists, or of those whom you trust. And these moral guides define morality and justice differently, and there are no hardcover law books to look up.

Russian society is soft, as we have noted on several occasions. Russians search for kindness, but cannot define it, and that makes kindness the true foundation of their society. As American society is based on law, you can take the word "kindness" out of the language entirely, and nothing would change: every action is either lawful or unlawful, and it is not measured in terms of kindness at all. If there were no law, American society would be thrown into chaos as its citizens' conception of kindness is strictly their private affair. Russian society can exist entirely without laws, and it also cannot agree on the definition of kindness; therefore, all that the Russians ever do is wait for a kind ruler, that is, one who combines kindness and power.

In Russia, the state actively demands that a citizen be kind, both socially (by denouncing or executing neighbors that have lost their way) and personally (by selflessly fighting the fascists or by creating great science or great art). And so it was that Stalin was killing millions and at the very same time allowing Boris Pasternak or Dmitry Shostakovich to create art that, in my view, embodies the human search for kindness.

The catastrophic failure of Russian civilization is that it forsook laws in favor of magnificent prose and verse. But poets cannot regulate, direct, or rule a human society: they can only shed tears over this misguided society after it had committed monstrous crimes against itself.

The Russians think that reading great literature will automatically turn them into good citizens. But literature by itself cannot cure a person of envy; for that, one needs the independence and self-sufficiency that come only from private property that is securely protected by law. Great literature was meant as the spiritual companion of free people, as their depository of wisdom and beauty, not as a tranquilizer for slaves.

LAW AND ORDER

Throughout their history Russians have always lived under strict external control. As a consequence, they had no need to develop the internal controls that turn people into independent yet law abiding citizens, who submit to (fair and reasonable) laws voluntarily. Internal controls make people law-abiding even when they are alone. But in Russia all controls have always been external, and Russians are likely to break the law once a policeman looks away.

A Russian is reluctant to ask the legislature to pass a law: it would seem as if he wants protection, implying that he is weak, and also implying that others are equally weak. Thus, there is either lawlessness or dictatorship (and these always go together). That makes the Rule of Law something very foreign to Russia.

The idea that dictatorship and lawlessness always go together needs to be especially emphasized, particularly as many Russians now want the return of "Stalinist" rule, claiming that then it was possible to achieve "order". External order, yes, very much so. But not real order, the order that comes from within. Under Stalin, beneath the thin veneer of "order", there was an absolute madness that caused extreme inefficiencies even when efficiency was earnestly meant. For example, many people were arrested and shot by mistake, even though the lists were supposed to be checked. (Note that it was not by accident that I chose efficiency in extermination as my example). Order is an internal thing, and neither good law nor bad law can bring order to Russia. Only law "of the people, by the people, and for the people" can do that. And for that, people must get organized, elect true representatives, pass laws that fit the situation, and live by these laws.

An industrial economy can function in a centralized, planned manner only for a short time, and with tremendous inefficiencies. An Information Age economy, which is decentralized and very complex, simply cannot be directed from a single center.

Russia did match the US in nuclear weaponry, and it did prove its ability to produce thousands of tanks, but the waste and inefficiency were so tremendous that they eventually left the country in ruins. A system based on an external semblance of order is most inefficient in utilizing positive human initiative, the creative potential of individuals, while negative human initiative, such as murders and denunciations, it utilizes all too well.

If there is no law, dictatorship is sure to follow. Dictatorship is good at imposing external order, and that only serves to hide, temporarily, the destruction of the very fabric of social life. Real order can come only from free cooperation of individuals with a win/win orientation.

Russian law is something external, a stick with which you are punished for no longer being a part of the system, for being unable to make the right phone call. That is why there can be no real order in Russia. In the West, citizens internalize the law, so that upholding the law and creating an orderly society comes to them naturally.

Russian state regards the citizen as a subject, as one who owes it certain services. At the same time the state does not see itself as owing anything to its citizens, and certainly does not see itself as a servant to their needs. That is why the Russian state is poor, oppressive, and weak. A state that regards each citizen as a repository of opportunities, some of which may need the state's help to be fully realized, is strong and rich, and certainly is not oppressive.

Russian laws are such that they push the citizen towards non-compliance. As a rule of thumb, Russians cross the street only on the red light, as to cross on the green light is either degrading or technically impossible. Russian laws forbid, so that nothing is possible when a policeman is looking at you, and everything is possible if the policeman is looking away or is below you in the social ranking. Western laws are universal, and everyone feels that they have to be upheld as they defend every person equally. Western laws tend to permit wherever possible and do not stifle individual initiative. As a consequence, if something is not permitted, the citizen knows that it is done for a reason and ultimately for his own benefit. In the West, breaking the law is seen by all citizens as a violation of their rights; in Russia, breaking the law is seen as a fight for citizens rights, and often it is actually so. Be it mob bosses or dissidents: few people have moral authority in Russia unless they did time in jail or are in danger of being jailed.

Why is there no real law in Russia? Because law combines rights and responsibilities. In Russia there are no rights (because gods do not need them) nor are there responsibilities (because gods do not accept them). In Russia, everyone wants to live like a god, and a god can be defined as an exception to the rule. A god is one whose power knows no limit, and as there are no laws in Russia, god is simply a Russian bureaucrat.

CHAPTER THIRTEEN. NECESSARY REFORMS
EIGHT BASIC ECONOMIC IDEAS

Economics is a very sophisticated science, and an oversimplified discussion may seem to be out of order. Still, I think it would be useful to list some of the reasons why some countries have annual per capita income of $30,000, while others have $300. What accounts for the hundredfold difference, soon to be a thousandfold difference? The question is all the more pertinent after the World Trade Center attacks, as it became clear that there is a real clash of values between the Third World and the First World. The destroyed buildings should have been called the "First World" Trade Center, as the Third World is too poor to trade, and yet the Third World was able to cause these buildings to collapse. We must repeat, yet again: envy is fully capable of destroying creativity, and on a planetary scale as well.

I would now like to list eight economic ideas that are so basic they are never discussed, as it is automatically assumed that everyone knows them and follows them. The mistakes that result from this assumption are truly horrendous. These eight basic economic ideas, if implemented together, would create a stable foundation for prosperity - in fact, they would ensure prosperity.

The First idea may be the most obvious, but it is surprisingly hard to implement.

Economics is production of goods and services. If so, the producer of goods and services should not be unduly impeded. Counterproductive and destructive work should be minimized.

The economic term "unemployment" is not really meaningful. You can employ everyone as a government bureaucrat, pickpocket, border guard, prison official, labor camp inmate, and religious cult leader – and create the poorest country on Earth. Those who want to produce should be allowed to work, but those whose "working day" causes destruction of resources should not be allowed to work.

Note that we have the luxury of making the assumption that humans lean towards goodness and creativity rather than towards evil and destruction, but we make this assumption only because this is not being written in 1940 or in Saddam's Iraq.

There are some producers who would produce regardless of the consequences, even if there were no profit. But the great majority of capitalists work for profit, and not just because of greed: profits are necessary for the enterprise to continue to work, to develop and grow.

The Second idea is: people must be paid for their labor. An economy is fueled by consumer spending, and true capitalists should realize that a higher wage level would work in their favor. Of course, wages should not be so high as to destroy competitiveness. But in Russia's perverted economy taxes are so high that nothing is left for investment and training anyway. Slave labor is not effective, and in Russia there are two large armies of slaves - soldiers and inmates - plus literally millions of workers who receive meager salaries and do not work productively. Creative and meaningful labor is one of the foundations of the vertical outlook. So if a person was raised with a horizontal outlook, as many Russians were, it is essential for them to work creatively to acquire the vertical outlook.

The Third idea is: the role of the State should be constitutionally limited. State enterprises cannot be effective economically, while a legal and legislative system without checks and balances will cause a real disaster.

The Fourth idea is: a country must have its own currency, and resources should be traded. In Russia, the population does not trust its own currency. No wonder: as we discussed, a currency is simply a unit of kindness and trust. Billions of dollars are hidden under mattresses, while penniless enterprises keep issuing debt obligations to one another. Resources must have their price, as a buyer always thinks he can use a resource more effectively than the seller. When huge resources such as land or real estate cannot be freely traded, the result is great inefficiency.

The Fifth idea is: the real currency in a country is not the ruble or the dollar, but kindness, honesty, and stability as well as their guarantor, law. Economics is based on promises, agreements, and exchange of goods and services, which is to say that ultimately economics is based on trust.

The Sixth idea is: it is wealthy individuals who push the economy forward, as they have money for investment and also because they buy the newest products when they are still very expensive to produce. When the laws of the state express envy towards the wealthy, most innovation stops, as the State Investment Board can only fund new tanks or eavesdropping devices, but never a new perfume.

The Seventh idea is: You are the master of your own fate. The Russians love to ask, "When will our lives be better?" But the answer is that your life will be better when you make it better, and nobody will make it better for you. Western advisors wanted to "bring democracy to Russia". But rights cannot be granted to people who are afraid to use them and/or have no use for them.

And finally here comes the **Eighth idea,** which in Russia is by far the most important: Every country is populated not just by its government, but also by its people. The Russian government employs millions upon millions of bureaucrats, and yet virtually nothing constructive gets done even though there is a lot of activity. But it is time for the people to also make their appearance: walk the streets, assert their rights, formulate and accomplish their personal goals. History should record that it took twenty-seven years to repair the flight of stairs leading to my apartment building in Moscow; apparently, for all this time, the more than one thousand people who live in my building had no need to reach their homes. Or were they there at all?

THE CURRENT SITUATION IN RUSSIA: TEN CRISES

The current situation in Russia can be described as comprising ten crises. They are:

A crisis of democracy. People do not wish to take part in governing the country, no matter how badly they live. People feel that they are unworthy of being consulted or taken into account. It does not occur to them that they can play a role in determining the course of the country, and it does not occur to them that the country is theirs. Just like an unwelcome guest, the people of Russia are grateful for being allowed to sleep on the couch. Worse yet, we must admit that this attitude is well founded: today, the Russian people are indeed unfit for self-government. People's morality has been thoroughly destroyed, they cannot tell good from bad, capitalism from socialism, democracy from dictatorship. Many loving parents dream of their sons growing up to be bandits and hope that their daughters will be attractive enough to work as prostitutes. Since physical survival in today's Russia requires a great deal of effort, it is no wonder that it has become the supreme value, and for some, the only value. Democratic political parties and movements do not exist, and thus there is no popular control over the political process. People expect everything from the state, but decline to contribute anything themselves.

An economic crisis. The Industrial Age economy is now outdated, and the recent lack of investment also means that the old equipment is now rusted and broken. The Information Age economy is developing in large cities, and it has a good foundation as the Soviet Union had excellent scientific and educational establishments. Yet the country lacks the advanced communication systems that are essential for the development of the Internet. Other problems include the weakness of the banking system, suicidal tax policies, the criminalization of the economy. There is no investment capital in the country, and only a very small domestic market as most of the people live hand to mouth.

A crisis of power. Since the Russian people resemble a baby that needs to be breastfed, the task that falls on the Russian bureaucracy can never be accomplished: since the state cannot wipe every nose, there are millions of those whose noses are dirty. The solution seems obvious: teach people to take care of their own noses. But the bureaucracy actively resists that: it would much rather see people fail than grant them independence from the yoke imposed on them by their own state.

A crisis of the legal system. Lack of the concept of law in the Western sense of the word; criminal "law" as an effective competitor with state law; a population that learned to hide from the law in order to survive; people convinced that they are entitled to nothing and have no rights; lack of historical experience of living in a law-abiding society – this is what Russia has today instead of a functioning legal system. Law should enjoy an elevated status and command respect, but the Russians respect only poetry, vodka, and raw force.

A geographical crisis. The population of Russia is sharply divided along religious and racial lines, and indeed is in the midst of a civil war. Japan, China, Turkey, Europe – all try to influence Russia and claim part of its territory or the right to influence those who live across the border from them. The revival of Islam and the creeping expansionism of the Chinese pose the most significant threats. The current borders of Russia may turn out to be untenable.

A resource crisis. There is an ecological crisis, and an inevitable future deficit of the raw materials on which the country's economy depends. Russia is tremendously wasteful and backward in its use of raw materials. Some Russian houses are centrally heated in such a fashion that the inhabitants are forced to open the windows to reduce the heat to tolerable levels. There is no effort to increase efficiency of resource use, and at the same time state utility subsidies are scheduled to be phased out, threatening a social explosion.

A health crisis. Growing (even though it hardly seems possible considering the sky-high current levels) alcohol consumption. A veritable explosion of drug abuse, with heroin being the drug of choice. Epidemics of tuberculosis, AIDS, hepatitis, venereal diseases, malnutrition, childhood diseases. Diseases that are traceable to extreme environmental hazards in some areas: radiation, chemical contamination, industrial pollution, poor water quality. The total collapse of the health care system. The lack of a real estate market, meaning that people cannot move away from contaminated areas. A demographic crisis. As a result, the population of Russia is decreasing dramatically.

A crisis of infrastructure. The last period of massive investment ended twenty years ago. Since then, there has been no new investment to speak of. Apartment blocks that have a projected lifespan of forty years are thirty five years old today, and they have never been properly maintained. Communications, factories, roads, and scientific establishments are all state of the art for the year 1975, but in the year 2003 they look pitiful.

A crisis of criminality. Massive unemployment, widespread poverty, lack of ideals, destruction of moral institutions such as the church, rapid expansion of drug culture, a well-developed criminal underworld that has acquired its own "rich and proud" cultural tradition, a totally corrupt and dispirited law enforcement, a medieval criminal justice system, a horrific prison system – this is why Yeltsin called Russia "a criminal superpower".

A crisis of professionalism. Millions of people pretend to be physicians, businessmen, engineers, democratic politicians, honest journalists. And these people do not just occupy their positions: they make sure that professionally qualified people do not and never will occupy these positions. Russia badly needs tests of professional competence administered to all its professionals. Such a law would never pass. Yet suppose the measure passed. Then it is likely that the best Russian professionals (and there are some excellent professionals in Russia, by any standard) might be exactly the ones that would not pass the test. To quote from Russian literature, "it all depends on who the judges are". We can make the following raw estimate: Russia has about ten million people who are functional from the point of view of the Information Age. The remaining one hundred and forty million cannot significantly contribute to an Information Age economy as they can barely provide for themselves.

The Russian state and the Russian people today are suffering from a severe and multifaceted systemic crisis. Yet the Russian people have been so weakened by decades of bloodletting, psychological remodeling, and Stalinist "genetic selection" that they cannot deal with this crisis by themselves. An earthquake or even a war can inflict horrendous destruction on people and on the social system. But the people who then start clearing up the rubble still speak the same language, and know the meaning of "good" and "bad". In Russia, from under the rubble of the communist state came people who are not just deeply shaken, but severely damaged, with a semi-destroyed language and a torn and uncertain morality.

And yet the country does have more than enough resources to turn itself into a prosperous Information Age society. The key to success is vertical orientation: creativity as opposed to envy.

TERMS THAT SHOULD BE REDEFINED

"What kind of bicycle do you have?" "I have a red one." For someone who knows what a bicycle is, this answer is adequate. But for someone who has never seen a bicycle, it is not. A bicycle is not a red thing: it has to have two wheels, pedals, and a seat. When we ask a naked tropical forest dweller to embrace "democracy", there is a considerable danger that he cannot quite point his arrow at what we really mean, and will miss the target. Again, let us not assume that the terms that depict the social technology that took the West its entire history to develop are self-evident and easy to define.

Bribery – use of power for personal gain in any form. A bureaucrat is there to implement a law that is fair and equitable to all. If the law is different, see corruption. When a bureaucrat bends the law for personal gain, he is taking a bribe. And this personal gain may be emotional, such as discriminating against those he happens to dislike, as well as monetary or social. When a bureaucrat allows his decision to be influenced by career considerations instead of giving the best possible performance, he clearly is accepting a non-monetary bribe. There are bureaucratic structures where no one is taking money, and yet they are utterly dysfunctional because each is putting as much as he can into his "political correctness and career advancement wallet".

Capitalist - one who uses the means of production to create goods and services in a market environment. Thus, a capitalist is not one who owns a factory, but one who both owns a factory and aims to put it to long-term productive use operating in a competitive market environment. In Russia, the factories ended up in the hands of former (or current!) Communist Party members. But if you obtained title to a factory through your bureaucratic connections and then sell it piecemeal to buy diamonds and limos for yourself, you are not a capitalist.

Corruption – destruction of the moral principles of human coexistence by state power. When the state's power is used by the few to control the many, and especially to control their ability to produce, to achieve their developmental goals, and to advance in society – this is corruption. Corruption is when you need to ask permission and/or pay a bribe to breathe air. In such circumstances, people do whatever it takes to get an exception for themselves, and that certainly includes giving bribes. But any bureaucrat who works for a patently unfair system of government should be seen as corrupt whether or not he is taking bribes, because all of them are taking away people's freedom and are in some way benefiting from this. In America, an official may take a bribe to rig a bid or to look the other way on a drug deal; this is bribery or criminal conspiracy, but not corruption because corruption has to do with the unfairness of the entire system.

Efficiency - when a bureaucracy gets smaller.

Elections – making a responsible and informed decision about the future course of the country. Since this decision now involves complicated economic and political issues, and since increasingly sophisticated techniques are being used to distort the issues and mislead the voter, it is doubtful that a voter should be defined as “each and every citizen who has reached 18 years of age”. Rather, there should be a maturity test of some sort, especially in a severely traumatized society. The Information Age is about decision making, and these decisions have wide-ranging consequences. From that comes the principle, “every decision must be made by those qualified to make it, and not by those who appear to be qualified according to some irrelevant criteria”.

Envy - a decision not to see one's situation in absolute terms ("I have $5"), but to see it in relation to someone else ("I have more (fewer) dollars than Joe") Once this method of viewing things is adopted, one becomes concerned with the amount of money (or whatever else) that Joe has, while one’s own situation becomes irrelevant. Once that happens, the effort to decrease the amount of whatever it is that Joe has becomes a way to improve one’s own situation, even if this effort is costly. Thus, envy is the desire to pay or to expend effort (to accept sacrifices) in order to worsen someone else’s situation. Thus, one’s absolute situation worsens, but the absolute situation of the other person worsens even more, *so the self-inflicted worsening of one’s own situation is seen as personal advancement.*

Democracy is not just a society that holds fair elections but a society where the majority of people are prepared to live according to the win/win principle. Only this type of society can be based on laws that are equitable for all. Only then will the strong be unable to abuse the laws to exploit the weak, and only then will the weak be willing to uphold the laws as their own. The win/win principle means that people live according to the vertical method, developing their own resources rather than claiming the resources of others. Since most of the people are independent, and do not ask the state to redistribute resources, the people become stronger than the state. That puts the law above the state, not above the poor. Democracy thus becomes a hierarchy where the law comes first, the people follow, and the state bureaucracy comes last.

Law. The law must be the same for all, because otherwise a bad law will not be changed, but will be used to exploit and to gain unfair advantage. The law must allow everything that does not encroach on the rights of others. In Russia, by contrast, the law is made to forbid, and thus it becomes an instrument of control and an instrument of state power. But the state should be given powers only to serve the people, never to subjugate them. We should not define law as "something that someone put on paper for others to unquestionably obey".

Order – a certain apparent predictability of events, which creates the illusion that the situation is under control. Order seeks to preserve the status quo, to capture stability by nailing it down. While harmony can last a long time, order has never been kept for more than an hour. You cannot create order without exterminating the entire population of Russia, so it is much better to go for harmony by creating laws that are fair and equitable to all, are based on creativity, and are implemented fairly, so that people accept and support them.

Owner – a vertically oriented person who has, in his secure and lawful possession, certain means of production that are currently in use. Means of production can fall in the hands of a horizontally-oriented person, such as a thief or a bureaucrat, but that does not make him an owner: an envious person cannot own, but can only formulate and process claims. Also, the use of means of production can be impeded artificially. This action turns an owner into a title-holder or a claim-holder. This is an important distinction for Russia: you seem to "own" but you cannot use.

Privatization –creation of a legal and psychological environment conducive to independent productive activity. This environment includes laws that defend producers from the claims of the envious, turn the means of production over to producers, and create a win/win environment. If there is the right and the opportunity to create, material production will follow. In Russia means of production that belonged to the state were arbitrarily and unfairly distributed to claimants connected to various power structures. Means of production (that which belongs to the vertical realm) ended up under control of the horizontal realm, in the hands of thieves and bureaucrats who are unable to think in terms of production. But the existing means of production are of secondary importance: the greatest failure was that there were no laws that protected producers. New means of production were not created; even more importantly, there was no new impulse to produce, no release of creative energies. Privatization is not distribution of property but implementation of laws that defend the producer and establish an environment conducive to private economic initiative.

Poverty. Inefficient use of resources. If a person is uneducated, his brain is not being efficiently used; if someone spends five hours to gather firewood to cook dinner, it is no wonder there is no meat in the pot. People who use resources inefficiently (which is often not their fault) appear to us as "poor", i.e. lacking resources. Rich countries, on the other hand, are rich because the resources they have are being used efficiently, be it in terms of education, labor productivity, mechanization, cooperation, or lack of civil war. Now we can really "combat poverty", by teaching the "poor" countries to use the resources available to them efficiently: not to work at cross-purposes destroying what has been built, not to be envious, to invest in health care and education, to use their natural wealth efficiently. There are no poor countries, but there are many countries that do all they can to make themselves poor, and Russia is one of them.

Taxes – the share of their income that people want to pay for public goods: not whatever the state can grab from people, and certainly not the money that is used to enslave and control people solely to perpetuate the power of bureaucrats. It is amazing to see international financial organizations being concerned about tax collection in a particular state, but never checking whether the public goods that are being delivered are worth anywhere near the amount extracted as taxes. In Russia, the existence of the state worsens the situation of the people rather than improving it. For example, it is quite likely that abolition of all law enforcement agencies in Russia, both the police and the courts, would actually improve the safety and security of citizens. The ultimate travesty is when taxation is used as an instrument of terror, when many businesses simply never open for fear of excessive taxation.

Redistribution. If you use the inanimate, non-time-sensitive term "haves and have-nots" and try to redistribute material wealth between those who, in this particular second, either have, or have not, you will fail. But if you use the time-sensitive terms "opportunity" or "ability", this is another matter. People do need to have equal access to opportunities and their ability to do things should be developed and protected. If opportunity is arbitrarily restricted, this is a roadblock that must be removed.

TWO METHODS OF TAXATION

As there are two outlooks, there are two corresponding methods of taxation, vertical and horizontal. Let us describe them using the following table.

TABLE. 5 THE VERTICAL AND HORIZONTAL METHODS OF TAXATION

VERTICAL	HORIZONTAL
The concept of time and the win/win principle are employed. The state cooperates with enterprises to maximize the long-term profit of the enterprise and long-term tax revenue.	There is no concept of time, no concern for maximization of long-term profit. Envy lurks under the relationship between state and business and the lose/lose principle is dominant. The state cannot decide what it wants more from enterprises: to exploit them for financial gain or to control and stifle them for political gain.
Property is private and protected by law.	Property is conditionally private and temporarily protected by an informal personal relationship to political power.

Tax credits for a new enterprise, or no taxation of an enterprise experiencing financial difficulty. The state protects enterprises from extortion.	The motto of the taxmen is the same as that of extortionists or racketeers: "Grab as much as you can until he runs away". First, a significant part of tax revenues does not reach the state budget. And then there is yet another theft, as the percentage of "taxes" of all kinds that returns to the people in the form of social services is negligible.
The tax system supports the underlying principle that "As a citizen, it is good for me to give a small part of my income so that the state can create necessary public goods." Taxes are good for business and the state.	The tax system supports the underlying principle that "As the state, I will grab all that I can, right to the point where businesses are taxed to death. But not to worry, somehow I'll always find a way to tax them further." By opting for maximum taxation, the state ultimately receives greatly reduced tax revenues. Taxes are bad for business and the state. The state seems to be testing the people: "Can you still live and work here, can you survive?"

Entrepreneurs have political power and actively participate in the administration of their respective industries.	Entrepreneurs have very little political power. Bureaucrats pride themselves on never having produced anything; yet they control everything and attempt to claim all the credit
Regulatory agencies and state agencies work in concert and in consultation with the businesses they regulate to achieve the goals of the state with maximum efficiency and lowest cost.	Regulatory agencies and state agencies do not take into account the interests of business at all, especially not the long-term interests of business. These agencies exist solely to control business and extract maximum tax revenue in the short term. Regulatory agencies and state agencies do not take into account the interests of the general population, but exist almost solely for their own sake, to stuff their own pockets.

Entrepreneurs are rewarded for investment and growth, supported in times of trouble, but otherwise left alone.	Entrepreneurs are tolerated only as a source of bribes or tax revenue, and the extortionists consider themselves morally superior to the entrepreneurs, as they have not dirtied their hands by producing goods and offering services. The entrepreneur's motives are always suspect, whether he invests, creates more jobs, or gives money to charity. When the entrepreneur spends some of his earnings on himself, it is a capital sin.
Being an entrepreneur is respectable and honorable, entrepreneurs assume visible roles as civic leaders.	Bureaucrats meet with entrepreneurs as little as possible, and mostly in secret. When an entrepreneur is killed, it is reported in a way that never makes clear whether the late businessman was a criminal or not. Bureaucrats "fight business on behalf of the people", and claim that it is the bureaucrats who create jobs and pay salaries. Economic success is credited to the bureaucrats, and not to businessmen.

Businessmen make plans, invest, expand their production lines, innovate, create new jobs.	If you cannot spend the money, the state will take it away. Investing in new technology is foolhardy and creating new jobs is very risky. Businessmen go to casinos, buy expensive properties, move money offshore. They wish they could do business elsewhere, but having succeeded in a dishonest and extra-legal environment, they cannot face fair competition and are mentally incapable of abiding by Western laws.
The state mimics the role of the entrepreneur in production and delivery of public and social goods. In return for taxes it builds roads, regulates business for maximum efficiency and safety, administers the state treasury, safeguards pensions, etc.	The state grabs tax revenue or takes bribes and gives nothing back. The state's "product", be it a road or a banking system, carries no guarantees whatsoever, and always breaks down in the shortest conceivable time.
The laws of the state are based on the principle of win/win and the productive morality created by business.	Laws are there only to give justification to the strong and the envious. People are alienated from the state. To search for productivity and social justice is suicidal; moreover, it is seen as morally questionable.

The Russian state is no longer completely in the right-hand column, but it is much farther from the left column than it is from the right. In Russia, as in no other country, it is important to write a low flat tax right into the Constitution: the Russian state must be cured from envy and pulled over into the productive octant, where it would be run like a business.

TAX REFORM

Economic reform could have only two clauses:

Stop rewarding destruction of resources

Create competitive businesses

A private enterprise spends certain resources to create a product. The product is then sold. The price received for the product should be more than the combined cost of all the inputs. If this is so, the enterprise works well. If the combined costs of inputs, labor, subsidies, and environmental damage is greater than the price received for the product, then the enterprise destroys resources. Russia has mines that produce coal that is pricier than gold, it has pulp and paper mills that destroy unique lakes and rivers, and Russia builds housing that collapses even before it is completed. A state populated by locusts simply cannot be green. Entrepreneurs should face business challenges, not bureaucratic regulations designed by extortionists. Directors must organize production, not desperately try to circumvent the laws.

The Russian tax system is such that the real value of all the inputs and all the outputs is arbitrarily distorted, and a monstrous destruction of resources is taking place while remaining hidden from sight. For example, I am convinced that Russian cars today are the most expensive cars in history. They sell for $2,000, are produced at a real cost of probably $20,000, and then require thousands of hours of repair, offer a very unpleasant ride, and are utterly unsafe. Russian men should find something better to do than to constantly repair their cars and die in crashes.

EDUCATION REFORMS

Young Russians today are in a truly unique situation: they cannot benefit from parental advice. If your father was a factory worker, you know there are no factories open. If you are an independent farmer, your father certainly was not. If you are a businessman, your father simply does not understand you and your grandfather is ashamed of you. That is why it is so important for Russia to educate its young generation; it is Russia's only hope, and yet, Russia is putting its young people through an antiquated and rotten educational system.

The Soviet school was a model of Stalinist society. On top, there was an all-knowing teacher, who spoke while everyone else had to remain silent. Everything that a pupil was allowed to say had but one justification: to obtain a good grade. That must be changed: teachers and students should be conducting a structured dialogue. There is so much information that nobody can be all knowing, and today the avenues of obtaining information are many. Moreover, today's Russian students are likely to be more knowledgeable than their teachers because the young are the ones who are connected to the Internet.

Students should be coming to school not so much to learn facts, but to learn about themselves, to develop the ability to use information for personal and professional growth, and to learn the information safety rules (how to protect yourself from the faulty and destructive information that disrupts scientific inquiry or, worse yet, enslaves your mind).

Independence, the ability to doubt and to learn, initiative, the ability to use information correctly and safely, and, above all, concentration on self-development, personal creativity and growth – this is what students should be learning at school. And of course, everyone should be fluent in English.

Russian schools still have no electives and teach the same basic disciplines that were taught in the 19th century. Even more worrisome is the total lack of parental involvement in school affairs and the lack of a volunteer spirit. No Russian parent would think about volunteering to coach a school sports team.

The situation at the university level is even worse. University students cannot change their major during the course of study, so a literature major cannot take a biology course. As high school students can apply to only one place during a particular year, most of the majors are chosen by their parents (i.e., by those who are often lost in the new economic conditions), and people often simply end up in the department where their parents know somebody who can rig the test results.

Once enrolled in a university, students face an atmosphere of total corruption. In many colleges, students cannot obtain good grades unless the professor receives a bribe or a sexual favor. Virtually all students cheat on their exams and plagiarize on their written assignments. Many students have to work to pay their school expenses, and as there is virtually no work for unskilled young people, prostitution and crime are rampant among students. For example, in the Siberian city of Irkutsk there are several firms that advertise "helping to put attractive young women through college": working as a call girl for three nights a week is all it takes.

This is intolerable for two reasons:

First, without moral renewal there is no hope for Russia, but here we see the opposite trend: total moral degradation. Russia needs to have upstanding citizens more than any other country, because the Russian legal system cannot serve as a moral guide, and yet its universities teach students to lie, cheat, and cover their incompetence, their lack of mastery over their own lives.

Secondly, Russia is getting millions of degreed professionals who have not mastered their chosen professions. There are millions of incompetent physicians, architects, and engineers. Yet there are no personal-liability laws, no professional codes of conduct, and no professional associations.

THE NEED TO CHANGE THE LAW

The fundamental problem is that Russia has horizontal laws and tends to choose horizontal "solutions". If there is a resource, it does not go to the one who can use it to create still more resources, but to the one who steals or destroys it.

Russia cannot live under its present laws, but it cannot live under the American or the French legal system either. The solution may be to have just ten fundamental laws that codify a vertically-oriented society in one page of simple text. This text would be understandable to people, and for the first time it would be clear to them what is bad and what is good. If there were just ten fundamental laws, everyone would be able to interpret and categorize every particular situation. Today, the Russian legal system is not of one mind on any single question, be it the sanctity of human life, inviolability of private property, protection of creativity, outlawing of envy. Task number one is to stop the civil war between envy and creativity, and that can be done only with the simplest and clearest set of "black and white" laws.

In physics, a law is something that always happens, without fail, no matter how many times you try. Two plus two is always four, a billion times out of a billion tries. Legal formulations are called laws when they are meant to apply to everybody, universally, every time. If we applied current Russian law universally almost all Russian businessmen would be arrested. But they could not be charged, as all the Russian prosecutors deserve to be arrested even more. Fortunately, there would be nobody to arrest the Russian businessmen, as many law enforcement officers are the thugs that should be arrested first. And such a law will never be passed, as many politicians deserve to be arrested as well. As Russia cannot arrest itself (and not just because there would be nobody to guard the arrested guards), it has to pick and choose whom to prosecute, making the entire process arbitrary and based on exception, whim, phone call, or what have you. And that means that by the definition of the word "law", Russia has none. And that happens to mean that, by definition, no one in Russia is guilty of anything. There are some who are in jail, of course, but they are no guiltier than the ones who put them there. Since no one in Russia can be prosecuted fairly (just look at the judges or the police), society lives arbitrarily, according to chance. And this is grossly, nightmarishly inefficient.

How do we solve this problem? My proposal is: starting today and forever and ever, "Thou shalt not kill – as of today" and "Thou shalt not steal – as of today". If we have that today, tomorrow we, for the first time, will have two kinds of people in Russia: those who killed and stole today or later, and those who did not. And then the second kind of people can legitimately and lawfully put the first kind in jail.

A deaf person learns to speak sound by sound, and learns to understand sign by sign. Being aware of that means showing respect for the deaf person. Assuming that a deaf person can hear human speech shows arrogance, ignorance, and stupidity and not one iota of respect for the deaf person. Those who discuss Russian law as if it were Western law written in the Russian language do not understand, or respect, Russia.

ON PROFESSIONAL CODES OF CONDUCT

Representatives of all professions should be united in professional associations with codes of conduct. These associations should be open to all who can pass their qualification procedures, but they should not have a monopoly on professional employment as restriction of entry and exit also engender abuses. These professional societies must not be governed by the state or be under the certification or licensing of a new or old bureaucracy. Russians would then be able to choose to be treated by a physician who is a member of a physicians' association. And that means a certain professional standard as well as certain guarantees in terms of insurance. Today a Russian physician bears no professional responsibility whatsoever, and can literally kill a patient without any adverse consequences for himself. In fact, for a mere $500 you can buy a ready-made doctor's diploma.

The point here is not just a certain standard of service, but a standard of citizenship, something that can slowly point Russian society the right way. If you are so bold as to say that an alcoholic cannot practice medicine it is not just the standard of medical service that you are talking about, but the standards of society as a whole. Russia just had a president who was an admitted alcoholic, one who missed official functions or attended them while drunk. Indeed, when Yeltsin once traveled on a pleasure ship, he ordered his Press Secretary thrown overboard, and the order was carried out. Later, this Press Secretary was made Russia's Ambassador to the Holy See, probably because he had been christened in such a dramatic fashion.

There is a war between the lose/lose outlook and the win/win outlook, and to win this war the win/win outlook must proclaim that it does everything possible to encourage achievement, that it recognizes and rewards achievement, distinguishing it very sharply from failure to achieve. Every failure to achieve must be recognized, analyzed, and corrected. September 11 illustrated the main point of the book very well: we stand for skyscrapers, for vertical growth; our adversaries stand for leveling them, for denying individual achievement.

In the Industrial Age there was a need for human labor and the only way to earn a living was through work. But in the Information Age, not every person's labor is valuable, as in the age of robots only information producers can add significant value. And that means that people should be provided for not in exchange for their labor, but in exchange for their agreement to forsake envy as a guiding force of their behavior.

Russia is the richest country in the world in terms of natural resources and a country that had a successful space program. Yet we should describe Russia as resource-poor and extremely technologically backward. We say so because we are referring to the resources that matter in the Information Age, not those that mattered in the Industrial Age. Russia is resource-poor because millions of its best people were exterminated and the rest were psychologically altered, so that today Russia lacks a well-educated, active, democratic, and envy-free population. Instead, Russia is saddled with an envy-ridden population that makes independent initiative almost impossible. This population cannot govern itself and is either aggressive or self-destructive. Russia is extremely technologically backward in terms of social technologies: technologies that protect enterprising individuals from the envy of others, technologies that allow the entire society to be managed effectively, to develop and grow without becoming aggressive and expansionist.

LIST OF NECESSARY REFORMS

People who have a vertical outlook should organize themselves in a political movement and take power in Russia. At present, Russia does not have functional democratic parties. Please excuse the pun, but people who attend parties where they talk about democracy do not amount to a democratic party.

Comprehensive legal reform and simplification of laws.

The entire system of government should be reformed on the basis of vertical principles, so that the government becomes envy-free, protects and recognizes achievement, and rewards envy-free behavior by its citizens while effectively discouraging all manifestations of envy.

A very significant reduction in the number of bureaucrats, as a consequence of the state becoming envy-free. But the state must not become permissive or lax, as the population of Russia requires very strict supervision.

Codes of professional behavior for public servants and for major professions. Professional associations, personal licenses, periodic professional examinations and evaluations by peers and consumers, not by government.

Comprehensive educational reform. The goal of education must be to create independent, envy-free people, able to correctly retrieve, interpret, and use information. Psychological education and civic education should be the major subjects as Russia is very backward in these areas. The Russian and English languages, as well as computer literacy, should come next. All other subjects could be optional as a psychologically healthy person is naturally curious and eager to learn.

Comprehensive privatization. With the exception of weapons, defense installations, and historical monuments, the state should not own any property.

Comprehensive public health and medical reform are urgently necessary, as Russia is in a midst of an enormous health crisis. It should be noted that this crisis is also largely a consequence of the envy that makes life in Russia is harsh and psychologically very distressing.

Abolition of everything that is "free", such as education and medical care. Introduction of vouchers and insurance for the poor. A "free" service, of course, is a dream of the envious; creators are ready to pay for every service what it really is worth.

LABOR PRODUCTIVITY

Economic success is said to depend on productivity of labor. In some countries, labor productivity is high, in others it is low. But why is this so, and what do these figures reveal? In the same vein, low unemployment is seen as a sign of a healthy economy. But this indicator also can be very misleading, if the underlying assumption that all human labor is used to create and none is used to destroy proves incorrect. Indeed, the Soviet Union had full employment and a very unproductive economy at the same time.

Here is an example. Children play in two sandboxes. In one sandbox, we see two pies, and in the other – only one. We conclude that the productivity of labor in the first sandbox is twice as great as in the second sandbox. But is this really so? In the first sandbox, Lisa made a pie and Hanna made a pie, so there are two pies altogether. In the second sandbox, Vic made ten pies, but Mike destroyed nine of them, and so only one pie remains. It takes the same amount of labor to make a pie as to destroy one, and that means that the boys could have made nineteen pies, nineteen times as many pies as we see. To make this example more lifelike, we should say that Vic could have made twice as many pies but didn't bother, as he knew that Mike was going to destroy them anyway. What does that tell us? It tells us that Vic's real productive capacity is twenty pies, while Mike's real destructive capacity is nineteen pies. The boys' real productivity is thus thirty nine pies, thirty nine times more than we originally thought.

A comparison between the American and the Russian GNP per capita would show that in Russia labor productivity is thirty times less than in the US. But this does not mean that the average Russian works for ten minutes a day, or that it takes five Russian men to lift a sack of potatoes weighting ten pounds. All it means is that one group of Russians succeeds in destroying ninety percent of whatever the other group of Russians succeeded in creating during the day. The Soviet Union collapsed because Russian families could not afford to own their own car, and there were thirty times as many cars in the US as in Russia. But there were ten times as many tanks in Russia as in the US: Russia's labor productivity was in fact quite comparable to that of the US.

The way to develop the economy is not to "employ" people, but to make sure that those who spend their working days trying to impede others either get employed productively or become unemployed. A country should have fewer controllers and claimants and more producers, and then it will succeed.

We have clearly shown that envy has limitless capacity for destruction of resources. If the United States were to transfer one half of its GNP to Russia, year after year for a hundred years, Russia would still be at least as poor as it is now: this enormous aid package is certain to have an overall negative effect. As for the United States, if it were compelled to give away half of its GNP for a hundred years, its economy would readjust in such a way that this loss would have almost no effect on the well-being and wealth of its population. In Russia, we have an unlimited capacity to destroy; in the US we have unlimited capacity to create. Hitler killed six million Jews, but could have killed twelve million of them just as easily; Picasso could have created even more paintings.

There are two ways of increasing GNP in a particular country. You can improve technology, education, and labor productivity. But if the envious keep up with you, you will fail. We can call this the Shah of Iran Rule. On the other hand, if we restrict envy and liberate creativity, the most barren land quickly turns into a paradise. This could be called the Taiwan Rule.

ON THE STATE

To create a successful economy, we must start by redefining the role of the state. The state is an organization that lets individual citizens achieve their personal goals, such as security, use of public goods, protection of the environment, international cooperation. This means that a particular nation may decide to be governed by a private firm, either domestic or foreign, and it simply would not need a national government. It is perfectly possible to have all the government offices of a particular state be located 1,000 miles away, and it is perfectly possible for one private firm to govern several states, or for one person to serve simultaneously as president or prime minister of several countries. We could also appoint a computer to run the state, and to run it in an authoritarian fashion, and it is certain that several states would hugely benefit from such an arrangement, as they are currently being run by self-destructive and rather irrational thugs.

Today a war is raging between win/win with lose/lose, and it is far from clear who is winning and who will prevail at the end. This war is on in every state and within each person. To win, we need to discover and restructure every manifestation of lose/lose.

The Russian economy has millions of bureaucrats, racketeers, assassins for hire, and security personnel. Unemployment in this sector is far too low, while productivity and incomes are far too high. At the same time, creators are risking their lives to pursue their chosen professions, and wasting their lives in order to obtain permission to create. Russia destroys resources at such a rapid clip that Russians would have probably been wealthier had all of them been legally forbidden to work.

A state that forbids creativity is very oppressive but at the same time very fragile, while a permissive state appears weak but is fundamentally sound. By impeding the creative impulses of its people, the Russian state not only impoverishes its citizens: it creates an area of instability, serves as a breeding ground for potential wars.

Both the Russian people and the Russian state must change. The people must stop formulating claims and excuses and get on with creative work. The state should abandon its attempts to control its citizens, which it does out of weakness, fear, and failure to perform its true functions. Instead, the state should be serving the people, and draw its strength from cooperation with the people. Today both the Russian people and the Russian state have an inferiority complex, both of them are ashamed of their inability to function as they should, their relationship is destructive, and there is a lot of cruelty and pain.

The Russian people must pass through the following stages:

Self-realization. You succeed as a creator and do not need to resort to destruction in order to assert yourself.

Independence. You have a sufficient economic base, skills, legal protection, and earning power to be a viable independent player on the economic field.

Initiative. You are psychologically ready to act and have the opportunity to act. You do not feel afraid or overly dependent; instead you see yourself as a citizen, with all the rights and responsibilities that this honorable title entails and carries.

Volunteer spirit. Society gives each citizen an opportunity to realize himself, and in return he assumes personal responsibility not only for himself but for the entire society.

Spirit of giving. A creative person creates for himself, but in fact it is for everybody's benefit. In other words, a creative person turns out to be selflessly giving to society, and that makes him happy, because in fact he is doing it for himself. In the same way, it appears that an envious person wants justice for himself, wants to have as much as his neighbors, but in fact his actions lead to uncontrollable and limitless destruction that goes far beyond what he could possibly have wanted for himself. A creator acts as if his goal were total harmony, whereas an envious person acts as if his goal were total destruction.

Self-Government. Individuals become such independent and self-sufficient parts of society that they take upon themselves certain social functions previously carried out by the state or not carried out at all. The state shrinks while the social services and the social safety net expand.

Political participation. To successfully carry out the functions of self-government, citizens must unite and act. Parties and movements should appear. Telephonocracy must end, and there should be open and fair government.

People power. The state and the people become one. The state no longer governs the people, but simply guarantees the laws and provides public goods.

ON PUTTING THE ECONOMY ON A PRODUCTIVE FOUNDATION

When we observe different countries, we see that in some countries people live well, while in others they live badly. And so we deliver grain and money to these countries, and yet they stay as poor as before. Here is the rule: in some countries people desire to live well, and in others they desire to live badly. They suffer from living badly, but they desire to live badly nonetheless. There are many people, such as smokers, who suffer from the negative effects of their behavior, and yet do not change. There is a two step solution: first, people need to be made aware of what kinds of behavior bring about negative effects (in our case, it is envy that breeds poverty), and then we need to rebuild their lives so that undesirable behavior no longer appears to be a "solution" and instead is seen as the cause of a multitude of problems that it is.

There is such a thing as an Index of Economic Freedom, and there is evidence that the higher this Index, the better the economic situation in a particular country. And this is indeed so. The trick is how to increase the Index of Economic Freedom. And here comes the main index, which I would call the Index of Psychological Readiness for an increase in the Index of Economic Freedom. As soon as Muscovites move into a new apartment building they cover the walls with graffiti and break all the lights. Some people want to live badly, and they are prepared to go to any length to achieve their goal. There are people who strongly prefer an ugly entrance because ugliness corresponds to how they feel inside and how they want others to feel.

ON THE FUNDAMENTAL REASONS FOR ECONOMIC BACKWARDNESS

We need to address the fundamental reasons, and not just the symptoms, of Russia's economic, political, and social decline. Here is the list of those fundamental reasons:

Envy. The judicial system should defend those who create against those who formulate claims against the possessions of others. There should be more workers than tax inspectors and others whose workday is dedicated to destruction of resources.

Phoniness. The Russians profess to love their native land, yet it is owned by no one and not well cared for at all. If there are phony, make-believe property rights, then the state, the morals, and the laws are also phony. But in Russia, make-believe is not limited to that: physicians have phony diplomas, traffic policemen do not give a damn about traffic safety, and public servants treat the public as their slaves. As a result, for the last 100 years the main topic of discussion in Russia has been that of Russia's future. There were times when it seemed that Russia had no future, and then there were times when it seemed that Russia's future would be glorious beyond compare. For the last 100 years Russia has not had a present the Russians were strong enough to face: they escaped into the future or into the past, escaped into the world of their dreams so as not to look at the life that was theirs at the present moment. And it is your actual present life that determines your future.

Lack of citizenry. A citizen is a person who enjoys protection of laws and in return assumes the full burden of civic responsibilities. As no one in Russia enjoys legal protection, Russia by definition has no citizens and is populated by inhabitants, by those who have no say in governing or administering it. In Russia this is called "birds' rights": indeed, the expression is apt as most birds are migratory, while chickens live in metal cages or try to pick something edible out of cow manure. A state that is not supported by its citizenry is cruel, arbitrary, aggressive, envy-ridden, insecure, and impoverished.

Limitlessness. Consider land separated into several plots belonging to different farmers. What is important here? Of course, the land itself, as this is what the harvest grows on. But there is another hugely important element, and this is the line separating the plots, the border between them. This line teaches us to cultivate our own gardens and not to interfere with the business of others. Borders prove to us that people are different and achieve different levels of success, usually, but not always, depending on the amount and quality of labor that they put in. If without land there would have been no harvest, without borders the harvest would have been impossible to use, as it would have had no owner. The land stands for labor, while the border stands for law and for morality. These borders are sacred because they separate whatever is mine from that which is not mine. In Russia, for geographical and historical reasons, there have traditionally been very few of those lines, and that has proved disastrous. The mission of the state is to make sure that no person crosses the dividing line between the various domains; in fact, the role of the state begins and ends with manning the borders. But in Russia there are no borders; the state lacks its proper place and, fighting for ground to stand on, steps on ground that it should not be stepping on. Consider a Russian bureaucrat: he demands a bribe for circumventing the law and he demands a bribe for implementing the law. You are the one who tells him what the rule should be, you employ him privately, make him your own "state" by paying him a bribe, and he will enforce your law. Why were you able to "privatize" this bureaucrat and the law he represents, why is he now your personal bureaucrat pushing your personal law? Because he did not have ground to stand on, there was no dividing line where he should have stood. As your guest, standing on your plot, he does your bidding.

A non-monetary economy. Money is what we give to strangers in exchange for their kindness to us, a good or a service. Thus, money is a unit of kindness accepted on the basis of the trust enjoyed by the issuer. Since kindness is a consequence of moral behavior, money is also a unit of morality. The less money there is in society, the more it is envy-based, immoral, primitive, or angry. Money by itself cannot make a society moral, because sometimes money is not earned (it could come from natural resources, for example, or be inherited), but wealth is usually a consequence of moral behavior. Where does money come from? It comes from a correct evaluation of the situation, from provision of necessary services, from productive labor, from cooperation between various creative people. The problem of Russia is that its economy is not based on money, as its currency is closeness to power; the richest Russians are far from being kind and none of them is a producer (they either sell their influence or exploit the natural resources of which they were appointed as owners).

Separation. A society can live on the basis of creativity, but a viable, if poor and aggressive, society can also be built on the basis of envy. This irreconcilable conflict is tearing Russia apart. Why have it continue? Russia is big enough, and could be separated into two states, Stalinia and Friedmania. Let one state have the envy-based laws and let all those who want to live under such laws move there. But the other part of Russia would have a genuinely free economy. Of course, the free part would pay the envy-based part tribute lest the envious die from hunger or resort to cannibalism or external aggression. No tribute is large enough for a genuinely free economy, and prosperity will come anyway. In this free part of Russia, the Russian nation, culture, and language (all of which are currently rapidly dying) will be preserved and developed. Again, an envious person is dangerous only if he is able to interfere with creative ones, and the creative ones should be willing to feed the envious ones as long as they agree to do nothing. Many Russians find they cannot live in Russia and seek to emigrate. This worries the Western European countries. But most of the Russians who want to emigrate do not want to leave behind the Russian language and culture: it is the Russian state and Russian law they are running away from. Many of these potential emigrants would gladly move to Free Russia, if such a territory existed. Russia has a piece of territory that does not border on Russia proper: the former East Prussia, including the city of Koenigsberg. The introduction of a different set of laws on this impoverished and small piece of land could show Russia the way. Russia is too big and too diverse to be boldly reformed in a relatively short period of time. East Prussia is small and could be reformed quickly.

Psychological dependence on the bad. A typical Russian expects bad things to happen to him. If you offer him $500, he will refuse as he will think that you surely want to steal his apartment. But this does not mean that he is cautious or suspicious: if you offer to sell him an apartment for $5, he will gladly give you five dollars yet, would not be surprised when he gets nothing back. It is the market that establishes fairness as the best way to deal with people and gives things their true value, and it is the market that was missing in Russia. In both cases, the Russian is really waiting for an opportunity to say, "Here, the scoundrels have tricked me again." Why? This is so because only free and creative labor gives a true measure of things. Just like the seller of the apartment, you have been working creatively, and that is why you know the true cost of an apartment, expect to pay a fair price, and are able to afford it.

Inability to succeed. First, you must want to succeed (we now know that there are people who actually want to fail). But the desire to succeed is not enough: you must have the opportunity to achieve the success for which you are psychologically ready. The Russian state does not encourage personal success but actively impedes it, thereby providing a universal excuse for personal failure, a service that Russian citizens continue to value and demand. The most important task of a well-functioning Russian state would be to organize a positive psychological reorientation of the population, to create a population that is healthy, functional, creative, and success-oriented.

Waiting for a miracle. If you are separated from property and not engaged in free and productive labor, you have no way of knowing what it takes to create. Thus, you wait for goods to appear magically. Since in times of famine food now falls from the sky in boxes, this phenomenon has earned the name of cargo-cult. In and around Russia there are lots of people predicting that the Russian economy is about to start growing just because it should. And that means only one thing: the economy has proved so utterly unable to create and produce it now relies entirely on miracles. But the oil price will come down, and the envy-based economy will one day have to be fundamentally reformed. Even with the price of oil as high as it is today, Russia fails to conduct essential daily maintenance: repairing housing, installing communications, providing for the needy. People who steal and waste resources are hard at work, while those who want to create are unable to do it.

Dependence of law on the (changing) status of the subject of law. The subjects of law must be equal before the law (otherwise this is not a real law). The law must be written by its future subjects (or their representatives), so that they willingly submit to it. A set of rules written for slaves by slave drivers is not law.

We should repeat again: all the phenomena discussed above have a common root: an envy-based social organization.

ON DICTATORSHIP

The Russian people like to destroy, but they now realize that this is not the best solution. As for creating, the Russians are not quite ready to do it on their own, but they would willingly submit if they were forced to become creative.

People are very reluctant to take their first cold shower, but then grow to love it and depend on it. The same is true of success: the Russians fear it now, but are equipped to achieve it and will grow to enjoy it. All it takes is to force them to taste success for the very first time. There are some successful and independent people in Russia already, but not nearly enough. If this is so, it means that we need to use force, to make the Russians do what they are reluctant to do.

What kinds of force are there, and what kind of force do we need?

The state can use force against the creative part of its citizenry. This course will spell the end of Russia and the Russians, a tragedy of planetary proportions;

The state can use force against the envious part of its citizenry while strongly defending and supporting those who are creative. This is necessary insofar as we permit the following process to establish itself;

The people must struggle against manifestations of envy within themselves, must struggle to strengthen their creativity as the only basis for their life.

Wherever there is envy, there should be a struggle with it, a struggle that uses all the force necessary to protect creativity and the creative. As this is a struggle for the creative in people, it could be a struggle on the side of a tiny minority. The thieves must understand that it is easier (and far more pleasant) to create and produce for themselves, but this understanding may need to be introduced by force.

Force that does not oppress people but liberates them from the constraints of envy and self-hatred in which they find themselves is an essential part of democracy. In Russia, this disciplining force will be heartily welcomed: Russia's territory has always been too great for the laws to work properly, and there have never been any laws that reliably defended the creative against the envious.

In a dysfunctional and traumatized society, a dictatorship of creativity over envy is an indispensable step towards genuine democracy, a step that the international aid organizations and Western policymakers continue to overlook.

We tend to forget that after 1945 both Japan and Germany were under military occupation. Democracy did not come right away: it was imposed from outside as both of these countries were given new constitutions. In Russia, there was no dictatorship of creativity over envy, and after 1991, Russia was led first by a reformed Communist and then by a reformed KGB officer.

INTERNAL CONTRADICTIONS IN THE DEVELOPMENT OF THE RUSSIAN ECONOMY

The Russian economy is a consequence of the following five destructive conflicts:

Envy and, as a consequence, fear of individual growth and development.

A government that is insecure and whose mission is perverted; government against the people.

The struggle of the envious against the creative; of citizens against one another, and the internal psychological struggle within each citizen.

The struggle of the law of the land against truth, justice, legality, public order, and humaneness.

Make-believe; reality is too scary, too uncomfortable, or too alien to be seen.

The vectors of Russian life are directed against one another, struggling and diminishing one another constantly. For a Russian man, success is to always have enough bread and vodka, live to be fifty, and avoid prison: these are low sights to set, and this is a great waste of human talent. Russians should be less cruel towards Russians if Russians are to survive. Instead of having an economy, the Russians play out the fight of hyenas over the half-rotten carcass of an animal that they couldn't even manage to kill themselves. The ratio of controllers to producers continues to increase in favor of the controllers.

Russians define power as that which controls everything, forbids arbitrarily, and is itself above the law. Power that forbids has no popular support and is extremely weak. Its arguments are those of a weak person:

lies, cowardly slayings, lame excuses, limitless cruelty. In the Information Age, a state that is governed this way is doomed.

In his inaugural address, Putin said that in Russia "the state is responsible for everything". A few months later he said, "we have a horrible mess everywhere we look". The point is that these two statements are identical. If there is no self-government, there is a horrible mess.

RUSSIA'S SECRET

Three people run a race. Here is the order in which they finish. First comes Ivanov, then Petrov, and Sidorov is last. Who won? Well, dear reader, careful now. If you are a Westerner, you will answer that Ivanov won, Petrov should train harder, and Sidorov is the loser. It Russia, the answer would be different. It would be good if you could close the book right now and think what this answer would be.

One answer would be that it is Sidorov who won. He was not rushing, he took it easy, and yet came to the finish line in the end, and made it to the bus with everybody else. Why kill yourself rushing? Other Russians would say Petrov won. He is a modest guy who hates to stick out. He came in in the middle, did not offend anyone, and did not make a laughingstock out of himself by losing or attracted envy by winning. Yet other Russians would say that it is Ivanov who won. He runs the fastest and was the first to sip a cold beer. And of course, many Russians would claim that the real winner was the observer. Why run at all, since you could spill your beer? Please note that in the West there is only one winner, but in Russia there are four of them. Well, how about the loser? In the West, it's an open and shut case: Sidorov can't run and he should be in tears. In Russia, the losers are four. Ivanov should be cut down to size, Petrov's ears stick out and catch too much wind, and Sidorov is a hopeless weakling. As far as the observer, this lazy fatso is far too clever for anybody's liking. In the West it is black and white, but in Russia it is all in the eye of the beholder. In the West, 99% of inmates are guilty of crimes. In Russia, since 99% of judges, prosecutors, and police are guilty of crimes, what percentage of inmates are being locked up fairly? You pick the number. In the West, you are either poor or rich, successful or not, happy or not. In Russia, you pour, you toast, you drink up, you pour the next one.

What does this mean? It means that Russia is unpredictable, amorphous, and lacks rules and regulations. Russia is invincible, as the Germans found out, because it lacks a definition of “too bad to bear”. Russia is not going to be democratic until there is a definition of “a politician who is unfit to serve”. Russia cannot become a market economy until there is a definition of “the winner”. Russia’s strongest firms of five years ago are no longer around; since there is no bankruptcy law, Russia’s weakest firms of five years ago are still with us. Russia’s winner is one who is getting beaten up and robbed right now, as you read these words.

CONCLUSION

Let us return to the illustration of the vertical and the horizontal law.

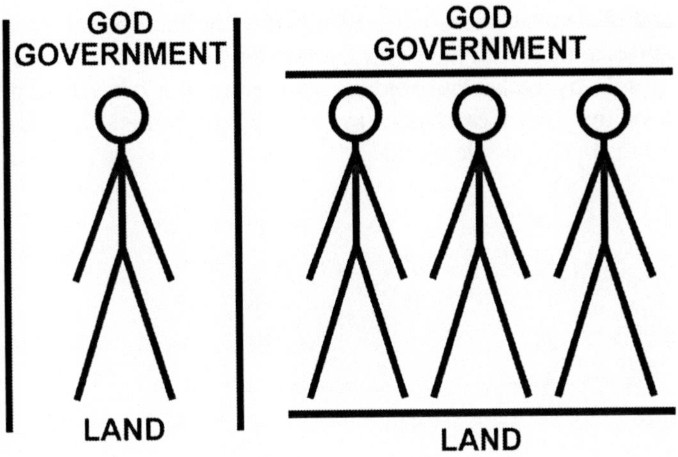

DRAWING 5. GOD, EARTH, AND VERTICAL AND HORIZONTAL LAW

If the law is horizontally oriented, it separates people from the land below and from God and the government above. Land stands for the means of production, for the opportunity to create. The separation of people from the land by the lower horizontal line of law means poverty, inability to put down roots, lack of opportunity to become a citizen in a true sense of the word, to master the land, to truly belong. Millions of people can disappear in Russia, as happened during the Stalinist purges, because they are not able to put down roots. The government is located above the upper horizontal line of law; a government that is above the law is uncontrollable, weak, cruel, and inefficient. The upper horizontal line of law also separates people from God, which stands for creativity, kindness, justice, and beauty. At the same time, the government presents itself as godlike. People expect miracles from it, and are always disappointed.

If the law is oriented vertically, it separates an individual from the claims of the envious with the fence of individual rights. Each person is standing on land, deep-rooted and secure, able to produce and create. There is no barrier separating the citizen from the government, and both the citizen and the government exist within the confines of the law. People are not separated from God: in fact, the law points them towards God. Now, simply by being law-abiding, they enjoy the protection of justice, discover the joy of creativity, and are able to make a personal contribution to the beauty of the world.

APPENDIX 1: NAMES OF THE ANGLES AND OF THE SIX AUXILIARY OCTANTS

Here is a table of all the angles:

Lines that make an angle	Name of the angle
Animate, past	library
individual, animate	each human being has opportunities
Animate, future	creativity
others, past	do as others do
others, inanimate	distribution
inanimate, past	everyone is dead
others, animate	people are talking
others, future	law
individual, past	memory
individual, future	tomorrow
individual, inanimate	life is over
inanimate, future	instruments and skills

Now we are ready to name the six remaining octants.

Octant "others, animate, future" is called "HUMANITY"

others, future	law
others, animate	people are talking
Animate, future	creativity

Octant "others, animate, past" is called "CIVILIZATION".

others, animate	people are talking
others, past	do as others do
Animate, past	library

Octant "others, inanimate, future" is called "PRODUCTION".

others, future	Law
others, inanimate	distribution
inanimate, future	instruments and skills

Octant "individual, past, animate" is called "KNOWLEDGE".

individual, animate	each human being has opportunities
individual, past	memory
Animate, past	library

Octant "individual, inanimate, future" is called "MIND".

individual, future	tomorrow
inanimate, future	instruments and skills
individual, inanimate	life is over

Octant "individual, inanimate, past" is called "DEATH".

individual, inanimate	life is over
inanimate, past	everyone is dead
individual, past	memory

ABOUT THE AUTHOR

I was born in 1958 in Moscow, Russia, and emigrated to the US in 1979, graduating from Columbia University in 1984 and receiving a Master's Degree in Sociology from Yale University in 1991. In 1985 I became a US citizen. I have lived in Russia and Ukraine since 1992. My first book, *Understanding Russia* (84 pages, in English) was originally published in 1995. My second book, *How to Make Russia a Normal Country* (320 pages, in Russian) was published in Moscow in 2000 and in Saint Petersburg in 2002. I have been an official adviser of the Russian Economics Ministry, worked for a venture capital fund, and served as the campaign strategist for the Ukrainian political party Women for the Future. I currently live in Kiev, Ukraine.

My e-mail is info@matthew-maly.ru
My website is http://www.matthew-maly.ru/index-eng.html

Lightning Source UK Ltd.
Milton Keynes UK
04 January 2010

148164UK00001B/84/A

9 781591 133919